Money
Theory, Policy and Institutions

Andrew Crockett

International Monetary Fund Washington

Money

Theory, Policy and Institutions

Nelson

Thomas Nelson and Sons Ltd
Lincoln Way Windmill Road Sunbury-on-Thames Middlesex TW16 7HP
PO Box 73146 Nairobi Kenya

Thomas Nelson (Australia) Ltd
19–39 Jeffcott Street West Melbourne Victoria 3003

Thomas Nelson and Sons (Canada) Ltd
81 Curlew Drive Don Mills Ontario

Thomas Nelson (Nigeria) Ltd
8 Ilupeju Bypass PMB 1303 Ikeja Lagos

First published in Great Britain by Thomas Nelson and Sons Ltd 1973

Reprinted 1974, 1976, 1978

ISBN 017 712206 4

Printed in Great Britain by The Camelot Press Ltd, Southampton

Contents

Preface

It is customary for an author to begin the preface to a book by explaining its purpose. In my case, the primary motivation was a desire to clear my own mind on a number of basic topics in monetary economics. Nothing clarifies a subject so much as the exercise of attempting to write about it in simple terms. Having struggled to write about the subject in terms which seemed to me to be as clear as I could manage, it naturally occurred to me that the result might be of use to others.

There are of course numerous books on money; and the mere existence of a manuscript would not justify publication unless it attempted to deal with the subject somewhat differently from other texts. The book tries to knit together, in a coherent way, the theoretical and the institutional approaches to teaching about money and banking. One of the main purposes in learning about monetary theory is to enable one to form opinions and make judgments about policy. But, to quote from a speech made in 1970 by the then Governor of the Bank of England, Sir Leslie O'Brien '... monetary policy is conducted within a particular framework of institutions and markets. This framework provides opportunities, of course, but it also creates constraints.'[1] Unless one has a firm understanding of the institutional framework within which policy operates, it is not possible to get full value for theoretical knowledge.

The book begins with a survey of received theory. Chapter 1 examines the nature of money, and the characteristic properties of assets used as money. Chapter 2 traces the evolution of credit money, the role of banks in the creation of money, and analyses the extent to which banks may be distinguished from other types of financial intermediary. Chapter 3 deals with the main theories of the rate of interest and the role of money in interest rate determination. Chapter 4 covers

[1] Jane Hodge Memorial Lecture, 7 Dec., 1970.

the debate between 'Keynesian' and 'monetarist' schools of thought about the importance of money. Chapters 3 and 4 contain a number of more difficult ideas, and the reader approaching them for the first time is urged to go slowly, re-reading where necessary.

Chapters 5, 6 and 7 deal with the formation and execution of monetary policy. Chapter 5 deals with the more philosophical questions of the objectives of monetary policy, and how to reconcile them. Chapter 6 analyses the various instruments which are available to monetary authorities as means of achieving policy objectives; and Chapter 7 looks at the market framework within which government and central bank financial operations must take place.

Part 3, covering Chapters 8–11 deals with the institutional framework of the British financial scene. These chapters treat, successively, the Bank of England; the main commercial banks; other banks within the banking system and non-bank financial intermediaries.

Part 4 makes use of both the theoretical and institutional sections to analyse the operation of monetary policy in Britain since the war. Chapter 12 deals with the development of policy in the period 1945–71; Chapter 13 assesses the nature and significance of the changes introduced in the 1971 credit reform.

Finally, Part 5 covers the International Monetary System. Chapter 14 is largely theoretical, treating the arguments for and against the different kinds of exchange system that have been proposed. Chapter 15 deals with the International Monetary Fund, the principal agency charged with responsibility for maintaining good order in the world's monetary arrangements. Chapter 16 traces the development of international monetary co-operation from the end of the war until the present (1972).

Clearly, a book of this kind owes much to many individuals. Among those who saw the manuscript in draft form and made many helpful suggestions, I owe a particular debt to Peter Bull, Charles Goodhart, Don Hodgman, Bo Karlstroem, David Laidler, David Walker and Bill White. In addition, a number of colleagues and former colleagues at the Bank of England and the International Monetary Fund were kind enough to point out errors and suggest improvements. To Marion Pennant-Williams, Barbara King and Simone Delavigne, I owe thanks for patient and efficient typing of successive drafts. To my wife Marjorie, and our children Alexander and Keith, even greater thanks are due for putting up with me during the evenings when I was preoccupied with the book.

A.D.C.

The author of this book is a former member of the Staff of the Bank of England who resigned (with an option to return) in order to take up the post of Personal Assistant to the Managing Director of the International Monetary Fund. The Bank of England and the International Monetary Fund have agreed to publication but the contents of the book are in all respects the responsibility of the author alone.

Part 1
Theory

1

The nature and uses of money

The theory of exchange

The development of a system of exchange is one of the earliest contrivances of organised society. It is through the exchange of goods that societies can move away from primitive subsistence agriculture toward an economy where the members of society can enjoy the advantages of division of labour and specialisation in production. People are not equally endowed with strength, skills, property and luck. It is by concentrating on those things he can do well, and exchanging the product of his labour for those things his neighbour can produce, that man in society makes material progress. The activity of exchanging goods is, therefore, at the very root of economic and social progress.

This proposition seems so self evident as to be scarcely worth considering further. But because it is fundamental to an understanding of economic processes, it is worth pausing to note the circumstances in which the exchange of goods will be worthwhile, and the mechanism which determines exactly what quantities of goods will be exchanged and at what prices.

Consider first a simple economy with only two products, say sheep and corn, in which every individual produces for himself, and no exchange takes place. Each member of society will try to produce that combination of sheep and corn which maximises his satisfaction. This combination will be determined by the interaction of two basic economic laws, the law of diminishing marginal returns in consumption, and the law of increasing marginal costs in production. In the context of our simple example, the law of diminishing marginal returns is simply a formal statement of the rather obvious point that the more sheep an individual has, the less value he will attach (i.e., the less corn he will be prepared to give up) to acquire an additional sheep. The law of increasing marginal costs of production reflects the fact that the more an individual concentrates on producing sheep, the more he will have to encroach on good corn-growing land and the greater will be the cost, in terms of corn output given up, of additional sheep production.

This argument is illustrated graphically in Fig. 1.1. The curve II represents those combinations of sheep and corn, available over the course of a year, which would leave the consumer's economic welfare

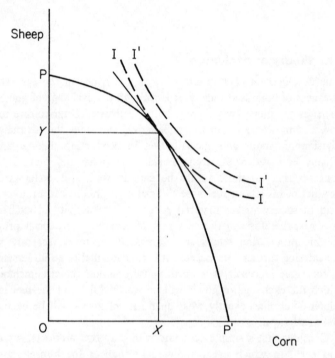

Fig. 1·1   Production possibility and indifference curves : one person

unchanged. (It is termed an indifference curve, because the consumer is 'indifferent' as between any of the combinations represented by points on the line.) The line is convex to the origin because of the property of diminishing marginal utility: when the individual has only a little corn he is prepared to give up more sheep to acquire an additional unit of corn than when he has a lot. Economic welfare would be increased by a move to a higher indifference curve (such as I′I′), representing a higher level of income, but not by a move *along* a curve.

The curve PP' is the individual's 'production possibility' curve. By concentrating all his efforts on sheep production, the individual could produce OP sheep. As he switched some land to corn, he would initially sacrifice very little in the way of sheep. This is because he would at first divert land that was very good for corn production but not very good for sheep. But as his corn output expanded, he would

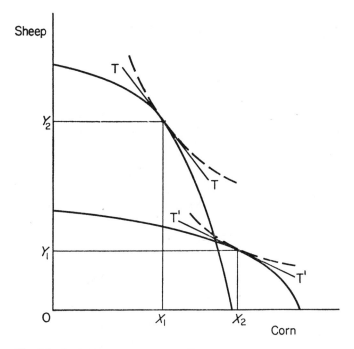

Fig. 1·2 Production possibility and indifference curves : two people, no exchange

find himself using land that was less and less suitable for corn and his sacrifice of sheep would be greater for each additional unit of corn.

Although each individual could produce at any point on the 'production possibility curve', he will naturally pick the combination of outputs which yields him the greatest satisfaction. In terms of our graphical analysis, he will pick the combination which enables him to be on the highest indifference curve. This point has an interesting property. The tangent to both curves is the same at this point, and its slope represents both the relative costs of production of each product in terms of the other, and the relative satisfaction derived from the consumption of a marginal unit of each. It is in fact the 'price' in an economic sense, even though no market exists.

Exchange becomes advantageous when the individuals in society have different tastes (i.e., different indifference curves) or different talents in producing (i.e., different production possibility curves), or

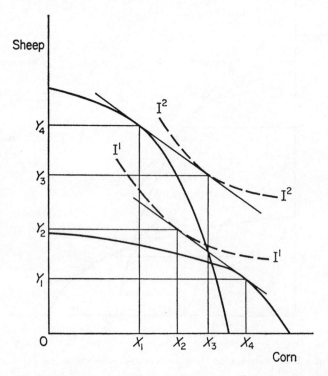

Fig. 1·3   Production possibility and indifference curves : two people with freedom to exchange

both. We can illustrate this simply by assuming an economy with two people, each with the same tastes, but one of whom lives in hilly country suitable for sheep farming, and the other of whom lives in flat land more suited to corn growing. Before any exchange takes place, they will produce and consume the combinations shown in Fig. 1.2.

For each individual, the price of sheep in terms of corn is represented by the amount of corn which must be given up to get additional sheep. This is the slope of the tangent lines TT and T'T'. At the margin the hill farmer values corn more highly than the flat-land farmer. If he concentrated on sheep, and exchanged his surplus sheep for corn, he would do better than if he tried to produce corn himself on his unsuitable land.

Figure 1.3 does more than just illustrate the principle involved. It can tell us exactly how far specialisation will proceed, and what will be the rate of exchange between the two commodities. Specialisation will proceed to the point at which the relative costs of production of the two commodities are equal for the two farmers. This will be where the tangent lines to the production possibility curves have the same slope. Each individual will then exchange goods at the price given by the slope of the tangent lines until he reaches his highest attainable indifference curve. In each case, it can be seen that exchange enables each individual to derive more satisfaction than if he were forced to rely only on what he could produce himself.

The need for vehicle commodities

The advantages of exchange do not themselves prove the need for money. In principle, the benefits of specialisation of production could be obtained through the direct exchange of goods. It is not hard to see, however, that there are serious drawbacks to a system of direct barter. If goods and services were not bought and sold for money, they would have to be traded against each other. In other words, if someone wanted to take advantage of his special ability to produce say, corn, he would have to try and find someone with whom he could barter his surplus output in exchange for the other necessities of life, building materials, clothes, meat, fuel, etc. The general disadvantage of a barter economy is that, in order to acquire an article he cannot make for himself, a man has first to find someone who can make it, and who is prepared to swap it for something he has available to give in exchange. Furthermore, both parties to the trade have to want the right quantities of the goods on offer and be prepared to exchange them at the same time. Finally, they have to agree on a mutually-acceptable rate of exchange for the commodities in question.[1]

These requirements can be stated as the need for a double coincidence of wants if a transaction is to take place. A moment's reflection reveals how unlikely it is that the condition of double coincidence of wants would hold in most transactions which take place

[1] The difficulties to which direct exchange gives rise are reflected in the fact hat the English word 'barter' is derived from the French 'bareter', to cheat.

in a modern economy. For example, what could a bank-clerk give a taxi-driver in return for the service of providing transportation? Even if the taxi-driver needed some banking services, he would not necessarily need the skill of that particular bank-clerk, nor would he probably want the services at that moment, nor would either party have any idea of how much of the bank-clerk's services should be exchanged for the services of the taxi-driver.

A pure barter economy is a theoretical construction, which is a useful analytical concept, but is never found in reality. All organised societies exhibit a tendency to develop monetary-type standards, through the development of commodities which are used, not only for their own intrinsic properties, but also as 'vehicles' to effect exchanges between other commodities. To take a simple example: if a villager wishes to exchange a horse for a cow, he may be unable to find someone who wishes to make precisely the same exchange in reverse. However, if there is someone who wants to exchange two sheep for a horse and someone else who wants to exchange a cow for two sheep, then three-way trade will enable exchanges to be made to the satisfaction of all three parties. It should be noted that one of the transactors has to make two exchanges to reach his desired position. To be technical, we would say he was using the purchase of sheep as a 'vehicle' to effect the exchange of a horse for a cow. He did not want sheep for themselves, but simply because they had a greater usefulness in exchange than did his horse. This is because the sheep were acceptable in exchange for the cow, where the horse was not. If only direct barter were possible, none of the parties to this exchange would have been able to obtain the animal he wanted.

Because of the drawbacks to direct barter, it is natural to expect that many transactions will tend to be made through intermediary, or vehicle, commodities. It is fairly easy to see that there will tend to be a 'bandwagon' effect encouraging the use of these vehicle commodities. The more people accept a commodity in exchange, the more acceptable it becomes to others, because they know they can always use it in trade. It is a bit like the telephone system. The first subscriber makes an act of faith, since there is nobody he can use his phone to speak to. The more people who acquire telephones, however, the more attractive the system becomes to new subscribers. Similarly with vehicle commodities, the first person to accept an untried commodity in exchange takes the risk that he may not be able to sell it on to someone else; once it attains a measure of acceptability, however, its usefulness becomes very much greater.

It is quite possible that more than one commodity would be used in societies as the 'vehicle' of exchange. In fact, however, there is a natural resistance to the proliferation of vehicle commodities. This is because, as soon as one commodity attains an ascendancy, it automatically becomes more acceptable because of its wider use. Only if someone is prepared to guarantee the convertibility of the inferior vehicle into the superior one can the inferior survive. Again, our analogy of the telephone system is useful. The new subscriber will normally want to join the system with the most existing subscribers, thus tipping the scales even more in favour of the larger system. Only if the smaller system can promise its subscribers access to the larger system will it be able to continue.

In an economic sense, we are justified in classifying as 'money' any vehicle commodity which serves the purpose of being a medium of exchange. This commodity will then become the standard by which the values of other commodities are judged. Instead of having separate exchange rates between horses and cows, cows and sheep, sheep and pigs, etc., every commodity will have a value expressed in terms of the vehicle commodity. Moreover, holdings of the vehicle commodity represent purchasing power. Transactors may choose to hold it in the interval between making a sale and using the proceeds to make a purchase, or to borrow it or lend it to someone else.

We may thus summarise the uses of a vehicle commodity as follows:

a as a medium of exchange
b as a store of value
c as a unit of account
d as a standard for future contracts

The types of money which were formerly used varied widely from society to society. Cattle, for example, have a long history as a medium of exchange. Their use is recorded in the classical world, and our word 'pecuniary' is derived ultimately from the Latin 'pecus' meaning cattle. More recently, cattle continued to be used as a means of exchanging wealth in parts of Africa and South America. Ornaments and craftwork have also been popular — small arrows, hooks and axes being used in parts of Northern Europe. A more recent example, illustrating the diversity of types of money, and the ingenuity of men in developing them, was the use of cigarettes as a medium of exchange in prisoner of war camps.

Precious metals have always been a favoured form of money, and the development of coinage (coins are metal cut to convenient shape and size) was made early. The coinage of China can be traced back for two and half thousand years; and silver was coined in the Hellenic world in the eighth century BC. Coins were known to have circulated in Britain before the arrival of the Romans, though Caesar notes that iron bars were a more popular means of exchange.

The properties of a medium of exchange

What are the characteristics which cause a particular commodity to emerge as 'money'? In the first place, unless there is some power that can enforce the acceptability of a money-commodity, it must have intrinsic worth. If it does not, it will not enter into exchange transactions in the first place, since no one will want to acquire it. (In a reasonably well-developed credit system, titles to goods of intrinsic worth will usually be equally acceptable; in this section, however, we are concerned with the development of a monetary standard where no financial system exists.)

What is meant by 'intrinsic' value? Simply that the commodity has some value apart from a value-in-exchange. It might have value because it is a commodity that satisfies physical wants (e.g., a food-stuff); it might have value because it enables one to produce goods that satisfy physical wants (e.g., a tool of some kind); it might have value because it satisfies psychological wants (e.g., a precious metal that satisfies the desire for display or adornment). To say that an item has intrinsic value is much the same thing as saying that it is a scarce commodity. Any commodity of which there is not enough to totally satisfy everyone's wants is, technically speaking, 'scarce', and, to get some of it, it will be necessary to pay a price. Commodities which are not scarce—sand in the desert, water in a lakeside community— will have no 'value' in an economic sense.

Intrinsic worth is not, however, the same as money value. Once an item begins to be used as a vehicle for exchanges, it will have a value-in-exchange as well as a value-in-use and this will increase the demand for it. To take an example: if two societies were alike in all respects, except that one used gold as its exchange commodity and the other used silver, one would expect to find that gold had a higher value in terms of other commodities in the first society, whereas silver had a higher value in the second society.

There are many commodities in every society which have intrinsic value. One therefore wants to know what other characteristics are desirable for a commodity to become a vehicle. *Durability* is an important property if the commodity is to serve the monetary function of being a store of value. Since there will normally be a gap in time between receipt of income and payment for expenditure, no transactor will wish to hold a wasting asset in this interval. Perishable foodstuffs would, therefore, make a very poor vehicle commodity, since their value is declining day by day. Precious metals, on the other hand, are very good in this respect, since they do not deteriorate at all.

Continuing with the need to serve as a store of value, a vehicle commodity should be subject to *stable supply and demand conditions*. This means that its value will not fluctuate greatly in terms of the average of other commodities. Those agricultural products which are particularly dependent on climatic conditions score low on this count, since a poor harvest sends prices shooting up, while a good one brings them tumbling down again. The most satisfactory vehicle commodity in this respect is one with a supply that is either fixed, or is augmented at a slow and predictable pace. Precious metals are again quite good, since the total quantity of, say, gold in existence is increasing at only a very slow rate. Stability of value can suffer, however, if the availability of newly-mined gold is suddenly increased or, in the other direction, if speculation suddenly increases the demand for the money commodity.

Another important attribute in a vehicle commodity is *homogeneity*. In other words, each unit of the vehicle commodity should be as like as possible to every other unit. If this were not the case, the vehicle commodity would lose the convenience of being a unit of account, since three inferior units of the commodity might only have the value of one standard unit. Thus, it would be impossible for a standard price-list to emerge. Each transaction would involve bargaining between the transactors. It would become much more difficult to compare relative values and the convenience value of having a money commodity would be correspondingly reduced. This again makes foodstuffs poor candidates for the vehicle commodity. An ounce of grain is not necessarily comparable in nutritional value with every other ounce. Where non-homogeneous assets have been used as monetary standard (e.g. cows in parts of Africa), one finds that the convenience of having a single unit of account dictates that all units of the money-commodity be deemed to have an equal value in exchange. Since the healthiest cow exchanges at the same rate as the thinnest, people naturally try to keep the healthy ones for meat and milk, and use only the scrawniest in exchange.

Precious metals and coins are somewhat better in this respect, but coins can be 'clipped' to reduce their metallic content, and precious metals are subject to debasement through being mixed in alloy form with base metals (this is the origin of the word 'debase'). Again there is a tendency to use in exchange those units of the monetary standard whose intrinsic value is least, the more valuable being either hoarded or converted to use as commodities. This process was characterised in Gresham's Law as the tendency for bad money to drive out good.

Divisibility is another important property. If a unit of money has a very high value, it will be of little use in making small purchases. In those parts of the world where livestock have been used as money, transactions have to be undertaken in large lumps. Let us take again the example of cows used as money. If one cow is equal to, say, three sacks of grain, then it becomes impossible to purchase small quantities of grain. This means that anyone who needs grain, assuming he has a cow to give in exchange, would have to buy more grain than he needed and incur the expense and inconvenience of storing the excess until it was required. Alternatively, he could try to swap the grain that was surplus to his requirements, but this would involve all the disadvantages of barter trading which were noted earlier.

Some commodity moneys measure up quite well to the criterion of divisibility. Salt, for example, can be divided into units of weight as small as could reasonably be required for purposes of exchange. Precious metals, such as gold, measure up rather less well, since, although gold can, in theory, be divided into very small units, the amount of gold needed to make a minor transaction would be inconveniently small. There are obvious impracticalities to carrying around a bag of gold dust and measuring out a few grains every time one needed to purchase a loaf of bread. For this reason, societies which came to use the precious metals as their basic money often used inferior metals as the standard for small transactions. Thus, in England and the US, there have been times when both gold and silver have been in circulation as monetary standards, and copper and nickel have also been used. The problem with this arrangement is that equal monetary units from the two monetary standards do not always retain the same value as commodities, and, as a consequence, the convenience of a single unit-of-account may be lost. If the government decrees that the relative values of the two standards remain the same, people tend to hoard the one that has the higher commodity value and to use in exchange only the one with the lower value as a commodity. This is yet another example of the application of Gresham's Law.

The list of attributes which a commodity money should have could probably be considerably extended. Here, we shall note only one more; the attribute of *portability*. In order to undertake transactions, buyers and sellers must come together, which means that the vehicle commodity must be carried to the exchange location (or market) by the buyer, and carried back by the seller. Livestock commodities have certain obvious attractions in this regard, since a cow can carry itself to market. This is not an unmixed blessing, however, since a cow can also carry itself away when its owner is not looking. In general, the attribute of portability requires something that is of relatively small bulk and weight compared with its value. Precious metals are again useful from this standpoint. It is even better if they can be converted into easily carryable form, such as coins. Gold and silver meet these requirements fairly well (though not perfectly, since pure gold and silver are rather soft; consequently coins are usually some kind of alloy). Portability may seem to be rather a trivial point, but if one considers the case of mercury—which is just as good as the other precious metals by most of the criteria we have noted, and inferior only in portability—it can be seen that it is important.

Thus far, we have considered the various reasons why certain commodities are more likely to emerge as the vehicles for exchanges than others. Precious metals have certain distinct advantages that help to explain why they have been so widely used in many different societies. In the first instance, gold and silver were valued as ornaments. Since these items were so widely desired, it was easy to give them in exchange for other commodities and as a result people came to want them, not only for themselves, but also as a store of value. This added to the 'value in exchange'. The increase in worth is illustrated by a comparison of the value of gold in societies where it was used as money, with its value in those societies (e.g., in the South American civilisations) where it was just another commodity.[2]

Money in modern economies

Commodity moneys are perfectly adequate to secure the advantages of being a unit of account and a standard for deferred payments. The intrinsic properties of the medium of exchange are not relevant in performing these functions; all that matters is that there should be a single agreed standard. But commodity moneys are less satisfactory as media of exchange and stores of value. They suffer the drawbacks of costs of production in their creation, and costs of transport and storage of the money commodity. Exchange systems based on commodity moneys therefore absorb real resources which might otherwise have been directly applied to the satisfaction of real wants.

The development of a banking system resulted from attempts to economise in the production and use of commodity monies. This

[2] Although the relatively low value of gold in South America reflects in part the more plentiful supply.

development was an evolutionary process, which will be examined in more detail in the next chapter. Its result has been a monetary system where the money stock consists primarily of bank deposits, but with notes and coin playing an important supporting role.

Bank notes and coins in the UK and in most other countries are legal tender. An economist might refer to them as 'representative money'. They are 'representative' because the paper and metal of which they are made do not usually have a value as great as the nominal value of the coin or note (this is not always the case; until 1966, US silver coins were 'full-bodied', i.e., the silver content was equal to the face value of the coins, and before the decimalisation of the UK currency, the old pennies contained more than a pennyworth of copper).

'Representative money' such as bank notes can be distinguished from 'token money', such as bank deposits. Bank notes, despite the promise to pay which they bear, are themselves legal tender which *must* be accepted in discharge of debts. Bank deposits are good only so long as there is confidence that they can easily be converted into legal tender money. Bank deposits are not legal tender for a very simple reason. If they were, no bank would be under any legal obligation to repay depositors. For, since it is always permissible to discharge a debt by using legal tender, a bank could repay a depositor by simply crediting another account at the same bank.

Having pointed out the difference between representative and token money, however, we must also note that this distinction is of very little practical significance to the individual holder of money. So long as there is general confidence in the ability of a bank to convert its deposit into legal tender money, its deposits will be just as acceptable in settlement of debts as legal tender money. Indeed, the greater convenience and security of bank deposits may well make them more acceptable for a wide range of transactions.

The precise conceptual definition of money (as any assets fulfilling the four functions noted on page 9) is far from being matched by equal precision in practice. No hard and fast line can be drawn between those assets which meet all of the four criteria and those which meet none of them. There are a large number of assets which fulfil some but not all the functions of money. Plenty of assets, for example, are stores of value, but this does not make them money. Some assets are a medium of exchange without being a unit of account (e.g., luncheon vouchers). A large volume of financial assets, e.g., deposits with non-bank financial institutions and time deposits with banks, are not media of exchange, since they cannot be transferred directly to make payments. Nevertheless they can quickly and easily be turned into cash and fulfil many of the same financial needs as current account deposits.

Some have suggested that money should be defined as those assets which are regarded by the holder as a 'temporary abode of purchasing power', e.g., those which he is holding for the *monetary* function of bridging the gap between receipts and payments of income, rather than for the *investment* function of transferring spending power into the future. On the practical level, however, this definition is even less helpful than the medium-of-exchange definition since there is no way of saying with certainty what has motivated the holding or disposal of a particular block of funds.

It is, therefore, widely agreed that whatever definition of money is used is bound to be somewhat arbitrary. There is no group of assets which economists would unanimously agree upon as constituting 'the stock of money'. Different definitions have advantages, depending on the purpose to which the statistics are to be put.

If, for example, one wishes to measure the quantity of money used as a medium of exchange, it would be natural to restrict the definition to notes and coin and bank deposits which can be drawn on by cheque. If, however, one is interested in those assets held as a 'temporary abode of purchasing power', a much wider definition would be appropriate, including probably all bank deposits and possibly the liabilities of some other financial institutions as well.

Further reading

Day, A. C. L., *Outline of Monetary Economics*, London, Oxford University Press, 1957, Chapters 1 and 2.

Hanson, J. L., *Monetary Theory and Policy*, London, Macdonald and Evans, 4th edition, 1970.

Harrod, R. F., *Money*, London, Macmillan, 1969, Chapters 1 and 2.

Hicks, J. R., *Critical Essays in Monetary Theory*, Oxford, Clarendon Press, 1967, Chapter 1.

Jevons, Stanley, 'Barter' reproduced in *Monetary Theory*, R. W. Clower (ed.), Harmondsworth, Penguin, 1969.

Pigon, A. C., *The Veil of Money*, London, Macmillan, 1949, Chapter 1.

Smith, Adam, *Wealth of Nations*, Volume 1, Chapter 2.

Questions for discussion

1 If everybody was paid an income in kind rather than in money, would there be any use for money?
2 In what ways is society better off as a result of the existence of money?

3 Assume a society in which gold was the only form of money. What would happen if a gold prospector found a mountain of pure gold?

4 Cowrie shells, cigarettes and metal ornaments have at different times been used as money. Assess their advantages and drawbacks in a modern industrial society.

5 'Money is one of those concepts which, like an umbrella or a teaspoon, but unlike an earthquake or a buttercup, are definable primarily by the use or purpose which they serve'. Comment.

2

The creation of money

Chapter 1 considered the functions of money and the nature of early commodity moneys. It ended by noting the fiduciary nature of the money which is used in all modern societies. The present chapter concerns itself with the way in which money is created. It traces the evolutionary process by which commodity money gradually gave way to fiduciary money; and deals with the factors which determine the quantity of money in existence at any one time; finally, it discusses the question of whether banks, as 'creators' of money, are qualitatively different from other financial institutions.

The creation of commodity money is a process which is relatively easy to understand. When the value of the commodity money in exchange for other goods exceeds its costs of production, more will be produced. It will enter into circulation as the producers of the money-commodity use their output to purchase real goods and services from other members of the economy. It is also fairly easy to see that there will be economic forces tending to limit the total volume in circulation. The more commodity money there is in circulation, the less will be the convenience value to individuals of having an additional unit. They will therefore be less willing to give up other commodities in exchange for money, and the value of money in terms of these other commodities will decline. (This is simply another way of saying money will buy less, i.e. that prices will rise.) In addition, as the producers of the money-commodities try to expand their output, they will run into increasing costs, as they have to use land, labour and capital which is less suitable for producing the money-commodity.

The stock of money is therefore limited by conventional supply and demand forces. The quantity of money will be given by the interaction of costs of production and the demand of economic units to hold money balances.

Bank money

In modern economies, money consists of promises to pay issued by financial institutions. The means by which these are created, and by which their quantity is limited, is considerably more complex than is the case with a commodity money. To understand this process, it will be convenient to trace the evolution of the monetary system from a commodity basis to a fiduciary basis. In order to make this development clearer, it will be considered as a series of rather stylised steps; in fact, of course, progress was rather more blurred, as one stage gradually gave way to the next.

Although gold had emerged as the primary vehicle commodity by the late middle ages, and although it had been widely coined into convenient units for exchange, it still had a number of drawbacks. Chief among these was the problem of storage. It was not that gold was physically difficult to store, but rather the danger of theft. It is usually the case with any commodity that has intrinsic value that owners will have to protect themselves against the danger of theft, and inevitably the case that such protection is costly.

Now, since the costs of protecting a large store of gold are little greater than those of protecting a small store, there is obvious advantage in the owners of wealth pooling their gold and sharing the protection costs. It happened that, in London in the seventeenth century, there was a group of merchants who already had vaults for the storing of gold and security precautions to protect themselves against theft. These were the goldsmiths. They were able to offer the services of safe-keeping of valuables for a very moderate charge. Thus, the owners of gold got into the habit of putting their gold in goldsmiths' vaults and keeping at home only pieces of paper showing title to gold, which were valueless to any thief. Whenever gold was needed to make a transaction, the owner could take his receipt to the goldsmith who would deliver up the gold that was required and amend the title accordingly.

This was a great improvement on the previous situation from the point of view of the owners of money. But it still was inconvenient in that, every time gold was needed to make a payment, the transactor had to go down to the goldsmiths' store, draw out the gold and return to the market to make a transaction. The receiver of gold would, like as not, then take it back to the goldsmith and redeposit it. Knowing, as we now do, the principles of deposit-banking, it is not a very difficult step to see how this process could be simplified. A transaction could be effected by exchanging title to gold, without anyone having to make a trip to the goldsmiths' store. So long as both parties to the transaction had complete confidence in the ability of the goldsmith to deliver gold in exchange for the title, the paper was literally 'as good as gold'.

There are two ways in which the exchange of title can be effected. The first is by means of a bearer certificate. If the goldsmith issues a note payable to the bearer in exchange for a gold deposit, this note can be tendered in payment of any debt, provided that the creditor has confidence in the ability of the goldsmith to meet his promise. A bearer note of this kind is just like an ordinary banknote today. It is highly practical and convenient, but it reintroduces the problem of theft and the need to guard against it.

The second method avoids the danger of theft by using an instruction given to the goldsmith by the owner of the gold. So long as the instruction is to make payment to a specific individual it is valueless to a third party. This kind of instrument is essentially the same as a cheque in the present day, by which the owner of a deposit instructs his banker to transfer a credit balance to the account of the payee. The disadvantage of this means of payment is that it requires that the recipient of the funds not only has confidence in the goldsmiths' solvency, but also in the value of the instruction issued. He must be confident that the cheque will not bounce.

With the emergence of the goldsmith-bankers gold ceased to be the principal *physical* medium of exchange. However, although paper might circulate, it still represented title to gold and was matched *pari passu* by coin and bullion lying in the goldsmiths' vaults. With more and more transactions being effected by means of bearer notes, or the writing of cheques, the goldsmiths realised that the net withdrawals from their stocks of gold were becoming very small in relation to the total amount they were holding. As they contemplated the gold lying in their vaults, it naturally occurred to them that they could make more profit from it than simply fees received for safe custody. They were sitting on vast quantities of idle wealth, at the same time as impecunious individuals were paying usurious rates of interest to moneylenders. Modern banking began when the goldsmiths exploited this combination of circumstances and began to lend out part of their holdings of gold against the promise to repay with interest.

This was an important step, and it is worth pausing to spell out in more detail the sequence of events that occurs. Let us assume goldsmiths' customers had, in total, entrusted £1000 worth of gold to their safekeeping. Before they undertook any lending, the combined balance sheet of goldsmiths would be as follows:

Liabilities	*Assets*
Gold deposits £1,000	Gold coin and bullion £1,000
———	———
1,000	1,000

Now assume that the goldsmiths decided to use the gold lying idle in their vaults, to make loans at interest. They lend £100 to a borrower, who takes his loan in the form of gold. The balance sheet is now as follows:

Liabilities	Assets	
Gold deposits £1,000	Gold coin and bullion £	900
	Loans to customers	100
		─────
		1,000

There has been no increase in goldsmiths' liabilities, but there is an increase of £100 in gold circulating outside the goldsmiths' vaults. When the borrower uses this gold to acquire goods and services, the likelihood is that the receivers of the money will deposit what they receive back with the goldsmiths. When this happens, the balance sheet would be this:

Liabilities	Assets	
Gold deposits £1,100	Gold coin and bullion £1,000	
	Loans to customers	100
─────		─────
1,100		1,100

The total quantity of deposits—that is to say, claims which can in theory be turned into gold on demand—has increased without any increase in the quantity of physical gold.

The next stage in this process is for the goldsmith to issue deposit receipts, not just against the delivery of physical gold, but against gold certificates. If an individual pays for goods with a cheque drawn on goldsmith A, and the seller of the goods takes the cheque to goldsmith B, goldsmith B will be quite willing to accept it so long as he has confidence in goldsmith A. He may ask goldsmith A to settle the indebtedness by a transfer of gold, but on the other hand he may be quite content to have a claim on A which he can use to settle a debt with C, D or E at some future date. With this refinement, the goldsmith, our pioneer banker, is enabled to 'create' money by a simple book entry, without a single coin being moved.

A monetary system based on banks depends on the acceptability of claims which are not fully backed by gold. Confidence, as we have seen, is of the essence. Every banker is subject to the over-riding requirement to retain confidence in his ability to redeem his liabilities. This means he must keep capital reserves and liquid assets. With time, and many bitter experiences, the banking system came to a general view on how much capital reserve was needed to run a deposit-banking business and what proportion of liquid assets should be held to ensure the ability to meet depositors' requirements. Even prudent bankers, however, were not immune to *all* crises of confidence. In a serious financial crash, every bank came under suspicion, and, since no bank kept 100% of its assets in the form of gold, all were exposed to some risk.

In London, in the early nineteenth century, there were a number of quite spectacular financial crashes in which banks which were being prudently run according to accepted criteria were pushed into insolvency, not because they were actually bankrupt (with liabilities in excess of assets) but because they were illiquid (unable to convert some of their assets into gold at short notice). It therefore came to be suggested that one bank, of unquestioned solidity, should act to support the rest of the financial system. This it could do by 'rediscounting' (i.e. buying) the assets of those banks which were short of ready cash. In London, the bank which emerged to fill this role was the Bank of England. Since this became the central bank of the system (though the term 'central bank' did not come into general usage until much later) the other banks gradually ceased to hold gold and centralised their cash reserves in holdings of notes and balances at the Bank of England.

At this stage in the development of money it was still an important aspect of bank balances that they were convertible into gold. Psychologically, gold represented the true store of value which backed the paper assets which, for the sake of convenience, were the principal medium of exchange. People knew from experience that banks could fail, and the criterion by which they judged a bank's soundness was its ability to supply gold to honour its promise to pay.

As the 19th century wore on, however, there were a number of developments which tended to reduce the importance of gold in the system. In the first place, the increased security of the banking system resulting from the gradual assumption by the Bank of England of responsibility for financial stability reduced the fear of banking crashes. Secondly, the growth of banks was much more rapid than the growth of the Bank of England's gold stock, and there were no serious adverse consequences. By the outbreak of World War I, gold had diminished considerably in importance and, during the war, the Bank of England suspended its promise to convert its notes into gold. It became apparent that the promise to convert into gold was unnecessary to the acceptability of paper money. So long as there was confidence in the financial system, paper money could exist without any backing of gold.

The fact that there is now no physical gold backing to money does not mean, however, that it is unbacked. A bank's assets must exceed its deposit liabilities or else it is insolvent. And it is the assets of a bank which form the backing for money. These assets are a fairly heterogeneous collection, of notes, coins, short-term bills, longer-term investments and advances to customers. These assets represent claims on present or future resources and are just as real and valuable as a gold bar—more so since they produce an interest return.

The expansion of bank deposits

Right from the early beginnings of goldsmith-bankers, concern had been expressed at the magic-like way in which banks' operations could increase the quantity of money in circulation. People could not see any means by which the indefinite expansion of credit could be halted. As a result of these fears, banks in most countries are subject to official regulations specifically designed to restrict their ability to create money. It will be argued later in this chapter that the nature of banks' power to create money has been misunderstood and its significance exaggerated. Nevertheless, the importance of the notion, both in the theoretical literature, and in the operation of monetary policy is such that it is worth considering exactly what is meant by the bank's money-creating rôle.

A commercial bank 'creates' bank money by accepting a deposit. It can do so *passively* by accepting the transfer of a claim on another bank, and the deposit of notes and coin over the counter. Or it can do so *actively* by purchasing securities from or lending to a client. In this latter case, the bank 'creates' money in its client's account by crediting the account with the value of the securities purchased, or the amount of the loan made.

With 'passive' deposit creation, there is no increase in the total quantity of money in the system, since one bank's deposit is created by a transfer away from another bank, or by the reduction of notes and coin in circulation. In the case of 'active' deposit creation, however, there will be an increase in the total quantity of bank deposits in the system as a whole.

In the normal course of business, bank customers will be transferring their claims on banks to other customers in settlement of debts between them. Thus any bank will be receiving and paying sums from and to other banks on behalf of its customers. Net positions are settled by a transfer of assets between banks—usually a transfer of balances at the Bank of England, where bankers keep their first-line cash reserves. If no bank has been engaging in 'active' deposit creation, it may be expected that the total of each bank's debits will be roughly equal to its credits, so that its cash balance with the Bank of England will be maintained roughly stable.

If, on the other hand, a bank is making loans or granting overdraft facilities to its customers, there is less likely to be an equality between debits and credits. People borrow money in order to spend. If the recipients of the funds which are spent are customers of another bank, the lending bank will tend to find its debits exceeding its credits in the daily settlement. As a result it will initially see a reduction in the cash balance it holds with the Bank of England; subsequently it may sell other assets or cut back on its lending. Because of the cash losses which may occur when a bank expands its lending activities, the amount of 'active' deposit creation it can undertake will be limited. Thus, for a single bank, taken in isolation, it is reasonably true to say that the amount of lending it can do is determined by the amount of deposits it succeeds in persuading people to hold with it.

But let us examine what happens elsewhere in the banking system when one bank begins 'actively' to create deposits. When a borrower spends the money lent to him by the bank, he transfers ownership of deposits to the sellers of the goods. Many of these sellers will be customers of other banks, although some will be customers of the same bank. If the bank has, say, 10% of the total deposits in the country, it is reasonable to suppose that out of each £100 spent by its customers, an average of £10 will pass into the hands of people who are also its customers. Thus the lending of £100 will result in a *net* loss of cash (i.e., notes and Bank of England balances) of £90. The other banks in the system will 'passively' receive an extra £90 in deposits. This extra cash will make them more willing to buy securities or to lend; and as they thus in their turn 'actively' create deposits, the first bank will find itself receiving more deposits.

Now if we assume that there is no way in which a deposit can be transferred out of the banking system and be lost to all banks—we shall see the importance of this assumption later—an interesting conclusion results. This is that, taking the banking system as a whole, the act of lending creates, as a direct consequence, deposits exactly equal to the amount of lending undertaken. Provided, therefore, banks all move forward in step, there appears to be no limit to the amount of bank money they can create. Even more than this, there would appear to be a basic instability in the banking system. As one bank increased its lending, for whatever reason, others would find themselves with more deposits and would increase their lending. This in turn would cause the first bank's deposits to rise further, and encourage it to do more lending.

This seeming power of the banking system to create apparently un-limited quantities of money has troubled economists and banking practitioners for many years. They have held up the spectre of an uncontrolled banking system creating money in such quantities that inflation would run riot and the value of money become debased. It was perceived, however, that the reason for the apparent instability of the volume of credit was the fact that the whole of any expansion in lending was assumed to become available to finance further loans. If, however, there was some leakage of funds out of the banking system, or if banks chose not to lend 100% of any additional deposits received, there would be a tendency for expansionary or contractionary impulses to be damped down. To ensure that this damping down actually takes place, most banking systems provide for a 'reserve requirement', which has the effect of freezing a proportion of the increment in deposits in a par-ticular form where it is not available for the making of loans.

In the next section, we shall see that the bogey of unlimited expansion (or contraction) of money stock is an artificial one. Banks cannot create unlimited quantities of money even without a reserve requirement, and indeed they are just as limited in their ability to generate money as other financial institutions are in their ability to generate their particular form of liability.

Commercial banks as creators of money

It is often suggested that banks alone among financial intermediaries should be subject to controls because only they have the power to create money. If money is defined as bank notes and bank deposits, and not extended to include any other financial assets, then it is obviously true that banks create money and other intermediaries do not. But we could equally well say that building societies create building society shares and life insurance companies create life insurance policies. The act of creation is not qualitatively different. If a building society borrows from individual A and lends to individual B, the total size of building society balance sheets has increased, but there has been no change in the quan-tity of money, nor will there necessarily be a change in the volume of any other financial asset.

The role of banks in creating money does not relieve them of any constraint which limits the size of other institutions. Admittedly banks can make a loan before actually borrowing funds, but this is a trivial distinction. Borrowers do not borrow in order to hold funds; they borrow to make payments, and when they do, a bank faces the same need for funds as any other kind of intermediary. In an efficiently functioning financial system, the size of a bank's business, or that of any other financial intermediary, depends on its ability to attract funds in competition with other institutions. This ability will depend on the attractiveness to depositors of the package of services it offers. This package will consist of the interest rate paid, security offered, convenience in account management facilities, financial advice, etc. And the ability of the bank or other financial intermediary to offer additional services in order to attract funds will clearly be determined by the yield it can obtain in the employment of its funds. So long as the margin between the return on lending and the cost of attracting deposits is sufficient to cover an intermediary's costs, it can expand its business whether it 'creates' money or not.

The individual bank clearly has an optimum balance sheet size dictated by its increasing marginal costs of attracting deposits and its diminishing marginal returns on loans. It is sometimes suggested that this kind of equilibrium does not exist when the banking system is viewed as a whole. It is argued that, since the making of loans generates deposits, the rising marginal cost of deposits is an illusion. Even if unlimited deposits could be generated at fixed cost, however, banks would still face diminishing returns as they expanded their loan portfolio, and these would ultimately impose a constraint on the further expansion of banks' business.

Much the same point can be made in another way. If the banks attempt to expand the scope of their operations when the rest of the economy and financial system are of given size, this means they must induce their customers, in the aggregate, to hold more bank deposits and borrow more by way of bank advances. To achieve this, they will have to offer more services on deposits and lower the rates at which they lend, i.e., to reduce the margin between the cost and yield of funds which covers their administrative expenses. Since banks are profit-making institutions which have operating costs, there will be a unique size to their business which maximises their profits. When a further expansion of business would reduce returns below costs, the banks' rôle as creators of money will not save them from incurring losses.

The foregoing implies that, in a freely competitive environment, the stock of money (defined as bank deposits) would be determined by the interaction of three main factors:

a the demand to hold banks' liabilities (i.e., to make deposits)
b the demand to hold banks' assets (i.e., to borrow from banks)
c banks' administrative costs.

Banks do not operate free from constraints, however, partly because the assumed need to regulate them in the interests of controlling the money stock makes them rather different from other institutions. Apart from anything else, this means that the policy actions of the monetary authorities are usually designed to act on the banking system in the first instance. Thus it is often simplest to judge the impact which official action is having on the system as a whole by its effect on the banking system and in particular on magnitudes such as the money supply.

The requirement that banks tie up a given ratio of assets in low-earning form constitutes an effective tax on banking that reduces the size of the banking system relative to what it otherwise would be. This creates a threshold in banks' lending activities. If the banks have more reserves than they are required to hold, then they will be prepared to lend at low rates since the alternative is a zero- or low-yielding reserve asset. If they have too few reserves, on the other hand, the existence of penalties (financial or otherwise) for a deficiency may drive the cost of funds far above the yield from employing them. Under these circumstances (which more nearly prevail in Germany and the US than the UK) the monetary authorities may be in a situation where they are able to manipulate the supply of money fairly precisely through variations in the availability of reserves.

We noted earlier that the mechanism by which money is 'created' by the banking system is not fundamentally different from the mechanism by which other assets are created by other financial intermediaries. There is no widow's cruse which enables bankers to create credit out of thin air but which prevents building societies undertaking credit creation based on their particular brand of financial instruments. But although the nature of the process by which credit is created is the same, the nature of the particular financial assets and liabilities that are generated are not. It is the unique nature of money as a financial asset that justifies special treatment of the banking system.

Actually, as will become apparent, particularly in Chapter 4, there is considerable dispute about how unique money really is. At the one extreme it is claimed that its properties as a medium of exchange differentiate it from other liquid financial assets to such an extent that it is really not possible to substitute the use of any other asset for money. The so-called 'new view' of money, on the other hand, sees it as standing at one end of a spectrum of financial assets, closely substitutable with other short-term instruments offering a high degree of liquidity, rather less substitutable with those assets of a longer-term nature.

Nowadays, however, all economists would agree there was some measure of substitutability of money for other assets and vice versa. The question is one of how great this substitutability is. The most comprehensive way to consider the question of substitutability, is to think of economic units as having some desired portfolio of assets (and liabilities) which they are continuously trying to achieve.

Theory of portfolio balance

Although they may not think about it in precisely these terms, individuals are continually making decisions about the total size of their wealth and the form in which it is held. Decisions about the total size of wealth are essentially decisions on whether to save or consume. We may note in passing that the line between saving and consuming is not so clear as it appears at first sight. Putting money in the bank is clearly saving; spending money on a meal or a holiday is clearly consumption. But what about the purchase of a car or a TV set? These are assets which continue to provide a service long after the date on which they were bought. It is much more appropriate to regard the purchase of a car as an act of investment, and its gradual depreciation over time as the true 'consumption of car services'. In Chapter 4, it will be shown that the difficulty of making an acceptable distinction between investment and consumption is important in analysing the channels by which monetary policy affects the economy generally.

Once the individual has decided how much he wishes to save, he then faces further decisions concerning the form in which he wishes to hold his wealth, and whether he wishes to incur liabilities (borrow) in order to hold additional assets. Each asset will have its particular attraction. A house will provide services of accommodation; a car, services of transportation; bonds, the service of a certain future yield; equities, the service of convenience and liquidity. The value to the individual of holdings of each of these forms of wealth is subject to the law of diminishing marginal returns. That is to say, the more of his wealth an individual holds in one form, the less the utility to him of spending another pound in the same way. This is fairly obvious. The first £1,000 spent on transportation makes the difference between a motor car and shoe-leather; whereas increasing expenditure from £1,000 to £2,000 only makes the difference between a perfectly adequate car and a rather superior one.

In monetary economics, we are perhaps more immediately interested in an individual's holding of financial assets, but the same principles apply. Financial assets have properties of expected yield, convenience, stability of value and so on. Each economic unit (individual or firm) will be seeking to structure his assets and liabilities in such a way that the last pound devoted to each employment produces equal satisfaction. This may entail issuing liabilities (i.e., borrowing) if the cost of doing this is less than the return, or satisfaction, derived from employing funds borrowed.

Money is normally a part of most people's portfolio, because it has a combination of properties that makes it a particularly convenient asset to hold for the purposes of financing day-to-day transactions. We may say that money produces a service of convenience and liquidity, but it must be noted that money holdings are also subject to the law of diminishing marginal returns. People can only be persuaded to hold a greater proportion of their portfolio in the form of money if it is made attractive to them to do so. In other words, either the return on money must be increased or that on other assets must be reduced.

Much the same kind of considerations govern the activities of banks. Because of the particular services they offer, however, banks are normally able to borrow on more favourable terms than they lend. As a result, their portfolio equilibrium is typically one in which their balance sheet is far in excess of their net worth (capital) and is financed by the issue of short-time liabilities (deposits). The gap between banks' borrowing and lending rates is accounted for by the fact that they provide services which simultaneously satisfy the portfolio preferences of borrowers and lenders. They provide the depositor with liquidity, convenience and security, and the borrower with funds on better terms than if he had to borrow directly on his own reputation. Banks can undertake this activity because they can pool risks—the risk of withdrawal in the case of deposits, and the risk of default in the case of loans —and because they can take advantage of specialised skills in credit assessment.

The law of diminishing marginal returns, or increasing marginal costs, will apply in determining both the total size of a bank's balance sheet and the disposition of assets and liabilities between various types. Let us take the effect on the overall size of banks' operations first. An individual bank will only be able to borrow more by offering higher interest rates, lower charges, better service or more advertising. Whichever course it follows, additional deposits can only be attracted with increasing costs. On the other side of the balance sheet, a bank will only be able to acquire more assets by lowering the yield it is prepared to accept or making loans of a lower quality. Either way its marginal return will decline as it expands the size of its business. The combination of increasing costs and diminishing returns will produce an equilibrium size for the banks' balance sheet where the additional return from making another loan is not sufficient to cover the additional cost of attracting the deposit to finance the loan. This is shown in Fig. 2.1.

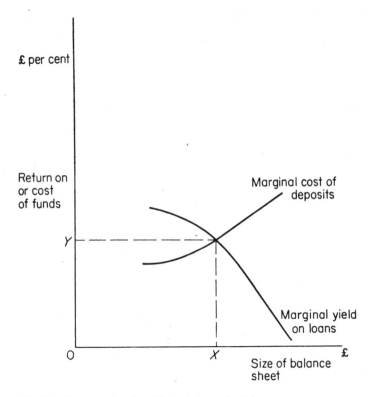

Fig. 2·1   Determination of equilibrium balance sheet size

In practice, banks' portfolio decisions are considerably more complex than simply balancing the cost of deposits against the return on loans. Their balance sheets contain a large number of different types of assets and liabilities. In allocating their portfolios, bank managements will be asking questions such as: Is the last £ of loans producing as great a return to us as the last £ in liquid assets? Is the last £ of savings deposits costing us more or less than the last £ of current account deposits?

These are not questions which can be answered by simply comparing relative interest rates. For as we have just seen, part of the return to a bank from holding liquid assets comes from the speed and certainty with which they can be turned into cash when needed. And part of the cost of accepting current accounts (which bear no interest) is the obligation to furnish cash to depositors on demand.

The value of these returns, or costs, in terms of interest rate equivalent, is a matter for judgment in the last analysis. We may say with certainty, however, that the more liquid assets a bank has, the less need it will feel to pay a premium to acquire additional liquidity. And the more it tries to increase its savings deposits at the expense of current account deposits, the greater yield it will have to offer. There will therefore be some equilibrium point, in a bank's portfolio structure, which balances the marginal costs and returns of all assets and liabilities.

From this very preliminary consideration of portfolio balance theory it can be seen that all financial assets can be treated in the same way, for *analytical purposes*. The public can only be persuaded to hold more of one asset if its yield is made more attractive. Banks will only issue more liabilities if they can make a profit by employing the funds thus obtained. Yields on the various forms of assets and liabilities have to move in such a way as to balance the supply and demand for all assets simultaneously. The yield on money is, of course, fairly static because of conventions regarding interest rates paid. But this simply means that the relative yield adjustment takes place through a change in the return on other assets. It is still the case that a change in relative quantities of assets with no change in the structure of demand for them must involve a price (i.e., interest rate) adjustment. Conversely, changes in price will bring about changes in the quantities of assets demanded and supplied.

However, although a similar analytical method can be employed for money and other financial assets, it makes a great deal of difference how great the substitutability is. If other assets are regarded as very poor substitutes for money, it will take a very large increase in the yield on these assets to compensate for a reduction in the supply of money. Under these circumstances, it would be permissible—though it is still a subjective judgment—to regard money as qualitatively different from other financial assets. This is because a change in its supply would have larger and more wide-ranging consequences for the financial system as a whole than an equivalent proportional change in some other financial asset.

Further reading

Dacey, W. Manning, *The British Banking Mechanism*, London, Hutchinson, 5th edition, 1964, Chapters 1–4.

Day, A. C. L., op. cit., Chapter 10.

Hanson, J. L., op. cit., Chapter 2.

Hicks, J. R., *Critical Essays in Monetary Theory*, Oxford, Clarendon Press, 1967, Chapter 2.

Moore, Basil J., *An Introduction to the Theory of Finance*, New York, Free Press, 1968.

Sayers, R. S., *Modern Banking*, Oxford, Clarendon Press, 1967, Chapter 1.

Tobin, James, Commercial banks as creators of money, in *Banking and Monetary Studies*, Carson (ed.), Homewood, Illinois, Irwin, 1963.

Tobin, James, A general equilibrium approach to monetary theory, *Journal of Money, Credit and Banking*, February 1969.

Questions for discussion

1 In what ways is money different from other financial assets?

2 If banks had no reserve requirements would there be any finite limit to the size of the money supply?

3 What is the cost to a bank of increasing its deposits?

4 What would happen to the level of bank deposits if building societies were to begin to offer cheque book facilities?

5 Why does most monetary theory distinguish between banks and other financial intermediaries?

3

Money and the rate of interest

The rate of interest is a price and, like other prices, its economic function is as a mechanism which balances supply and demand. Over the years, however, there has been a considerable amount of dispute about what it is that the rate of interest balances the supply and demand for. This chapter reviews the two main theories of interest, the 'real' and the 'monetary', and considers how and in what circumstances they can be consistent with one another. It ends by considering the influences which cause securities of different maturities to yield different returns.

Since interest is usually a price paid to borrow money, it might seem obvious that interest is a monetary phenomenon. But looked at another way, when one person borrows money, another is purchasing a claim on the future, whether it be an equity share, a bond, or simply a promise to repay. We can regard the borrowing of money as the sale of future claim and the lending of money as the purchase of future claim. The rate of interest can therefore be viewed as the price established by the interaction of the supply and demand for future resources, in the same way as the price of potatoes is determined by the supply and demand for potatoes.

Many classical economists saw money as a 'veil' which did not fundamentally affect economic transactions, but merely clothed them in a system of prices. They argued that the quantities in which goods were exchanged for each other were determined by basic factors of utility on the one hand, and costs of production on the other; and that the use of money was merely a convenient numeraire, and medium of exchange, which lubricated the economic mechanism but was not necessary to understand how the mechanism worked. This view was, perhaps, put most clearly by John Stuart Mill:[1]

[1] Mill, J. S. *Principles of Political Economy*, Longmans, 6th Edition, Book III, Chapter 7.

The introduction of money does not interfere with the operation of any of the Laws of Value laid down in the preceding chapters. The reasons which make the temporary or market value of things depend on their demand and supply, and their average or permanent values upon their cost of production are as applicable to a money system as to a system of barter. Things which by barter would exchange for one another, will, if sold for money, sell for an equal amount of it, and so will exchange for one another still, though the process of exchanging them will consist of two operations instead of only one.

Looking at the economy in this way, money could not be demanded for itself but only as a vehicle for obtaining something else. Therefore, if people paid interest to borrow money, this must reflect the demand for the assets that the borrowed money was used to purchase. Likewise, the supply of funds to lend must represent the willingness to forgo the goods that the money which was lent could otherwise be used to buy. Interest rates were therefore seen as balancing the desire for future resources against present resources, and equating the community's saving with its capital investment.

It must be emphasized that the 'neutrality' of money, as it was called, was something that only obtained when the economic system was working smoothly. It was widely recognised that if the supply of money was altered at short notice, e.g., through the activities of banks expanding their lending, changes in the availability of funds could have an effect on interest rates. Under the classical schemes of things, however, this was a strictly temporary disequilibrium phenomenon.

Keynes claimed that the influence of money on the level of interest rates could be more than simply transitory. He pointed out that people could want to hold money for its own properties, and not simply as a bridge between income and expenditures. It therefore became important to look more closely into why people would want to hold money. And once money was viewed as an *asset*, rather than simply as a medium of exchange, it became natural to regard the interest forgone on other assets as the price paid for holding money. Interest rates in the Keynesian view of the world are therefore determined by the supply of and demand for money; in other words, by the 'liquidity preference' of the public faced by a stock of money fixed by the action of monetary authorities.

Despite their greatly different emphasis, these two theories of the rate of interest, the real and the monetary, are not necessarily incompatible with one another. The desire to acquire money must reflect a desire to dispose of some other asset in exchange. And the holding of durable assets—whether real or financial—represents a means of deferring consumption from the present into the future. It can be seen, therefore, that the liquidity-preference theory does not rule out the time-preference element of the classical theory. In a later section we will explore the conditions under which the two theories are compatible.

Nevertheless, they represent very different ways of looking at the question of how interest rates are determined. If the rate of interest is seen as being determined by the interaction of the demand for and supply of future resources, our attention is focused on factors underlying these demand and supply functions, namely productivity and thrift. Both of these are real factors, not directly affected by the money supply or the absolute level of prices. On the other hand, if interest rates are seen as equating the supply and demand for money, our attention is immediately focused on the factors determining the supply and demand relationships for money.

'Real', or non-monetary, theories of interest

It is perhaps as well to begin with a cautionary note: there are a large number of 'theories of interest' differing in emphasis or in detail. It would be unnecessarily complex to detail them all here; what is attempted is to give a general outline of the two main types of theory in order to illustrate the relative role of money in each.

The non-monetary theory of interest sees the rate of interest as being determined by the interaction of forces of thrift on the one hand, and the relative productivity of investment on the other. The mere fact that interest rates emerge from markets in which money is the medium of exchange does not imply that money itself is particularly important. Because money is used as the medium of exchange, the act of saving is reflected in the supply of money, the act of borrowing in the demand for money.

The volume of saving is likely to be dependent on the strength of people's desire, at the margin, to make provision for the future. This in turn will be dependent on the degree of uncertainty about future incomes, the wisdom and foresight of people in appraising their future needs, and the amount of provision that they have already made. The desire to invest will be determined by the amount of additional resources which can be obtained in the future by refraining from current consumption and producing capital goods instead. Neither the desire to invest nor the desire to save is necessarily dependent on the quantity, or even the existence, of money as two examples will show.

First, consider the case of Robinson Crusoe. As a one-man economy, he had no need of money. But he did continually have to make decisions concerning time preference. If he went fishing using his bare hands, he might with luck catch one or two fish per day. But if he took time off from fishing to make himself a rod and line, he would be enabled :ater on to catch many more fish. If he took even

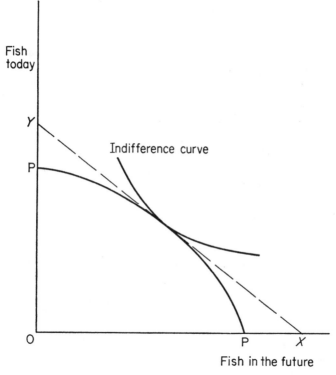

Fig. 3·1   Robinson Crusoe's fish consumption

more time off and constructed a boat and nets, his catch would become even greater. Thus Robinson Crusoe faces a choice between consumption now and consumption in the future. The more saving he does (by refraining from consumption and staying at home to make equipment) the more consumption he can have in the future. However, the more time he spends at home, the less fish he will have to consume in the present, and consequently the more valuable will be each unit of consumption he does have. He will have an indifference curve which reflects the diminishing marginal returns to be derived from shifting consumption from the present into the future and vice versa. At the same time, the more effort he devotes to 'investing' in the construction of fishing equipment, the more he will find himself engaging in projects with smaller returns. He will have diminishing marginal returns on his investment. Figure 3.1 shows that the combination of present and future fish consumption which yields him the greatest satisfaction is when the relative cost (and relative satisfaction) and present and future consumption are in the proportion OX/OY. This future return per unit of current savings can be regarded as an interest rate earned on investment and paid on savings.

Robinson Crusoe is admittedly a rather far-fetched example, but he does illustrate how the *concept* of the rate of interest can be applied even when there are no banks, financial markets, money-lenders, etc. In a money economy, money is the vehicle of exchange, and therefore enters as one side of most transactions. Lending and borrowing, which represent exchanges of present against future resources, are no exception. However, as we have noted, simply because the rate of interest is what a borrower has to pay for money it is not necessarily a monetary phenomenon.

The second example we consider, therefore, is where the quantity of money in the economy is increased or reduced at a stroke. One can think of the case of France in 1960, when one hundred old francs were declared to be worth one new franc, largely in order to save writing so many zeros, or the case of countries which decimalised their currencies on the basis of a unit having a value half that of the old unit. In all these cases, prices in shops were altered by exactly the amount of the change in value of the currency, incomes changed by a proportionate amount, and there was virtually no effect on the economy as a whole. In particular, there was no change in the rate of interest.

Where there is simply an administrative change in the unit of account following decimalisation, one would hardly expect there to be any economic consequence. By extension from this simple case, however, it could be argued that if the quantity of money were exactly doubled through the creation of new money, rather than by administrative change in the unit of account, the end result would be the same. It would be recognised that there would be distributional effects, since all members of the economy would not necessarily be affected to the same extent as a result of money creation. And it would also be recognised that there might be lags, during which the change in the quantity of money might have real effects. For example, a sudden increase in the quantity of money might cause spending to increase before prices rose sufficiently to offset the higher money balances. But in the end classical economists would expect the price level to adjust fairly quickly to the higher money stock, and equilibrium prices—including the rate of interest—to be restored.

Thus although most economists recognised a role for money in the determination of interest rates, it is probably true to say that, until the time of Keynes, they saw monetary phenomena as causing only temporary deviations from the 'natural' rate established by the interaction of 'real' economic forces. These 'real' forces of productivity and thrift, however, are essentially long-run, and the drawback to this kind of analysis is that it is not very useful in analysing real-world problems. 'In the long run, we are all dead', wrote Keynes, 'Economists set themselves too easy, too useless a task if in tempestuous seasons they can only tell us that when the storm is long past the ocean is flat again'.

Liquidity preference, or monetary, theories

Keynes stated his dissatisfaction with existing theories of interest in forthright terms: 'The rate of interest is not the price which brings into equilibrium the demand for resources to invest with the readiness to abstain from present consumption. It is the price which equilibrates the desire to hold cash with the available quantity of cash'.

Received doctrine was couched largely in terms of the *flow* of savings and the *flow* of investment demands. The question of how to allocate *stocks* of assets was largely ignored. Keynes pointed out that there were two different categories of decision that people made. In the first place they had to decide how much of their income to consume and how much to save; secondly they had to decide the form in which their savings (both the new saving and existing assets) should be held.

Transactions representing new saving and borrowing are, over any short period, necessarily small relative to transactions in the outstanding stock of assets. Changes in the desire to save and invest are, therefore, not likely to have a very great impact on total sales and purchases of securities. Transactions in existing securities, however, can in principle involve the whole stock of financial assets, and as a result have much more profound effects on interest rates. The distinctive feature of the Keynesian way of looking at interest-rate determination is its emphasis on the role of the rate of interest in balancing the supply and demand of assets to *hold*. If, for example, the quantity of money is increased and the quantity of bonds reduced, interest rates will have to change in such a way that people are prepared to hold more money and fewer bonds. In other words, the attractiveness of bonds will have to decline, which is the same thing as saying that their yield will have to fall.

In the liquidity preference theory, the supply and demand which the interest rate balances is the supply and demand for liquidity, or money. If it is assumed that the quantity of money is somehow independently determined—whether through the limited availability of a physical commodity money, or as a result of the control of a monetary authority—then the theory will concentrate largely on the factors determining the demand for money.

In assessing the elements which make up the demand for money, Keynes made another important departure from earlier theory. In its simplest form, the classical notion had it that, since money was wanted only as a medium of exchange and not for its own properties, the demand would be directly related to the volume of transactions to be financed. In the liquidity preference theory, the demand for money is derived from a consideration of the properties of money as an asset in its own right, rather than simply as a lubricant for 'real' transactions.

Why should people wish to hold money as an asset? Would they not be better off holding their wealth in an interest-bearing form and transferring it into money only when they need to make a transaction? To answer these questions we need to look a little more closely at the traditional functions of money as a medium of exchange and a store of value.

The function of money as a medium of exchange gives rise to the need to hold transactions balances. The size of transactions balances will naturally depend in large part on the level of income and expenditure, and on institutional practices such as how frequently people are paid and whether or not they are allowed to overdraw their accounts. It will also depend in part, however, on a weighing up of the relative costs of keeping a low balance, which requires frequent replenishment and careful management, against the loss of interest involved in keeping a high balance. The higher the rate of interest, the greater the incentive to minimise the proportion of assets held in non-interest bearing form. As rates rise, it will become more worthwhile to hold bonds for short periods, since the return will rise relative to the transactions costs incurred in buying and selling. The stock of money held as a medium of exchange will therefore depend, at least in part, on the rate of interest. Another way of putting this is to say that holdings of money are subject to the law of diminishing marginal returns. People can only be persuaded to hold more money if it becomes cheaper to do so; i.e., the cost in terms of interest forgone must fall.

The other main reason for which balances are held is a reflection of money's function as a store of value. Although money generally has a lower yield than other stores of value, it has the advantage of being more predictable in terms of its capital value. Other financial assets, such as fixed-interest bonds and equity securities, can fluctuate in value with the general economic climate. Since individuals wish, by and large, to minimise uncertainty in their financial affairs, they will only be persuaded to reduce their holdings of money if the yield on other assets, whose value fluctuates more than that of money, is increased. In equilibrium, the value to a wealth owner of the convenience and certainty of his last unit of money holdings will be just equal to the financial yield of his last unit of securities-holdings. The lower the yield on securities, the more money will be held; the higher the yield, the more securities people can be persuaded to hold.

This yield comparison is complicated, but not essentially changed, when there is a prevailing expectation that interest rates will move up or down. If interest rates rise, the price of bonds and equities will fall, and the capital loss from holding this kind of asset may offset or even wipe out completely the interest return. In these conditions money, though earning no interest, may be the most attractive asset to hold, since it is the only one that avoids the possibility of incurring an actual loss. Money held for this reason is said to be held for speculative purposes; the holder takes a view about future bond prices. Again it is clear that the size of balances depends on the rate of interest. The lower the rate of interest, other things being equal, the lower the cost, in terms of interest forgone, of holding one's wealth in money form. At the same time, if a lower rate of interest is considered to increase the chances of a future upward movement in interest rates (and thus a fall in bond prices) it provides an additional reason for holding money rather than securities.

The volatility of speculative balances is much greater than that of transactions balances. Individual economic units require fairly fixed minimum balances in order to finance their day-to-day transactions, but additional wealth can be transferred between assets with very little inconvenience. Figure 3.2 illustrates the relative volatility of transactions and speculative demands. The line TT represents the demand for transactions balances and is rather insensitive to changes in interest rates. The line SS, representing the demand for speculative balances, is much more elastic. The line (TS)–(TS) is the overall demand for money formed by the sum of the demand for the two different kinds of balances.

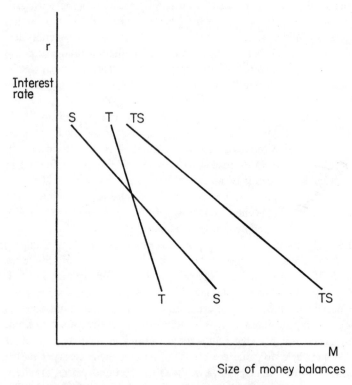

Fig. 3·2 Response of money balances to changes in interest rates

The demand of individuals and firms to hold money balances, therefore, depends on the rate of interest. But the rate of interest, as we have noted, has to balance the overall supply of money with the overall demand to hold money balances. If the monetary authorities use the various techniques at their disposal (described in more detail in Chapter 6) to create a given quantity of money, then an equilibrium will only be restored when interest rates have moved to a level where the combined demand for money of all economic units just exhausts the available supply. Given other factors, such as the level of national income, there is therefore a unique relationship between the quantity of money and the rate of interest. The authorities can control one or the other, but not both.[2]

---

[2] For the moment we ignore devices designed to distort the demand for, or supply of, funds such as administrative ceilings on bank lending or interest rates.

Consistency of the two theories

In the pure non-monetary theory of interest, changes in the quantity of money have no effect at all on interest rates and influence only the price level. In the extreme version of the Keynesian theory, as can be seen from the earlier quotation from the 'General Theory', it is the demand for money that is all important, with thrift and productivity playing no role.

But these rather stylised extreme positions conceal a much greater consistency in the two approaches than appears on the surface. The classical economists who stressed the importance of the supply and demand for 'loanable funds' recognised that sudden changes in the quantity of money might cause the desire to save and invest to get out of line. They also recognised that hoarding and dishoarding of money would add to the supply and demand for money which reflected normal saving and investment. They were not so naive as to imagine that all prices would adapt immediately to monetary changes, noting that there would be lags in the adjustment of the economy with effects on the level of demand in the interim.

From the other side, most Keynesians accepted that any divergence between the rate of interest needed to balance the supply and demand for money and that needed to secure a balance between saving and investment at full employment would set up pressures tending to bring the two rates together. An increase in the quantity of money would, as we have noted, initially result in a decline in the rate of interest. The fall in the money rate of interest would cause the desire to invest to run ahead of the desire to save. This would set up inflationary pressures which would tend to cause prices and money incomes to rise. As money incomes rose, however, some of the increased quantity of money would be needed to finance the higher level of current transactions, and the demand to borrow funds from banks would increase. As a result the interest rate would tend to rise back towards its original level, thus tending to reduce the inflationary pressures.

The broad mechanism by which interest rates adjust to monetary and real factors is implicit in both the loanable funds and liquidity preference theories. The main difference between the two formulations is that the liquidity preference theory gives much more explicit emphasis to the process by which one state of long-term equilibrium merges into another. By treating the question in terms of the demand and supply for money, it concentrates on the determination of interest rates in the market at each point in time. Loanable funds theory, on the other hand, directs its main attention to the level of interest rates which will emerge once transitory disturbances have been eliminated.

It is already clear that forces will exist which tend to bring market interest rates towards the level which will balance saving and investment in the longer term. But we can go further than this and show that, in equilibrium, the interest rate which balances the supply and demand for loanable funds (for simplicity, 'bonds') must be the same as that which balances the supply and demand for money.

Consider first an economy with only two goods, say potatoes and beef. In such an economy anyone who wants to buy beef must by definition want to give potatoes in exchange (there is no money). If the supply and demand for beef are in balance, then by definition the supply and demand for potatoes (which is the other side of the coin) must also be in balance. If we add another product, say wheat, then anyone seeking to buy beef must be offering either wheat or potatoes. If the supply and demand for wheat and beef are both in balance then by definition the supply and demand for potatoes must be in balance. By extension it can be seen that, if there are n products in an economy, the fact that the markets for $(n-1)$ goods are in balance means that the nth market must be too.

The relevance of this to the determination of interest rates is as follows: if an economy has n commodities, plus money, plus bonds, there will be $(n+2)$ items entering into transactions. However, there will only be $(n+1)$ independently determined prices. Given the money price of the n commodities, only one of the remaining two prices, of money and bonds, can be determined independently. From a purely mathematical point of view, it does not matter which. If we regard the rate of interest as the price which equates the supply and demand for money, and all commodity markets are in balance, then by definition the supply and demand for bonds must be in balance too. On the other hand, if the supply and demand for commodities are in balance, and the rate of interest is seen as the price equating the supply and demand for bonds, the supply and demand for money must be in balance. It must be the case that one and the same interest rate balances supply and demand for money *and* bonds when the economy is in an equilibrium state.

Another way of showing the equivalence of the two theories is to consider the ingredients of the demand and supply functions for money and bonds respectively. In a given period the demand for bonds (loosely defined as all claims on the future) consists of: current net saving, plus any reduction (less any increase) in desired money balances. The supply of bonds is net borrowing to finance investment, plus desired conversions of existing bonds into money form. Since new saving and investment must turn out to be equal *ex post*,[3] any net increase in the desire to hold bonds must reflect a net decline in the desire to hold money. It may be seen that the demand and supply for bonds is the other side of the coin from the supply and demand for money.

However, simply to show that in a formal sense the two theories of interest produce the same result does not necessarily mean that they are equally useful as a means of understanding economic processes. To say that the supply and demand for bonds must be equated by the rate of interest is only useful if we can identify and measure the factors governing the supply and demand for bonds. In the loanable funds theory, productivity and thrift are the two main factors. As we have shown, however, the flow of new saving going into bonds is, in the short run, small relative to the stock of outstanding financial assets which can be converted into bonds. The supply and demand for bonds is therefore composed not simply of flows of new assets, but of preferences for existing assets. In the short run, it is probably more realistic to think of the interest rate as being determined by factors which dictate the allocation of existing wealth between money and bonds, i.e., by the demand to hold a given stock of money.

The longer the period we are considering, however, the more realistic it becomes to think in terms of flows. If the supply and demand for money interact to produce a rate of interest where the desire to invest exceeds the desire to save, the demand for resources at existing prices will exceed the supply. To restore balance, prices will have to rise. As the level of money national income increases, the desire to hold transactions balances will be higher, so that the demand for money will be greater. With no change in the quantity of money, higher demand will cause its price (the rate of interest) to rise, and this process will go on until an interest rate is reached at which desired investment and saving are equal. Then money national income will stop rising.

A similar process will restore equilibrium when the initial cause of disturbance is a rate of interest that is too high. At the high rate of

[3] This derives from the so-called national income identity. All expenditure can be divided into consumption and investment; and all income can be divided into that part which is spent on consumption and that part which is saved. But the expenditure of one economic unit is the income of another, so that savings must equal investment. Formally:

$$\text{Expenditure} = \text{current spending} + \text{capital spending}$$
$$\text{Income} = \text{current spending} + \text{saving}$$
$$\text{Income} = \text{expenditure}$$
$$\text{therefore, Saving} = \text{capital spending (investment).}$$

interest, the desire to invest will fall short of the desire to save, so that demand will fall, causing unemployment leading to deflation. As a result, prices will tend to fall, causing the quantity of money to become larger as a proportion of money national income. The greater relative availability of money will cause rates to decline, and investment will gradually pick up.

The foregoing can be summarised as follows: in the short run, the market rate of interest can be different from the level necessary to balance savings and investment at full employment. There is, however, a mechanism which tends, at least in theory, to push interest rates back towards an equilibrium level where desired savings equal desired investment. This mechanism, however, is a long-run tendency, which may not be particularly strong in the short-run periods of most interest to policy-makers.

The term structure of interest rates

So far we have talked of *the* rate of interest; and traditionally much of the theory of interest has assumed that there is one rate of interest. In fact, of course, there are numerous rates of interest, and differences cannot simply be explained by the credit risk of different borrowers. The term structure of interest rates is significant because different rates may be performing different economic functions. If, for example, it is short-term rates of interest which balance the supply and demand for money, and long-term rates which affect savings and investment decisions, it is clearly important for monetary policy to know how the two rates are related to one another.

In a world of perfect foresight and firmly held expectations, the long-term rate of interest would simply be the average of expected future short-term rates. If the rate for one-year borrowing is 5%, and the rate for two-year borrowing is 6%, this implies that people expect the one-year interest rate during the second year to be 7%. If they thought that the rate would be more than 7%, nobody would hold a two-year bond, since he could do better by holding a one-year bond and then buying one yielding 7% + a year later. On the other hand, if the rate in a year's time was expected to be less than 7%, say 6½%, nobody would hold a one-year bond, since they could do better by holding the two-year bond, and selling it after a year.[4] In general, we

---

[4] This is because the two-year bond would yield an income of 6% during the first year, and would at the end of the year stand at a discount on its redemption price of roughly ½%). Thus the total yield (income plus capital appreciation) would be something over the 5% that would be yielded by the one-year bond.

can say that people will switch between longer and shorter bonds in order to equalise the expected yields over the period for which they wish to hold their wealth in financial assets; and that this will be achieved when the rate on long-term bonds is equal to the average of expected short-period yields.

This is the so-called 'expectations' theory of the determination of the yield curve. (The yield curve is the relationship between yields on similar assets with different terms to maturity.) It is intuitively appealing, and indeed incontrovertible in a world of perfect foresight and certainty. Modifications need to be introduced, however, to adapt the theory to real world conditions. In the first place, extraneous conditions such as differential taxes and credit-worthiness will tend to distort the smoothness of the curve. Secondly, and more importantly, it is of the nature of expectations about the future that they are held with less than perfect certainty. Uncertainty is a cost which investors (other than gamblers) are prepared to pay a premium to avoid. In the case of financial assets with a long life, the risk that investors face is of an unforeseen change in interest rates during the life of the asset. This will result in a change in the capital value of the asset concerned; in case the bond has to be sold before maturity, this would have to be reckoned along with the interest yield as part of the return. The return on assets of different term may therefore reflect the uncertainty with which the return is expected.

Unfortunately, this does not tell us very much about what shape we should expect the yield curve to have. Those investors who want to have a steady long-term income would regard a long-term bond as safer than holding a succession of short-term securities whose yield cannot be accurately forecast at the time the initial purchase is made. On the other hand, wealth-holders who set store by having a stable value of their investment would regard short-period assets as safer. The existence of the two different types of investor will have off-setting effects on the shape of the yield curve, to a certain extent. If, however, the yield curve shows a tendency to slope upwards, or downwards, this would indicate a predominance of investors with one kind of preference. The fact that long-term yields are higher than short-term more frequently than vice versa would seem to indicate that capital-certainty is more highly valued than income-certainty. (Figure 3.3)

Apart from modifications to theory made necessary by the existence of uncertainty, further changes are necessary when the existence of market imperfections and the imperfect substitutability of assets are recognised. There are costs and inconvenience in moving between sectors of the capital market to take advantage of shifts in rates. The

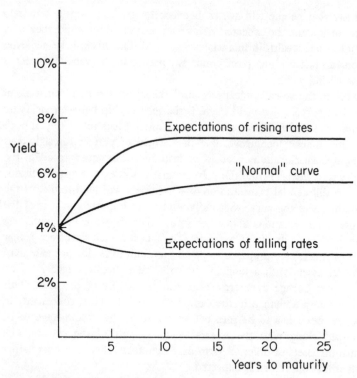

Fig. 3·3   Typical time – yield curves

frequent revision of asset portfolios requires continuous expert surveillance, and the activity of buying and selling will involve costs in the form of commissions, etc. For these reasons, it is believed that there is probably a certain amount of 'segmentation' in markets. A change in yield on assets of a certain maturity will induce a substantial change in price on assets of similar term, but rather less change as one moves further away on the maturity spectrum.

Segmentation may also be induced by institutional factors. Certain investors (e.g., trustees) may be required by their articles to hold only a certain kind of security. Also, market conventions, e.g., the classification of bonds under 5 years as 'shorts' and those under one year as 'reserve assets' may push wealth-holders into asset preferences not strictly based on the inherent properties of the assets. Finally, taxation patterns will also influence the resultant picture.

Some economists have suggested that central banks could use the apparent 'segmentation' of markets to 'twist' the yield curve deliberately to fit in with official policies. Purchases of long-term bonds combined with sales of shorter dated securities should tend to reduce prices of short stocks relative to longs. This will cause longer-term rates to be lower than would otherwise be the case, and short-term rates to be higher. If the government wished to have low long-term rates to encourage fixed capital investment and high short-term rates to discourage an outflow of mobile funds abroad, such a policy would, at least in principle, have much to recommend it.

Further reading

Axilrod, S. and Young, R., Interest rates and monetary policy, *Federal Reserve Bulletin*, September 1962.

Conard, J. W., *An Introduction to the Theory of Interest*. University of California Press, 1959.

Day, A. C. L., op. cit., Chapters 4–8.

Harrod, R. F., op. cit., Chapter 3.

Lutz, F., *The Theory of Interest*, University of Chicago Press, 1967, especially Chapters 10 and 11.

Meiselman, David, *The Term Structure of Interest Rates*, Englewood Cliffs, N.J., Prentice Hall, 1962.

Malkiel, Burton, *The Term Structure of Interest Rates*, Princeton University Press, 1966.

Robinson, Joan, The rate of interest, in *The Rate of Interest and Other Essays*, London, Macmillan, 1936.

Wicksell, Knut, *Interest and Prices*, London, Macmillan, 1936.

Questions for discussion

1 What effect does the existence of financial intermediaries have on the rate of interest?

2 In what ways does a budget deficit affect the rate of interest?

3 What effect would you expect the discovery of a major new industrial process to have on interest rates?

4 Can interest rates be negative?

5 Under what circumstances would long-term rates of interest be below short-term rates?

4

The importance of money

Having in the first two chapters discussed what money is and how it comes into existence, and in the third discussed its relationship with the rate of interest, it is time to investigate what significance money has for the working of the economy at large. The question we shall examine can be more precisely put as being the manner and extent to which changes in the quantity of money affect the size and distribution of national income and the price level.

This is a subject that has been a topic for debate in academic circles and outside for two centuries or more; and at the present time the debate is raging as fiercely as ever. The fact that the most distinguished theoreticians are unable to come to agreement on major points must serve as a warning that the following brief survey cannot expect to resolve the issue.

We shall trace three main developments in theory. The starting point must be the classical Quantity Theory of Money. This held sway as an interpretation unchallenged in theory for many years, but of little practical use. The Keynesian revolution proposed a different and in most respects much more fruitful way of looking at the economic system, which has come to be known as the Income–Expenditure Theory. This method of analysis continues to have quite wide adherence among professional economists, though naturally not all Keynesians agree on details. Finally, in the 1960s, there has emerged a 'monetarist' school, led by Professor Milton Friedman of Chicago, which puts forward a doctrine resembling the old quantity theory in some essentials, but avoiding its more simplistic assumptions.

The first part of what follows is primarily of historical interest, as no economists now subscribe to the old quantity theory; but it nevertheless serves as a useful introduction to set in perspective the two views which are now most widely held—Keynesianism and Monetarism. Later in the chapter, we have a look at the ways in which research has narrowed the area of difference between the two schools.

The quantity theory

If money is solely a medium of exchange, the classical theorists argued, it should not affect the relative prices of other goods. If it costs twice as much to rear a cow as to rear a sheep, the fact that money is used to facilitate the exchange should not alter the ratio in which the goods are traded. If a cow costs £10, then a sheep must cost £5; if a cow is worth £100, then a sheep will be £50. Money facilitates exchanges by avoiding the need for barter and by providing a numeraire which permits people to compare prices more easily. This, however, does not affect the *relative* prices of goods and services, nor should it affect the total amount of goods and services that is produced.

Since relative prices depend on real factors, it was argued by the classical economists that money could affect only the overall price level. This line of reasoning was reflected in the classical quantity theory equation:

$$MV = PT$$

M is the quantity of the medium of exchange, or money, and V is the velocity of circulation, or the number of times each unit of money is 'turned over' in expenditure, as an average during a given period of time. The product MV is therefore the total value of expenditure in that time period. On the other side of the equation, T represents some measure of the physical volume of transactions in the economy, and P is the average value of each transaction. It is easy to see that PT is also equal to the total value of expenditure, so that MV must by definition equal PT.

An identity such as this is not particularly helpful as an *explanation* of what is happening in the economy, and the quantity theory is only significant because of the assumptions which it makes about the various ingredients of the equation. The particular assumptions made by the quantity theory were that V and T were independent of what was happening to the quantity of money, so that changes in M had a direct effect on P. The reasons for the independence of V were as follows: Since money was not wanted for itself, but only as a means of effecting exchanges, the amount people held against a given level of income and expenditure would be determined by institutional factors in making payments and receipts, and this would not change in the short run. For example, it was accepted that a society where the majority of income earners were paid weekly would need a smaller 'float' of circulating currency than one where all other factors were the same but the prevailing custom was to pay workers monthly. But it was assumed that institutional custom would not be subject to sudden change over a short period.

It will be seen that the value of T represents the size of the economy's real output. The independence of T was the result of assuming that full employment was the natural state of the economy so that a change in M could not change T. If any resources were left unemployed, or goods left unsold, the forces of competition were assumed to drive wages or prices down until supply and demand were brought back into balance. Of course, simple observation showed that this did not always happen in practice, but generally speaking unemployment was regarded as a temporary aberration from the normal state.

Thus the importance of money, from the classical quantity theorist's viewpoint, was simply as the determinant of the price level. Changes in the quantity of money were not seen as having any lasting effect on the size or distribution of real income. If all wages and prices changed to the same extent, so that there was no alteration in relative prices, or in the purchasing power of incomes and wealth, the change in the price level would be no more significant than the administrative change effected by the French government in declaring 100 old francs to be worth 1 new franc. In such a case, the quantity of money would be 'neutral' with respect to the size and distribution of real income.

The 'neutrality' of money and hence the whole of the classical quantity theory depend on a set of assumptions about how the economy works that is rather unrealistic and thus not much use as an aid to practical policy making. Some of these assumptions are:

a Wage and price flexibility. In order for money to be neutral, wages and prices must be able to adjust as fast as the quantity of money changes. If they do not, then any change in demand to which a change in the quantity of money gives rise will not be fully felt in an equivalent change in the price level, but will also have an effect on unemployment and the level of economic activity. There are obviously difficulties in wages and prices responding immediately to *every* small change in the money stock, but in a more general way there may be rigidities, particularly in the downward direction, which make wages and prices very inflexible in certain circumstances. In terms of the quantity equation $MV=PT$, the fact that P is not completely flexible means that T, the level of real output, will have to have an element of flexibility.

b There must be no 'distribution effects'. People will have a variety of different assets and liabilities, some of which will be denominated in money terms (e.g., fixed interest securities) and some of which will be in real terms (e.g., fixed assets and equity securities). An increase in the quantity of money which results in a rise in the price level will reduce the value of claims expressed in money terms, and this will tend to benefit debtors and work to the disadvantage of creditors. Not only will this tend to redistribute wealth from lenders to borrowers, it may also have an effect on the overall level of spending. This will occur if the contraction in spending by lenders—brought about by their reduced wealth—is not exactly matched by the increased spending of borrowers. If there exists a large national debt, for example, the real value of the securities held by the private sector will decline as a result of inflation. If people feel poorer as a result, they may well curtail their expenditure, but it is much less likely that the government will, at least in the short term, be prompted to increase its spending.

c Inelastic expectations. If a change in the price level induces expectations of further change—either in the same direction or back towards the old price level—people will adjust their behaviour to anticipate this. If they think prices will go on rising, they will clearly try to economise on money assets, which will be depreciating in real value. Conversely, if they expect the price level to fall back again to its old level, they will want to hold more assets with a fixed money value. In the former case, the velocity of circulation will rise, while in the latter, it will fall.

d There must be no 'money illusion', i.e., people must respond to changes in their real incomes rather than to money incomes. If they do not, the kind of situation can arise where the effect of higher money incomes in encouraging spending is not exactly matched by the effect of higher prices in discouraging spending.

From this brief review, it can easily be seen that the conditions for perfect neutrality are never likely to hold exactly. And simple observation tells us that the economy is very rarely at a point of precise full employment equilibrium, even though it may be continuously tending towards such a point. It is therefore much more than just an academic question to ask how monetary factors are likely to affect the way in which the economy moves towards its equilibrium position. This subject is often referred to as the 'transmission mechanism' by which the influence of monetary factors is felt on the real economy. We examine first the Keynesian version of the transmission mechanism.

Keynesian theory

For a long time before Keynes published his major work, *The General Theory of Employment, Interest and Money*, it had been recognised that the old style quantity theory did not provide a very good explanation of the way the economy worked in practice. Various economists, notably Wicksell, evolved explanations of why the achievement of a quantity theory equilibrium would be delayed by the existence of friction in the economic system. But it was not until Keynes that a serious attempt was made to grapple with the consequences of the fact that modern economies did not appear to move at all quickly towards the assumed equilibrium. Since Keynes wrote, of course, theory has been refined and modified, and what follows is a rather stylised version of the general method of analysis of income–expenditure, or Keynesian, theorists.

One of the main points at which the Keynesian conception of money's role differs from that of the old quantity theory is in the emphasis on its importance as an *asset* to hold as well as its role of a medium of exchange. Once money is seen as being held for its own sake, it can be treated in terms of ordinary demand and supply analysis. The holders of money measure its usefulness on the one hand —in terms of convenience and liquidity—against its cost on the other, —the return they could have had by holding other assets.

When the supply of a commodity is increased, conventional analysis tells us that its relative price must go down if the increased supply is to be absorbed. For an ordinary commodity, this means a reduction in the money price of the commodity in increased supply, while the money price of all other commodities stays more or less unchanged. But what happens when the commodity whose supply changes is money itself? Since it is *relative* prices which determine the amount of a commodity demanded, the price of commodities other than money must rise, so that the amount of money desired can rise to meet the now higher supply. So far, there is little difference between the quantity theorists and Keynesians. But Keynesians point out that, if money is viewed as an *asset*, certain commodities will be closer substitutes for it than others. Therefore the relative price of these close substitutes will exercise a greater impact on the demand for money than changes in the price of commodities which are not good substitutes for money. This point can perhaps be made more clearly by an example from the realm of real goods. If the price of oranges is for some reason fixed, and we want to increase the demand for oranges by varying the money price of other commodities, we shall achieve the largest result by buying a lot of tangerines and thus forcing their price up. Since tangerines and oranges are close substitutes, any substantial discrepancy in relative price will cause a switch in demand to the cheaper commodity. A change in the price of, say, newspapers, even if it was quite substantial, would not have much effect on the demand for oranges. (Eventually, of course, the price of tangerines would come down again, as growers responded to the greater profitability of tangerine production. But this would require time for investment in new tangerine orchards.)

When the supply of money changes, therefore, Keynesians believe that the most immediate impact of the change will be on the price of substitutes. The closest substitute for money is a short-term financial asset. Let us take the case where the monetary authorities allow a government deficit to add to the money supply. The result will be the creation of money balances in excess of what is desired by wealth-holders at existing prices and interest rates. Portfolios are thus no longer in equilibrium, and the holders of the excess money balances will in the first instance try to switch into short-term financial assets. The additional demand for these assets will drive their price up (and therefore push the interest yield received per £ paid for them down). If the yield on short-term financial assets goes down, some holders will try and switch out into longer-term assets, thus depressing the yield on these assets also. Equilibrium in financial markets will be restored when relative interest rates on the various financial assets make wealth-holders just satisfied with the distribution of these assets.

This can be expressed formally by saying that the demand for money is a function of income levels (which determine the need for transactions balances) and the rate of interest (which determines the relative attractiveness of money and alternative financial assets). Mathematically,

$$M_d = a_1 + a_2 Y - a_3 r$$

where M_d = demand for money, Y = incomes, r = rate of interest, and a_1, a_2 and a_3 are coefficients whose values reflect the relationship between the demand for money and the value of the other variables.

From the above equation, it may be seen that changes in Y and r may be offsetting from the point of view of the demand for money. A rise in income levels will increase people's desire to hold money; while a rise in the interest rate paid on other financial assets will encourage people to economise on their holdings of money. A given quantity of money will, therefore, just satisfy the demand for it with a number of combinations of incomes and interest rates. In Fig. 4.1, the line LL represents all those points at which the demand for money is in equilibrium, assuming a fixed stock of money. An increase in income from X_1 to X_2 would be exactly balanced, in terms of its effect on the demand for money, by a rise in interest rates from r_1 to r_2. An increase in the stock of money would be reflected in the diagram by a new curve below and to the right of LL (say L'L'). It will be seen that an increase in the money stock is associated with higher national income, or lower interest rates, or both.

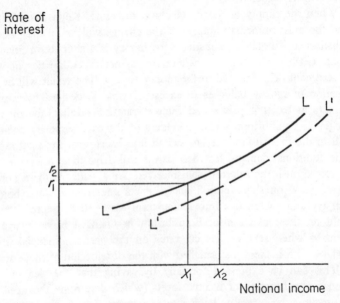

Fig. 4·1 Factors influencing the demand for money

If a change in the quantity of money is not immediately associated with a change in income levels (i.e., it does not result from additional spending), its initial effect is seen by Keynesians as being on short-term interest rates, and through them right along the spectrum of financial assets. The size and predictability of the impact, however, is thought to become less, the further one goes along the chain of asset switches which the initial disturbance sets in motion.

The interest rate, however, is not only the yield necessary to per-suade an investor to hold his funds in a particular security; it is also the cost of borrowing, and for a businessman an element in the cost of his capital investment. For the economy to be in equilibrium, the marginal cost of investment to a businessman must equal the marginal return on investment. Otherwise it would pay him to expand or cut back his spending programme. Starting from an equilibrium position, a change in interest rates brings about a divergence between the cost of investment and the return on investment and either encourages or restrains capital formation. This is shown in Fig. 4.2, where the line

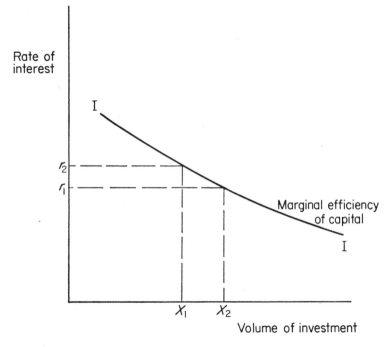

Fig. 4·2   Marginal efficiency of capital

II represents the declining profitability of investment, or 'marginal efficiency of capital', to use the Keynesian jargon. If the interest rate drops from r_2 to r_1 in this chart, the amount of investment which it is profitable to undertake will rise from X_1 to X_2.

Changes in the amount of capital formation, or investment, have, in the income–expenditure theory, a multiple effect on total demand. This comes about in the following way: If there is an increase of £1 million in investment, this will increase the incomes (including profits) of suppliers of goods by that amount. Out of their increased incomes, a proportion, x, will go in higher taxes and savings, leaving £$(1 - x)$ million to be spent at the second round. If the recipients of this expenditure save the same proportion of their new income, they will have £ $(1 - x)(1 - x)$ million to spend.[1]

What this means is that in income–expenditure analysis there is a predictable relationship, acting through the quantity of investment, between interest rates and the level of the national income. This means that in Fig. 4.2, we can substitute national income for investment on the horizontal axis. But if we do this the axes are the same as in Fig. 4.1, giving the result shown in Fig. 4.3.

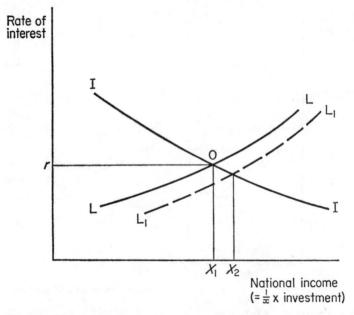

Fig. 4.3 Determination of national income

This shows a single equilibrium point for national income. Point O is the only place on the diagram which is able to reconcile equilibrium in the financial market (which would obtain anywhere along the line LL) with equilibrium in the market for real goods (which occurs anywhere on the line II). It should be noted that 'equilibrium' in the market for real goods is not necessarily a point at which there will

[1] When a new equilibrium is restored, total incomes will be higher by $1 + (1 - x) + (1 - x)^2 \ldots$, etc., which can be shown to equal $1/x$ times the initial investment, which is sometimes known as the investment multiplier.

be full employment. If the equilibrium interest rate established by the interaction of the two curves causes the demand for real resources to fall short of the available supply at existing prices, most Keynesians believe the initial consequence will be underemployment.

Increasing the quantity of money would have the effect of shifting the LL curve to the right, say to L'L'. This would lower interest rates and the cheaper cost of borrowing would in turn stimulate investment demand and cause national income to rise to X_2.

Although interest rates are seen by Keynesians as the main route whereby monetary changes affect the real economy, there are two other factors worthy of mention. First, a change in interest rates affects the capital value of financial assets, and may thus make people feel richer or poorer, causing them to adjust their expenditure. This is known as a 'wealth effect'. To the extent that financial assets held by one group of people are the liabilities of another, there is no change in net wealth. There may nevertheless be a change in overall expenditure if the spending patterns of creditors respond to changes in wealth differently from those of debtors. This is likely to be the case with assets which are the liabilities of the government, where any change in the value of the assets held by the owners of government debt is matched only by a rather intangible change in taxpayer's future liabilities.

Secondly, there may be institutional rigidities, which cause actual interest rates to diverge from freely determined market rates. For example, the Building Societies Association attaches importance to rate stability, and prefers to recommend changes in rates to members as infrequently as possible. In the periods between rate changes, Building Societies may have to ration the funds they have available, not by the price mechanism, but in some other way. Some potential borrowers who are prepared to pay the going rate are unsatisfied. A similar 'rationing' process takes place when banks operate under officially imposed lending ceilings or interest-rate ceilings. This rationing is known as a 'credit availability effect'.

Although Keynesian theory does postulate a role for monetary factors, it should be noted at once that their influence is usually seen as a subordinate one. In terms of Fig. 4.3, it is clear that the impact of changes in the quantity of money on the level of national income depends on the relative slopes of the two curves. Since increasing the quantity of money initially causes the curve LL to move to the right, the flatter the curve, the less vertical movement will take place, and therefore the smaller will be the interest rate consequences. Turning to the II curve, the steeper it is, the less responsive investment (and therefore income) will be to such changes in interest rates as do occur. At the limit, either a vertical II curve or a horizontal LL curve would mean that monetary changes would have no effect at all on the real economy.

The subordinate role which most Keynesians usually assign to monetary policy reflects their view of the relative slopes of the two curves. Since monetary policy operates through interest rates, it can only affect those decisions where interest rates are a significant element in the cost calculation. The choice between spending and saving has been thought to be virtually unaffected by interest rate considerations, and in many investment decisions interest payments make up only a small proportion of total costs. It is only the longer-lived investments where interest becomes really significant, and in not all of these cases are decision-makers responsive to interest changes. In the public sector, for example, investment programmes are decided at intervals and, in the UK, not normally varied for interest rate considerations. House purchase, which involves a very long-lived investment, is in Britain traditionally financed by loans whose interest rate fluctuates with short-term rates. House buyers are not more than marginally deterred by currently high levels of interest rates because they know the rate of interest on their loan will revert to a lower level when interest rates fall.[2]

The kind of fluctuations in interest rates that would be needed to have a significant impact on the level of demand would be so wide, many Keynesians believe, that they would cause wide variations in the capital value of portfolios of assets. The result might be occasional crises of confidence in the financial system, and possibly bankruptcies. In any event, whether or not these catastrophic consequences occurred, the uncertainty as to the capital value of claims and liabilities at future dates would undermine the effectiveness of the financial system by tending to discourage both lenders and borrowers.

To recapitulate, the effectiveness of a policy of controlling the money stock depends, in Keynesian analysis, on:

a a change in the quantity of money having a substantial effect on interest rates.

b a change in interest rates having a substantial effect on demand.

Ten or fifteen years ago, it would have been possible to find a large number of economists who doubted whether either of these conditions

[2] In the US, where it is customary for mortgage rates to be fixed for the life of the loan, monetary policy may have a considerably greater effect.

would hold in practice. The Radcliffe Committee doubted the power of money supply to affect interest rates: 'In a highly developed financial system ... there are many highly liquid assets which are close substitutes for money.... If there is less money to go around ... rates of interest will rise. But they will not, unaided, rise by much....' (Para 392). And inquiries made of businessmen, both by the Radcliffe Committee and by earlier investigators (especially some famous studies undertaken at Oxford in 1939) appeared to indicate that the very people who were supposed to be financially sophisticated enough to respond to interest rate variations in practice paid little attention to them.

Because they do not have much faith in the efficacy of monetary policy, most Keynesians have tended to emphasise other means of controlling the economy, such as fiscal policy. Fiscal policy, by changing levels of government spending and taxation across the board can act directly on the size of disposable incomes. Assuming, as Keynesians do, that after-tax income is the main determinant of spending, a tax cut can thus have a quicker and much more predictable effect on economic activity than changes in the stock of money.

The 'new' quantity theory

The new quantity theory is a school of thought generally associated with the name of Professor Friedman of Chicago, and often called monetarism. Unlike the old quantity theorists, the new monetarists have abandoned the assumption that the economy will automatically operate at full employment. In other words, they accept the effective demand approach to income determination in the short term. Where they differ from Keynesians is in believing the velocity of circulation to be predictable (not necessarily constant). In terms of the old quantity theory equation ($MV = PT$) they therefore see changes in M as having an effect on the value of PT.

Because they stress this relationship between the quantity of money and the level of effective demand, it is sometimes asserted that monetarists do not believe the impact of monetary policy to be transmitted through interest rates. This is not strictly true, as the following quotation from an important monetarist work shows:

> The crucial issue that corresponds to the distinction between the 'credit' (i.e. the Keynesian) and 'monetary' effects of monetary policy is not whether changes in the stock of money operate through interest rates but rather, the range of interest rates considered. On the 'credit' view, monetary policy impinges on a narrow and well-defined range

of capital assets and a correspondingly narrow range of associated expenditures. . . . On the 'monetary' view, monetary policy impinges on a much broader range of capital assets and correspondingly broader range of associated expenditures.[3]

Where Keynesians see money as being just one among several liquid financial assets, and therefore quite a close substitute for them, it is in the nature of monetarist theory to regard money as unique — the one asset that is not wanted for itself but as a repository for wealth waiting to be spent — a 'temporary abode of purchasing power'. Because of this, the degree to which a change in the quantity of money will induce people to try and move into alternative liquid financial assets is strictly limited. Money is no more a substitute for one asset than for any other. And people are just as likely to use excess money balances to buy real goods as to purchase financial securities.

How does this tie in with Friedman's statement above that monetary policy operates through interest rates? To see this, we must divorce the concept of interest from the financial markets, in the context of which we usually think of interest as being paid. Interest as a concept is simply a way of relating a flow of returns over time to a present value. A house, for example, yields services of accommodation, and the value of this future stream of services can be related to the cost of the house as an 'interest' yield. The same applies to cars, TV sets, clothes, and indeed any commodity which is not consumed at the time of purchase.

In a notional equilibrium situation, everyone would have exactly those quantities of assets so that the 'return' to the last £'s worth of each asset was the same. But while Keynesians would expect a change in the supply of money to affect first the price of 'near-money' assets and the demand for real assets only via this effect, monetarists see the influence as direct. As the money increases, the convenience yield of the last unit of money balances falls (as holdings are subject to diminishing marginal returns), and holders of money find themselves out of equilibrium. The effect of this disequilibrium will be to cause a small but pervasive change in planned expenditures on all assets. Monetarists therefore believe that the response of expenditure to a change in relative yields on money and other assets is quite sensitive. In this rather broad sense, 'interest' effects are more important in monetarist theory than in Keynesian.

If this is so, why do monetarists not give more explicit attention to

[3] Friedman and Meiselman, in *Stabilisation Policies*, published by the Commission on Money and Credit.

interest rates, and include them in their models? This is partly because many of the interest rates which monetarists believe are important in affecting expenditure are not observable, and are thought to move differently from the observable ones. Even if there was a reliable index of relative yields on all these non-financial assets, this still might not be a good guide to real interest rates. If prices are rising rapidly, interest rates will be high simply in anticipation of continued inflation, and the real rate of interest need not be very high at all.

Furthermore, if the effect of monetary policy is, as has just been suggested, widely spread over the generality of all assets, the impact in *particular* markets will be small and may not be measurable with the statistical tools economists have available. So instead of pursuing a will-o'-the-wisp effect through a complicated series of statistical equations, monetarist theorists prefer to stick to one or two basic relationships which quite simply link the level of the money supply with the value of national output.

Although it is common ground amongst monetarists that the stock of money is the main (though not necessarily the only) determinant of the level of national income, many believe that the main effect of changes in the money stock is delayed, possibly by as much as a year or so after a policy action is taken. Because of this, and because they believe the lag to be a variable one, these monetarists believe it is dangerous to use monetary policy to try and smooth out the trade cycle. The risk is that the policy that seems to be needed at a particular point in time may be the exact opposite of what is needed when it begins to take effect. This risk can be averted by prescribing a simple rule for a steady expansion of the money stock, with little or no discretion allowed to the monetary authorities to vary it.

Some evidence from statistical tests

Economics being a subject where theories are, at least in principle, capable of being statistically tested, there has been no shortage of attempts to distinguish whether the Keynesian or monetarist approach fits the facts best. To some extent, the most significant result of much of the work that has been done has been to reveal the inability of various statistical methods to distinguish conclusively between the hypotheses. However, although the work has not been wholly successful in producing an accepted consensus view, it has narrowed the area of disagreement, and is worthy of study.

Perhaps the most straightforward test of the impact which money has on the economy is to look at the evidence of historical experience to see whether fluctuations in the stock of money have been followed by fluctuations in the level of national income. This exercise was done for the US economy by Professors Friedman and Schwartz with, it appeared, quite striking results. Fluctuations in the level of national income seemed to follow quite closely fluctuations in the rate of growth of the money supply, though with a lag of somewhere between six and eighteen months. This seemed to show that money was the driving force. In another piece of work, Professors Friedman and Meiselman attempted to compare the predictive power of monetarist and income–expenditure hypotheses. Essentially, they did this by testing the relative stability of the investment multiplier and the money/income relationship over a long historical period. Their findings seemed to indicate that money was more important than investment in determining income levels.

Keynesians, however, soon pointed out that these various findings were consistent with several explanations. The lag which Friedman and Schwartz had discovered, for example, was largely the result of comparing the *level* of national output with the *rate of growth* of the money supply. It is a natural phenomenon of any cyclical series that its rate of growth reaches a peak before its absolute value. Once it was compared with the level of money stock, the lag more or less disappeared, and Keynesians were able to demonstrate that the remaining connection between money and national income could be the result not only of money influencing economic activity, but of expanding economic activity generating a need for additional money balances which were passively created. This latter explanation seemed to be quite plausible since for many years central banks had devoted greater emphasis to keeping an even keel in financial markets, and therefore providing cash when needed, than to keeping a tight hold on the money supply.

As far as Friedman and Meiselman's test was concerned, the principal objection was that it involved a very artificial version of the income–expenditure model. This model, as normally formulated, involves a series of equations which reflect the interaction of a number of economic processes. To test the performance of a single equation in isolation, it was argued, did not constitute a fair test of the Keynesian hypothesis.

Objections were also raised to a series of studies undertaken in the Federal Reserve Bank of St Louis. These compared the responsiveness of the economy to fiscal and monetary policy actions respectively. Although this study showed a much higher correlation and a much more immediate response between monetary actions and the real economy than was the case for fiscal policy, the nature of the causation mechanism was still open to question. It was possible, for example, that the money supply was being allowed to adjust passively to changes in the demand for money caused by movements in economic activity unrelated to financial factors.

Nevertheless, the historical association between money and national income is striking. And the link has been demonstrated for a wide variety of countries and in quite widely different time periods. Therefore, although it is possible to entertain doubts about the precise factors which initiate changes in the money value of national income, it is scarcely possible to deny that changes in the stock of money play at least a *permissive* role in determining the level of national income.

Because of the objections to direct tests of the predictive power of Keynesian and monetarist models, attention has been focused on the more technical question of the precise mechanism by which money affects the economy; whether indirectly, through causing changes in interest rates, or directly by causing people to buy or sell real assets. As we have seen in the quotation noted earlier, this is not quite such a fundamental divergence of view as it appears at first sight. Both views imply an interest rate effect; the difference is a question of the *range* of interest rates through which expenditure decisions are influenced.

Early attempts to discover a role for interest rates in expenditure decisions were markedly unsuccessful. Surveys were carried out which appeared to show that in fact the rate of interest played a relatively minor role in businessmen's decisions to invest. The problem with surveys, however, is that the response very often depends on the manner in which a question is asked. Also, although interest rates may be a minor contributory factor in each decision, and thus disregarded by an individual respondent, if they systematically enter each decision their cumulative impact may be quite large.

Statistical studies avoid the 'subjectiveness' problem involved in surveys, but they pose problems of their own. When changes in spending are correlated with changes in interest rates, the result is usually either inconclusive, or actually perverse (i.e., an increase in interest rates appears to be associated with an increase in spending). The reason for this is not far to seek. An increase in spending brought about for some external reason (say a change in tax rates) may increase the demand for borrowed funds, and thus push up the interest rate. In such a case the change in demand is affecting interest rates to a greater extent than the other way around. Another intractable problem is that only nominal interest rates are measurable, whereas it is 'real' interest rates (i.e., nominal rates adjusted to take account of anticipated inflation) that are presumably more important in determining expenditure decisions.

More fruitful methods of ascertaining the importance of money have therefore had to proceed by a more roundabout route. One such route is to ask why people hold the money balances they do. Friedman has in fact defined the quantity theory as a theory of the demand for money. His theory requires that there should be a stable relationship between money and income and that it should be unresponsive to changes in interest rates on financial assets. If this turned out to be the case, it would show that when the money was increased, equilibrium could only be restored by an increase in income. Changes in interest rates in financial markets would not alone be sufficiently powerful to do the trick, and so the effect would have to take place through some kind of 'direct' substitution between money balances and real goods. As people tried to use their excess money balances to buy real goods, their expenditure would increase until economic activity reached a level where sufficient demand to hold the higher level of money was generated.

Keynesians, on the other hand, believe that the relationship between the demand for money and the rate of interest will be quite a strong one. Indeed, the Radcliffe Committee, as we have seen, thought that a small change in interest rates would be sufficient to cause a substantial change in the demand for money. Other Keynesians, while not going to quite the same lengths, nevertheless believe that interest rates will play the primary role in determining the demand for money.

The evidence here contradicts the extreme versions of the two theories. There are any number of statistical studies to show that the demand for money does respond to changes in interest rates on financial assets, though the elasticity is nowhere near so great as the Radcliffe Committee imagined. Again, however, the evidence is not unambiguous. It is clear that both incomes and interest rates affect the demand for money; but since both tend to move together over the cycle, it is far from easy to distinguish the relative role of each. Furthermore, there is always the thorny problem of whether the interest rate and the money supply that are being used for statistical tests are the appropriate ones. Do we measure the interest rate as the flat yield on a security? Or should we take into account expectations of capital gain and the likelihood of inflation?

Another problem is to know the policy framework that has existed in the past and produced the observed results. Are we observing the response of the economic system to a quantity of money predetermined by the central bank? Or has the central bank attempted to peg interest rates and allowed the money supply to be whatever it turned out to be? If the latter, it is not permissible to draw conclusions about what would happen if a policy of more determined control of the money supply were embarked on. The demand for pound notes has grown closely in step with national income; but nobody supposes the country would be plunged into depression if the Bank of England were ordered to stop producing pound notes and concentrate on £5 notes instead.

Finally, the existence of lags has posed a separate set of problems for researchers. Theory does not help in telling us what sort of lags to expect. Some investigators have suggested that the main effect of a change in policy should be felt immediately, and that its impact should die away gradually over time. Others expect policy not to have any effect until a certain time has passed, then to build up in its impact to reach a peak before dying away again. The representation of these lags in statistical form can often be a very formidable mathematical problem; and for technical reasons which need not detain us here, what appears to be a good and stable relationship to one investigator can disappear when subjected to different tests.

Further reading

Bank of England, The importance of money, *Bank of England Quarterly Bulletin*, June 1970.

Friedman, Milton, The quantity theory of money—a restatement, in *Studies in the Quantity Theory of Money*, Friedman (ed.), University of Chicago Press, 1956.

Friedman, Milton, The role of monetary policy, *American Economic Review*, March 1968.

Harrod, R. F., op. cit., Part II.

Johnson, H. G., Monetary theory and policy, *American Economic Review*, June 1962.

Meigs, A. James, *Money Matters*, New York, Harper and Row, 1972.

Robertson, D. H., *Money*, London, Nisbet, 1948, Chapter 2.

Tobin, James, The monetary interpretation of history. *American Economic Review*, June 1965.

Walters, Alan A., *Money in Boom and Slump*, Institute for Economic Affairs, Hobart Paper No. 44, 1969.

Questions for discussion

1 What was wrong with the old Quantity Theory of Money?

2 In what sense does Monetarist theory postulate an interest-rate mechanism?

3 Every major inflation has been accompanied by an increase in the quantity of money. Therefore, every inflation is caused by an increase in the quantity of money. Does this follow?

4 If we knew the factors which influenced people's desire to hold money, how would that help us to understand the importance of money in determining national income?

Part 2
Policy

5

Monetary policy

If financial factors such as the quantity of money and the level of interest rates have an effect on such magnitudes as economic activity and the balance of payments, it is only natural that governments should seek to exercise control over the monetary mechanism. The methods by which this control can be exercised will be the subject of Chapter 6. Before going on to this, however, it is necessary to review some more basic questions about how monetary policy works, and the circumstances in which it should be employed.

Perhaps the most fruitful way of viewing the impact of monetary policy on the economy is to see it as affecting the private sector's preferred holdings of real and financial assets. By their actions in financial markets, changing interest rates or the relative quantities of financial assets, the monetary authorities can bring about a divergence between the private sector's desired portfolio of assets and its actual portfolio. Subsequent attempts by the private sector to restore the desired portfolio balance will involve sales and purchases of assets, both financial and real, which will have repercussions on income flows.

This much is common ground. There is much less agreement on how monetary policy should be applied. There is debate about what objectives monetary policy should seek to achieve; what means can or ought to be applied to achieve these ends; how we can tell at any given time whether policy is tight or easy; what the relative roles of fiscal and monetary policy should be, and what are the lags which intervene before the policy takes effect. This chapter reviews each of these issues in turn.

Targets and instruments

It is useful to divide monetary variables into those which the authorities would like to influence but cannot directly control (targets) and those which they only control as a means to influencing some other variable (instruments). In between these come intermediate variables which often serve the purpose of being the channel through which the instruments have their effect on the targets. Finally, there may be other variables which are purely indicators, in the sense that they reflect the impact of policy but they do not form part of the channel of causation.

An example may serve to make this clearer. The driver of a car may have as his objective (target) to make the car go at 50 miles per hour. He does not control the speed of the car, however, only the settings of the gears and accelerator pedal. The achievement of a speed of 50 m.p.h. is therefore the target, the setting of the accelerator and gears the instrument. An intermediate variable would be engine revolutions. The accelerator only affects the speed of the car by increasing or reducing the number of engine revolutions. Finally, the speedometer is the indicator. If accurate, it is a good guide to the speed that is being achieved, and if it was unreliable, one would be less likely to achieve a steady 50 m.p.h. Nevertheless, it is not crucial to the process which links accelerator setting, engine revolutions and actual speed.

The targets of monetary policy are the same as those of economic policy generally, namely, full employment, economic growth, price stability and balance of payments equilibrium. Of course even these are not ultimate goals. Balance of payments equilibrium and price stability do not in themselves add to economic welfare and the level of GNP is only one element in the overall well-being of the community. Nevertheless, it is reasonable to suppose that economic policy makers, as opposed to social planners, do not look much beyond the targets we have listed.

The existence of various different targets is the first problem of all economic policy. For the different objectives may be in conflict. Everyone is familiar with the dilemma presented to policy-makers when unemployment is high and prices are rising. To stimulate demand may help to bring down the level of unemployment, but it will merely serve to aggravate the problem of rising prices. To hold back demand may help to check the rise in prices, but will cause unemployment to increase. The problem of conflicting objectives is particularly acute when there is a large number of targets.

Faced with conflicting objectives, the economic authorities have two possibilities: in the first place, they may accept the existence of an irreconcilable conflict and 'trade-off' the achievement of one objective against the achievement of another. A successful 'trade-off' is one which produces the preferred combination of policy objectives, even though no single objective is fully attained. In the case of the trade-off between unemployment and inflation, the amount of additional inflation needed to secure a cut in unemployment gets greater the lower the level of unemployment. This is illustrated in Fig. 5.1 where it will be noted that the curve (called the Phillips curve, after the economist who first investigated the relationship) is convex to the origin. This diagram (which is hypothetical) tells us that a 2%

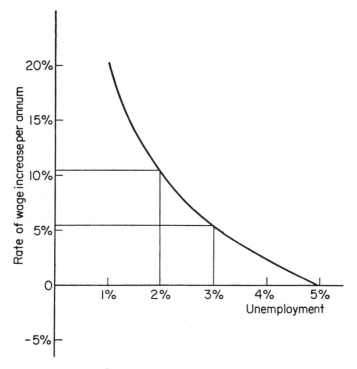

Fig. 5·1 Typical 'Phillips' curve

unemployment rate would be consistent with annual wage increases of just over 10%, while a 3% unemployment rate would reduce wage increases to just over 5%. The task of politicians is to choose the point on the curve where the particular combination of inflation and unemployment is least painful.

The second, and potentially more satisfying way of resolving a conflict between objectives is to devise additional instruments which are specific to the targets being aimed at. The motor car, for example, has a steering wheel to control direction and an accelerator to control speed. In the case of the car there is one instrument specifically designed to achieve each target; in the economic system, where policy instruments have consequences for a number of targets, it is still true to say that, in order to achieve a given number of independent objectives, one needs at least an equivalent number of independent instruments.

The problem of policy mix

The possibility of using different instruments in order to hit a variety of economic targets raises the question of the appropriate 'mix' of policy. The problem is rather more complicated than in the case of the car, where the steering wheel exclusively affects direction, and the accelerator exclusively speed. Typically, an economic policy instrument will affect quite a large number of economic variables, though not all to the same extent. Monetary policy has an effect on the overall level of demand and therefore on unemployment; it may have an effect on the distribution of demand between investment and consumption and therefore on the rate of economic growth; and it will have an effect on the balance of payments, both on current and capital account. Similarly, fiscal policy, incomes policy, and policies of direct intervention in industry may also have wide-ranging consequences.

It might seem that this would take it impossible to use instruments selectively to achieve desired objectives in several different directions. In fact, however, this is still possible if each policy instrument affects the various objectives in different ways. For example, monetary policy is thought by Keynesians to have a lagged and probably rather minor effect on the level of domestic demand but, through interest rates, a rapid and sizeable effect on the capital account of the balance of payments. Fiscal policy, on the other hand, is thought to have fairly rapid and predictable effects on the level of the domestic economy, but to influence the balance of payments mainly through changes in the current account. So long as external trade is not a large proportion of the economy, the effect of fiscal policy on the balance of payments will therefore be small relative to that on domestic demand.

This line of reasoning leads to the conclusion that if a country wants, say, both to increase domestic employment and to improve the balance of payments, it should have an expansionary fiscal policy and a tight monetary policy. The tight monetary policy will work against the expansionary fiscal policy on the domestic front, and fiscal policy will work against monetary policy on the external front. But the important point is that the offset will only be partial, and can be dealt with by increasing the strength of each policy.

This is a comforting conclusion, and indeed has been widely canvassed as a recipe for policy. There is, however, considerable scepticism as to whether the policy would work as smoothly and easily as its advocates claim. In the first place, and this would be accepted by all shades of opinion, an improvement in the balance of payments which relies entirely on attracting mobile capital through high interest rates is essentially temporary. Once the funds have come in, the balance of payments will revert to its former state unless there is a further rise in interest rates. Indeed, since the expansionary fiscal policy will have caused an increase in imports, it is probable that after a short time, the balance of payments will be worse than before the policy mix was adopted.

A second reason why there is doubt about this particular mix is that many people believe the importance of monetary policy for the domestic economy is underestimated. At the extreme, some economists believe monetary policy is all-important in the determination of the level of domestic demand, with budgetary policies affecting only the *distribution* of income and expenditure.

Although at the theoretical level the assigning of instruments to targets is straightforward, it is clear that there are formidable complications in practice. Nevertheless, policy in many countries has reflected an attempt to use different instruments selectively, and this is explored in more detail later. Generally speaking, fiscal policy in the UK has been used to achieve the goal of full employment. Monetary policy has normally been used in support of fiscal policy, but occasionally has been operated independently to affect inflows and outflows of funds. For the most part, however, policy-makers in the UK appear to have accepted the inevitability of a trade-off between domestic demand and the balance of payments which has frequently resulted in neither being wholly satisfactory. In 1967, however, the conflict became too great and, to resolve it, devaluation was resorted to.

Some observers believe that exchange rate policy should be used more actively, perhaps even to the extent of a floating exchange rate, as a means of keeping the balance of payments in equilibrium, so that the other weapons of policy can be concentrated on achieving domestic economic objectives. This has considerable attractions from the point of view of domestic economic management, and indeed the UK authorities allowed sterling to float in 1972. In Chapter 14, however, we examine some of the difficulties that might be encountered if there was general floating of exchange rates.

Before leaving the problem of policy mix, it is perhaps worth noting that the conflict between full employment and balance of payments equilibrium is only one among several such conflicts faced by policy-makers. Within the domestic economy, there is the problem of combining full employment with stable prices. It is not clear that the choice between monetary policy and fiscal policy is very helpful here. If, as many economists believe, both kinds of policy have their effect on employment and prices only insofar as they affect the level of demand, then they cannot be used to achieve two targets. We may say that, although they are *separate* policy instruments, they are not *independent* policy instruments—at least not so far as their effects on output and prices are concerned. It is sometimes claimed that monetary policy can be more effective in reducing prices, so that there is a degree of independence, but these claims rest on ad hoc statistical observation rather than on any strong analytical foundation.

The problem of combining targets for unemployment and inflation, therefore, comes down to a question of either 'trading-off' one goal against the other, or seeking an additional policy instrument that is truly independent. The latter is the motive of those who advocate using some form of administrative influence over wages and prices as a means of achieving stable prices. (It can be noted, however, that although this may resolve an economic policy conflict, it may create a political conflict if importance is also attached to the maintenance of free wage-bargaining.)

The indicator problem

So far we have talked of monetary policy largely in the abstract. If it is independent of other types of policy, it increases the freedom of the economic authorities to pursue separate objectives simultaneously. If it is not independent, it will not increase this freedom, but it can nevertheless be used in conjunction with other policies to increase the speed and certainty with which an important objective is reached. In order to judge these questions, we need to be able to say in more detail just what the effects of monetary policy are.

As we have seen in the previous chapter, neither theoretical nor empirical work has yet been successful in producing a firm consensus to answer this question. Part of the difficulty lies in not being able to say just what monetary policy is, or to measure how it is being

applied. There is no simple index of whether monetary policy is tight
or easy. Do we, for example, regard an interest rate of 4% as representing an easier monetary policy than one of 8%? Presumably not, if
the former exists in the middle of a slump when prices are falling,
and the latter in the middle of an inflationary boom when prices are
rising at 10% a year.

An alternative is to look instead at the rate of growth of the
monetary aggregates, such as the stock of money. If people are borrowing and spending more and the money supply is rising, this must
imply that monetary policy is somehow easier than before borrowing
and spending started to go up. This is intuitively appealing, but also
not an unimpeachable guide to the thrust of policy. If, for example,
the government undertakes a fiscal policy which leads investors to
expect, say, a 2% greater return from investment and at the same time
the central bank causes interest rates to rise by 1%, presumably the
volume of borrowing will go up, since the margin between the cost
of capital and the return on capital will have widened. But the purely
monetary part of the policy package will have been restrictive. Simply
because monetary policy only partially offsets a stimulus to the
economy coming from elsewhere this is not, it may be argued, a
reason to call it expansionary.

Interest rates and the money supply are, therefore, alternative
indicators of the impact of monetary policy. They are also alternative
intermediate variables from the point of view of the monetary
authorities. That is to say that the authorities can adjust their basic
instruments of control in order to achieve a certain level and structure
of interest rates or a certain rate of growth in the money supply. But
they cannot do both.[1] If the supply of money is fixed, then interest rates
will tend to adjust to a level where the demand to hold money balances
just matches the available supply. If the interest rate is fixed, then the
authorities will be called upon to supply at the fixed rate whatever
quantity holders of money wish to have.

One of the important questions facing policy-makers, and anyone
seeking to analyse the impact of policy, is whether the authorities

[1] This is not strictly true. The authorities can take administrative action to
directly control interest rates (e.g., through setting a legal ceiling on deposit
rates, as under Regulation Q in the US); or they can directly influence the
money supply through placing ceilings on, say, bank lending. This, however,
merely conceals the basic relationship between money supply and interest rates,
by creating or exploiting imperfections in the market for funds between ultimate
borrowers and ultimate lenders.

should attempt to control interest rates or the stock of money.[2] The question may be put thus: 'Is the economy more likely to follow a stable path of development if the authorities attempt to fix interest rates than if they attempt to fix the rate of growth of the money supply?' In a world of perfect certainty, and where portfolios were adjusted instantaneously, there would be no problem. The relationship between the stock of money and the rate of interest would be fixed and known and the choice of a target value for either the money stock or the rate of interest would necessarily imply a given value for the other. Under conditions of certain knowledge, there would also be a fixed relationship between the rate of interest and the level of economic activity, so that the policy decision would be purely mechanical. In terms of Fig. 4.3, the two lines II and LL would be fixed (i.e., not subject to uncertainty).

However, economics is an uncertain science, and it is this that introduces the problems, and the fascination, to matters of policy. The rate of interest depends not only on the stock of money relative to national income, but also on other factors which cannot be predicted. Thus a given stock of money will imply a certain level of interest rates, *subject to a margin of error*. Similarly, interest rates affect the level of economic activity, but the size of the effect cannot be exactly predicted. Again in terms of Fig. 4.3, the line LL is simply the best estimate of the relationship between the variables.

The relative stability of the two relationships—between velocity and interest rates on the one hand, and between interest rates and final demand on the other—is of great importance to the choice of which intermediate policy variable the monetary authorities should adopt. If there is a very loose relationship between velocity and interest rates, and a very close relationship between interest rates and the level of demand (national income), it is fairly obvious that it is more satisfactory, both as an instrument and an indicator of policy, to concentrate on controlling the level of the rate of interest and to leave the money supply to be whatever it turns out to be.

If, on the other hand, the relationship between velocity and interest rates is a stable one, while that between interest rates and the level of demand is subject to unpredictable fluctuations, then it can be shown

---

[2] An additional problem, which is ignored here, is that there is debate about *which* interest rate and *which* money supply is appropriate. There are several different definitions of the money supply and of course numerous interest rates. For the purposes of this discussion, however, it is sufficient to assume there is one interest rate and one figure for the money stock which serve as a reasonable approximation to the theoretical magnitudes.

that it is more desirable to concentrate on controlling the money. This is less obvious at first sight, but can be illustrated fairly simply.

If the relationship between interest rates and national income is unstable, this means that the economy is subject to other influences which may cause the level of activity to rise or fall for reasons unconnected with the rate of interest. Let us assume that demand increases because, say, something happens that causes consumers to fear a rise in prices (e.g., devaluation). With a fixed money stock, an increase in the level of demand will require an increase in velocity which in turn leads to a rise in interest rates. (It will be remembered that a stable relationship between velocity and interest rates has been assumed.) The rise in interest rates will exercise a deflationary effect, thus partially offsetting the initial stimulus to demand. If the monetary authorities had followed a course of stabilising interest rates, however, there would have been no such offsetting effect.

The problem of lags

It has already been noted that monetary policy has its effect on the economy by creating a situation of disequilibrium in the portfolios of individuals and firms. They respond to this by buying and selling assets in order to restore an equilibrium where the marginal unit of each asset gives an equal yield (of interest or satisfaction) and there is no advantage to be gained by shifting holdings between assets. It is implicit from what has already been said that there will be lags in the operation of policy. If this were not so, there would be no such thing as a disequilibrium, since asset holders would be able to adjust their portfolios immediately.

In fact, of course, people do not adjust immediately to changed circumstances, and this may be for one of two reasons. In the first place they may take time to become aware of the new conditions. Secondly, once they have become aware of imbalance in their portfolio, it may take time to correct it. It is virtually impossible to increase or reduce the holdings of some assets immediately and, even in the case of those where immediate sale or purchase is possible, hasty action may impose extra costs.

Most of the research that has been done on the demand for money shows that it responds with a lag to changes in interest rates. In other words, if interest rates go up, this will generate some tendency to economise on money balances straight away, but the tendency will build up fairly slowly and only reach its full strength after a considerable time interval. A consequence of this is that a much larger increase

in interest rates is needed to get a quick change in the equilibrium
stock of money than if a longer period is allowed.

If this is indeed the case, then a policy of controlling growth of
the money supply on a day-to-day basis could lead to sharp fluctuations
in interest rates. Let us take a simple example. Suppose the relationship between velocity and interest rates is such that, when equilibrium
is restored, a reduction of £1,000 million in the money stock is
accompanied by a 1% rise in interest rates. To secure a reduction of
a full £1,000 million within, say, a single month a rise in interest
rates of much more than 1% would be needed. Later, as the lagged
effects of the initial rise in rates began to take effect, current yields
could gradually fall back, until in equilibrium, the money stock would
be £1,000 million less and interest rates only 1% above their original
level. The achievement in the short term of a new target for the money
supply will thus imply a sharp up and down movement in interest rates.

This consequence of the existence of lags suggests two possible
strategies for the monetary authorities. In the first place, they might
abandon an actively interventionist monetary policy and simply aim
at steady growth in the quantity of money. Secondly, they might direct
their activities to controlling interest rates and not bother about the
money supply.

The policy of pursuing a steady growth in the money supply has
been advocated by Professor Friedman. But since it involves eschewing any attempt to use monetary policy in support of counter-cyclical
policy, it seems unlikely to be adopted. Even if it were, it is far from
certain that it would necessarily avoid the fluctuations in interest rates
mentioned earlier. For economies may be subject to unforeseen changes
in the demand for money too and, to the extent that the authorities
fail to adjust the supply to accommodate, the strain of adjustment will
be thrown on interest rates.

The foregoing would seem to imply that the monetary authorities
should direct their activities to controlling interest rates and not
bother about the money supply. If it is an interest rate mechanism
that is influencing expenditure decisions, sharp swings in interest
rates, however caused, may result in unnecessary disruptions to savings
and investment flows before a new equilibrium position is reached. In
terms of the example given above the monetary authorities could alter
their dealing prices so as to cause yields to rise immediately by 1%.
In the first month after the change, the money stock would only fall
by, say, £100 million or so; and with the passage of time the effect of
the higher rates would build up until ultimately the money stock
would be £1,000 million below its original level.

A pure interest-rate target can itself be misleading, however, since it is not easy for the monetary authorities to know what is an appropriate target for interest rates in particular circumstances. The incentive to spend is generated when the rate charged on borrowing falls relative to the yield expected from the acquisition of assets. And while it is possible to observe the money cost of borrowing very precisely, it is not possible to do more than guess at the other side of the equation. The expected money return from investment may rise because the general economic climate is improving, or because expectations of continuing or accelerated inflation cause anticipations of price increases in real goods.

It should be noted, furthermore, that an interest-rate target, expressed as a fixed long-term rate, is potentially very destabilising. For a policy expressed in this way means that credit becomes cheaper, in real terms, the greater the rate of inflation. This produces a vicious circle. As the rate of inflation goes up, credit becomes cheaper; and cheaper credit stimulates the level of investment thus fuelling further inflation. And the vicious spiral will work in the other direction if the initial problem is deflation; falling prices will make a fixed rate of interest more expensive in real terms, thus cutting demand further and leading to more deflation and unemployment.

When measuring credit conditions, the proof of the pudding is in the eating. If people are continuing to borrow and the money supply is going up, then conditions are, in some meaningful sense, 'easy' no matter what the interest rate is. It is a useful compromise to say that monetary policy works through *interest* rates, but that the rate of growth of the money supply provides a useful index as to whether the interest rate is right or not. One could perhaps summarise the policy implications of this by saying that the authorities should have a long-term money supply target, but be prepared to move towards it gradually so as not to cause large fluctuations in interest rates.

In addition to lags between movements in interest rates and changes in the quantity of money, there may be other kinds of lag which intervene between the time when a change in policy becomes necessary and the time when a policy action becomes effective. We may categorise these lags as follows:

a An information lag. It will take time for the information showing that a change in policy is necessary to be collected and placed in the hands of the policy-makers. In the UK, for example, information on national income during the course of a quarter does not become available in a complete form until two months or more after the end of a quarter. More seriously, information which does appear may reflect chance factors as well as basic trends. It may not be until two or three sets of figures are available that the authorities are able to tell with any certainty that an observed change represents a new trend and not just a random fluctuation in the statistics.

b An implementation lag. Once policy-makers have become aware that there is a change in underlying circumstances, there will be a further lag while they formulate an appropriate policy to deal with the new conditions. This lag can be quite short if there exist contingency plans ready to be put into operation. Normally, however, even the most carefully thought out set of contingency plans will overlook a special feature of a particular policy problem that makes it different from what was anticipated. The sheer mechanics of discussing the possible alternatives and agreeing on an appropriate policy between the responsible departments is a time-consuming process.

c An instrument response lag. It will be remembered that we noted earlier that the authorities control directly certain 'instrument variables', such as bank rate and special deposits, which they use to achieve a certain value for the more significant 'intermediate variables' such as the money supply and long-term rates. An 'instrument response' lag arises because these 'intermediate variables' do not respond immediately to changes in the instrument variables. Holders of money, for example, do not immediately increase their stock of money if there is a fall in interest rates. Nor do dealers in long-term bonds automatically change their dealing prices in response to a change in the Bank of England's dealing tactics.

d A reaction lag. Finally, there is a lag involved in the response of the target variables to changes in the intermediate variables. Once interest rates or the money stock have moved to the level desired by the authorities, there will be a further delay while individuals and companies revise their investment and saving plans. For example, if credit conditions change in such a way that they encourage an individual to buy a new car, the chances are that the actual acquisition of the car will not take place for several weeks. A choice of model has to be made, finance has to be arranged and his old car has to be sold. For an industrial company contemplating new investment the lags will typically be very much longer. There may also be one final lag, between a change in demand and a change in production, if companies respond to an upswing in demand by initially supplying goods from stocks and not undertaking additional output.

There is no very broad consensus about the length of these lags. The longer they are, however, the more difficult it is to use monetary policy as a weapon of short-term counter-cyclical control. At one extreme, Professor Friedman believes the operational lag may be as long as a year or more which, combined with the fact that the policy-maker may be acting on information that is three months or so out of date, makes fine-tuning almost impossible. As we have noted, Friedman's recipe for this dilemma is to eschew the idea of counter-cyclical action altogether, the attempted implementation of which, he believes, has actually caused the economy to be more unstable than it would otherwise have been. Instead, he suggests that the monetary authorities should follow a fixed rule requiring the money supply to grow at a certain prescribed rate.

Unfortunately for the policy-maker, however, there is very far from being general agreement with Professor Friedman on this matter. Amongst those who believe in the power of monetary policy, there are many who believe it is very quick acting, and that it can therefore be used as an element, indeed the main element, of counter-cyclical economic policy. The support for this hypothesis was at its strongest in 1969 and 1970, before the policy was tried in the US and shown not to work in quite the fashion expected.

Further reading

Axilrod, S. and Young, R., Interest rates and monetary policy, *Federal Reserve Bulletin*, September 1962.

Bain, A. D., *The Control of the Money Supply*, Harmondsworth, Penguin, 1970, Chapter 6.

Brunner, Karl, *Targets and Indicators of Monetary Policy*, San Francisco, Chandler, 1969.

Croome, D., and Johnson, H. G., *Money in Britain*. London, Oxford University Press, 1970.

Federal Reserve Bank of Boston, *Controlling Monetary Aggregates*, 1969.

Mundell, R. A., *The Appropriate use of Monetary and Fiscal Policy for Internal and External Stability*, IMF Staff Papers, March 1962.

Radcliffe Committee, *Report on the Working of the Monetary System*, Cmnd 827, London, HMSO, 1959, Chapter 2.

Questions for discussion

1 What would you consider the appropriate policy for a country with:

(a) Unemployment and a payments deficit.

(b) The desired level of employment, and a payments deficit?

2 In what ways can a restrictive monetary policy have an effect different from that of a restrictive fiscal policy?

3 Is a country's exchange rate a target or an instrument of policy?

4 In what ways does the existence of lags complicate the problems of monetary management?

5 Which is more likely to stabilise the economy: a constant rate of growth of the money supply, or a constant level of interest rates?

6
Techniques of monetary control

We have seen in the previous chapter that monetary policy can be expressed in terms of an attempt to influence certain 'intermediate' variables, such as interest rates, or the money supply. The present chapter reviews the main techniques by which a central bank may achieve these policy objectives.

It is important to note at the outset, however, that none of these techniques can enable the central bank to control directly the quantity of money, nor can they permit it to precisely determine the interest rates at which persons and institutions in the private sector lend to one another. The stock of money consists largely of bank deposits, and the quantity of these in existence is at least partly determined by the desire of banks' customers to borrow and the willingness of banks to make loans. As far as interest rates are concerned, those which most directly determine spending and investment decisions are arrived at in markets for funds in which the central bank does not participate. If the monetary authorities have objectives for the rate of growth of the money supply, or for the pattern of interest rates, they must therefore seek to achieve them by indirect methods.

This involves the use of instruments which *are* directly under the authorities' control and which can be used to induce private institutions to act in the desired fashion. These instruments are of two main types—market intervention and portfolio constraints. Market intervention instruments rely on the power of the central bank as a dealer in financial markets to influence the availability and rate of return on assets in a general way, thus affecting both the desire of the public to hold money balances and the willingness of banks to take deposits and lend. Portfolio constraints place restrictions on a particular group of institutions (usually banks) limiting their freedom to organise their own portfolios.

It is helpful to discuss the main policy instruments under the following headings:

Market Operations
   Discount rate
   Open market operations

Portfolio Constraints
   Reserve requirements
   Moral suasion
   Direct controls.

Discount rate

A central bank's discount rate (bank rate) is the rate at which it is prepared to lend to the banking system when the latter is short of liquid funds. In most countries, this is done by lending direct to the banks themselves, though in the UK, as explained in a later chapter, assistance is provided *via* the discount market. By setting the terms on which it is prepared to provide this last resort lending, a central bank can, under certain conditions, exercise a pervasive effect on financial markets. The most important aspect of these terms is the rate of interest charged, but other factors may also be varied, e.g., whether assistance is provided by the discounting (i.e., purchase) of assets, or by loans against collateral; the nature of the collateral accepted; guidelines governing frequency of access to central bank facilities; limits on borrowing, etc.

It is normal for a central bank to declare publicly its rediscount rate and to change it periodically at its own discretion. It is also possible, however, for a central bank to express its discount rate as being a fixed margin above some market-determined rate. This latter method, which was used in Canada from 1956–62, and was introduced in the UK in 1972, removes the element of discretion in fixing the rate.

It is quite easy to see how a discretionary bank rate can in principle act as the pivot in the overall spectrum of rates. Rates on securities (usually bills) eligible to be used as collateral cannot rise above bank rate by very much or for very long, otherwise it would be profitable for the banking system[1] to borrow unlimited quantities from the central bank on the security of bills which yielded them a higher running return. If there was no restriction on the amounts the banking system could borrow—an important proviso—then any tendency for bill rates

---

[1] In the UK, the central bank traditionally lends to the banking system through the discount market. This refinement, which is not material in the present context, is explored more fully in Chapters 9 and 10.

to rise above bank rate would give rise to a heavy demand for bills, which would bring their yields down again. Rates will not fall too far below bank rate, either, because of the costs involved in covering a shortage by last resort borrowing at a penal rate from the central bank. The influence of bank rate on the yields of eligible bills can therefore be fairly direct; and because these money markets assets are competitive with other forms of financial assets, this influence can in principle be generally disseminated throughout the financial system.

Thus the effect of the discount rate is clear if the authorities are frequent lenders at this rate. But in fact the influence may still be felt, even though not much actual lending is done. If the banking system believes that the central bank will enforce penal borrowing whenever interest rates fall more than the authorities wish, they will take care not to let rates move to such an extent. (The threat of a penalty may thus be just as effective in inducing the banking system to behave in the desired way as the use of the penalty.)

The influence of the rediscount rate on other rates, however, depends ultimately on the willingness of the authorities to 'make the rate effective' by using it as a basis for operations. In Britain in the later part of the 1960s it became increasingly doubtful whether the authorities were really willing to use the bank rate instrument in the traditional way. Because of the political consequences of the publicity surrounding bank rate changes, they became reluctant to change the rate, particularly in an upward direction. Bank rate consequently slipped out of line with market rates, and the Bank of England stopped using lending at bank rate as a normal means of relieving cash shortages in the banking system. To a considerable extent, changes in bank rate came to be of primarily psychological importance.

Even in this diminished role, however, bank rate changes could still be a significant component of policy. Expectations are of the very greatest importance in many financial decisions, and bank rate changes could occasionally have a profound influence on market psychology. By its very nature, however, the use of a bank rate change to achieve a psychological result was something that could only be effective occasionally, not as a continuous element of policy. And, of course, a psychological weapon is hard to use with a controlled effect; it may have little or no effect on expectations if used too lightly, but a dramatic effect if used somewhat more strongly. There can even be a perverse effect: a large change in bank rate may serve to emphasise the seriousness of a crisis even more than the resolution of the Government in dealing with it.

Partly because the use of discount rate changes had tended to become invested with a political significance out of proportion to their economic importance, the Bank of England in 1972 abandoned its discretionary bank rate (after 270 years). In its place it substituted a floating bank rate, to be set $\frac{1}{2}\%$ above the Treasury bill rate. The advantage of the new system is that it 'depoliticizes' bank rate, and allows it to adjust more or less automatically to market pressures. The disadvantage, of course, is that it deprives the authorities of the option of initiating a change in rates through a discretionary bank rate change. Too much should not be made of this shortcoming, however. The Bank of England can still exert upward pressure on rates by enforcing penal borrowing. In this way it can cause bank rate to be pushed up by a rising rate on Treasury bills.

Open market operations

In addition to setting the terms and conditions on which it is prepared to lend to the banking system a central bank can intervene directly in financial markets by buying and selling securities. Most central banks control a very large portfolio of securities, used as backing for the note issue, which they can use, to a greater or lesser extent, to influence financial conditions. By buying and selling securities in the open market, the monetary authorities can have an effect on interest rates and the money supply by changing the availability of the various financial assets in which they operate.

If the authorities are buying securities, they will be adding to demand for these assets, pushing up their prices and lowering yields. At the same time, these official purchases will provide cash in exchange for securities which will add to the reserve assets of the banks and make them more willing to grant advances. This will tend to cause the money supply to increase, and will also lower interest rates.

The precise manner in which central banks intervene in the markets depends on the nature of the financial system in the country in question and the other objectives of the central bank in promoting a smooth and efficient system of financial intermediation. Open market operations are really only possible where there is a well developed financial system, with a widely held, and relatively large, national debt.

One of the main ways in which open-market operations affect the economy is through their influence on the portfolio composition of the banking system. In those countries where the banks have a reserve requirement expressed in terms of cash, purchases and sales of short-term assets such as Treasury bills are sufficient to change the reserve holdings of the banks. In these countries (e.g., the United States) one finds that the bulk of open-market operations are conducted in short-term markets. The central bank decides each week on the volume of bills it will offer for sale for the coming week, and the size of the offering will influence the rate reached at the tender; subsequently, the central bank can deal in the day-to-day market for bills if it wishes to modify the impact of the tender on the banking system's holdings of reserves.

To some extent, influence over Treasury bill rates implies a measure of control over other rates as well. As we have just noted, it affects the willingness of banks to lend and, as was pointed out in Chapter 3, rates on long-term securities are to some extent influenced by current and expected short-term yields. However, if Treasury bills form part of the required reserves of the banking system, as is the case in the UK, purchases and sales of them will not alone be sufficient to influence the overall reserve position of the banking system. They will affect the composition of reserve assets, but not the total quantity. To have an effect on the quantity of reserve assets it will be necessary to extend open-market operations to securities which are not reserve assets. Such a move may be desirable anyway if the authorities wish to have a more direct means of influencing longer-term interest rates.

In the UK, the Bank of England is a continuous and active participant in the market for gilt-edged securities (i.e., long-term government bonds). From the point of view of demand management, the Bank's operations in the gilt-edged market should be counter-cyclical. That is to say, when restraint of demand is needed, the Bank should be selling longer-dated stock, thus reducing liquidity and the money supply and pushing up interest rates. When the problem is one of underemployment, purchases of stock should be used to expand the money supply and bring down interest rates.

Although there is broad agreement that this is appropriate general strategy for central banks to pursue in their open market operations, there is much less agreement about short-term tactics. In the short-term, markets may be importantly affected by expectations which may cause the normal inverse relationship between the supply of an asset and its price not to hold. The UK authorities believe that the gilt-edged market is subject to these destabilising expectations. '... the market response to a moderate price change for gilt-edged has been found to be unstable and often perverse in the short-term.'[2] It is also believed—though less strongly than formerly—that if these destabilising tendencies are allowed to express themselves in sharp price

[2] *Bank of England Quarterly Bulletin*, December 1969, p. 456.

fluctuations, the long-term willingness of investors to hold gilt-edged will be impaired.

This view of investor psychology has meant that a certain amount of price stability has been an additional objective of the Bank of England's market operations. In principle this is a perfectly legitimate goal of market management; in practice, however, it presents the authorities with a difficult question of judgment in distinguishing between price movements which are short-term and should be smoothed out, and those which reflect an underlying trend. As explained in Chapter 13, these difficulties have made for increased reluctance to intervene actively in the longer-term bond market.

Reserve requirements

Reserve requirements are a particular example of a more general weapon of central bank policy, namely the imposition of constraints on banks' asset portfolios. Most governments impose some sort of formal or informal rules on portfolio structure at an early stage in the development of the banking system. The initial motive has often been to encourage prudent management and to secure the solvency of the banking system against the possibility of a run on the banks. Later, when banking systems became more stably based, rules about portfolio structure were usually retained because of their usefulness as control instruments.

The rule is usually expressed as a requirement to hold a fixed proportion of assets in a certain form. In most countries there is a minimum ratio of cash to deposits. Sometimes cash is defined as just deposits with the central bank, sometimes it includes currency notes and coin. In some countries, including the UK, the ratio that is used includes near-cash assets as well. When banks find that their ratios of reserve assets have fallen to their minimum permitted levels, they will either have to stop increasing their holding of non-reserve assets (i.e., stop lending), or try and borrow more from their depositors. Either course of action will tend to raise interest rates and restrict the growth in the money supply. In order to hold back the growth of non-reserve assets, the banks will have to push up their lending rates so as to discourage borrowers. If, on the other hand, they try to acquire additional reserves by bidding more actively for deposits, they will drive up the cost of funds, which in turn will push up leading rates and thus check borrowing. And in the aggregate, of course, banks can only increase their holding of reserve assets by acquiring additional reserves from outside the banking system. If the authorities are able to control the supply of reserve assets, they can impose an infallible constraint on the size of the banking system.

The preciseness of the control which can be achieved over the money supply by means of reserve ratios depends on two factors:

a the ability of the monetary authorities to control the total volume of reserve assets in the hands of the banking system, and

b the stability of the ratio of reserve assets to total deposits.

Each of these two factors will introduce a certain amount of 'play' into the relation between official actions and the money supply. As far as the first is concerned, there will be transactions in reserve assets between the banking system and outsiders; for the second, there will be a fluctuating 'cushion' of reserve assets which banks hold in excess of the required minimum.

The margin of uncertainty in control of the money supply cannot be removed entirely, but it can be reduced by making reserve assets unattractive to hold in their own right. This will ensure that outsiders do not wish to hold more than they strictly need for transaction purposes, and that banks strive to keep as close to the required minimum as possible. The drawback to this technique is that the holding of reserve assets constitutes a form of 'tax' on banking activities which may have adverse consequences for the allocation of resources. In particular, it may encourage the growth of other, intrinsically less efficient, means of financial intermediation.

We have already seen one way in which pressure can be brought to bear on reserve ratios—by open market operations designed to reduce the total quantity of reserve assets in circulation. Another means of achieving the same result is through changing the required reserve ratio. This can be done, either by changing the proportion of assets which must be held in the form of reserves, or by calling for 'special deposits' to be made by banks in addition to normal reserves. In either case, the result will be to make the banking system short of reserve assets—either because it is actually below the minimum required quantity or, more likely, because the prudential 'cushion' of reserve assets which it holds above the minimum has become uncomfortably small. Whichever it is, individual banks can set about rectifying the situation in two ways. In the first place they can bid more actively for deposits, thus pushing up rates in that market. Secondly, they may attempt to switch out of holding non-reserve assets into reserve assets.

Now while an individual bank can acquire a reserve asset by bidding for it in the free market, the aggregate of banks can only increase their holdings of reserve assets if either additional reserves are created or individuals and institutions outside the banking system are persuaded to give up some of their holdings. If we assume that no new reserve assets are being created and that holdings of reserve assets outside the banking system are static, then attempts by banks to get back into portfolio balance after a call for special deposits can be achieved only through a reduction in the total of bank deposits.

To illustrate this, consider the following simple combined balance sheet of the banking system.

Liabilities		Assets	
Deposits	100	Reserves	$12\frac{1}{2}$
		Bonds	$37\frac{1}{2}$
		Other Assets	50
			100

Now assume that the required reserve ratio is raised to 15%. The typical bank will respond by offering $2\frac{1}{2}$ of bonds for sale, which will be taken up partly by its own customers, and partly by customers of other banks. The bonds will be paid for by a reduction in the customers' bank balances—and interest rates will have to adjust by an amount sufficient to make wealthholders content to hold $2\frac{1}{2}$ more bonds and $2\frac{1}{2}$ less money. The banks' combined balance sheet will now be:

Liabilities		Assets	
Deposits	$97\frac{1}{2}$	Reserves	$12\frac{1}{2}$
		Bonds	35
		Other Assets	50
			$97\frac{1}{2}$

It will be noted that the banks have been unable to increase the sum total of their reserves, because the money they received from the sale of their bonds to their customers was exactly matched by the funds they had to provide their customers with to enable them to pay for the bonds. The reserve ratio is still less than 15%, so the banks have to sell more bonds. This process continues until an equilibrium is reached where the reserve ratio is 15%. This will be when the balance sheet is as follows:

Liabilities		*Assets*	
Deposits	83⅓	Reserves	12½
		Bonds	10⅝
		Other Assets	50
			——
			83⅓

(Subsequently, there may be an adjustment in the banks' relative holdings of bonds and 'other assets', but this will not affect the equilibrium size of the overall balance sheet.)

It is important to note that special deposits work by pushing up interest rates and thus inducing people to hold less cash and more bonds. In this respect, the mechanism of special deposits is very little different from that of open market operations. The difference lies not so much in the end result, when the system has returned to an equilibrium position, but in the way in which the equilibrium is reached. If the banking system had a large quantity of extra reserve assets, the authorities could mop them up by selling large quantities of bonds. If the demand for bonds was relatively price-inelastic in the short term, however, these bonds could only be sold by accepting a substantial drop in price. The consequent rise in interest rates necessary to persuade the public to hold the bonds in the short term might be greater than was necessary in the long term. Thus rates would rise sharply, then fall back again possibly upsetting the smooth flow of saving and investment.

If the extra reserve assets were mopped up by a call for special deposits, however, there need be no market operations by the authorities. The banks would have lost their cushion of reserve assets and they might try to reconstitute this by selling secondary liquid assets. But they would probably do this gradually over time, as and when the market could absorb their sales. Interest rates would rise smoothly and gradually to their new equilibrium instead of oscillating. Special deposits are therefore a useful adjunct to open market operations, for use when the need is to cancel out excess liquidity quickly.

Moral suasion

Market operations and reserve requirements are, broadly speaking, instruments of control which are aimed at the overall size of banks' balance sheets. They are not really capable of discriminating between different kinds of lending activity. It is in order to try and practice this kind of discrimination that central banks have often attempted to use their influence and prestige in the financial community to persuade banks to restrain their lending or allocate it in a different way. They are, in fact, trying to induce banks, in the national interest, to abandon the aim of profit maximisation in the short-term.

Moral suasion has frequently been a matter of suggesting priorities in lending, with finance for exports getting top priority, investment also coming high up on the list, and importing and private consumption receiving lowest priority. It has also embraced more general appeals for restraint in lending, and has been used to prevent an outflow of funds. In the US, large corporations were asked by President Johnson to observe restraint in their overseas investment programmes, and in the UK there were similar voluntary curbs on investment in the four developed countries of the overseas sterling area between 1966 and 1972.

Moral suasion is normally employed when it is felt that the ordinary market mechanism does not, and cannot easily be made to, take full account of the public interest. Under these circumstances, allocation of resources to the bidder prepared to pay the highest price does not necessarily secure the best distribution. If the monetary authorities are capable of improving the allocation of financial resources—say by directing lending to activities where there are 'spin-off' advantages to other sectors of the economy—then the community's economic welfare will benefit if the banks can be induced to follow the authorities' wishes.

The advantage of moral suasion over direct controls, which are treated later, is that it is a highly flexible control and does not need legal implementation. Because of this, there is less need for detailed and costly administrative regulation and, if the national interest is clear, then there should be less trouble about a divergence between observing the letter and the spirit of guidelines. Moral suasion works best in a closely-knit financial community with a relatively small number of institutions and where there is easy and regular communication between private institutions and the authorities. In this way, the private institutions can become aware of the reasons behind official guidelines and, for their part, the authorities can exert pressure on the unwilling.

Moral suasion does not work particularly well in a system with a large number of institutions (such as the US), geographically far removed from the seat of government, and possibly out of sympathy with official objectives. The major difficulty is that as soon as one institution appears to breach the guidelines, all others suffer a competitive disadvantage. The directors of a bank then have a difficult conflict of loyalties to resolve—to the national interest on the one hand, to the shareholders on the other. The more the guidelines are breached, the more difficult it becomes for other banks to remain within them. Moral suasion is therefore best applied as a temporary weapon. But even if moral suasion is changed into direct legal controls in order to prevent backsliding, problems still exist. The fact that controls have to be used to induce banks to act in a certain way means, in essence, that the monetary authorities are assuming that they can ensure a better allocation of resources than would occur as a result of the play of market forces. It is possible that in some circumstances this may be the case; but since the use of such controls is inevitably subject to political pressure, it is by no means likely that this will always be so.

Direct controls

The line between moral suasion and direct controls is a difficult one to draw. Moral suasion tends to develop into direct controls because in a competitive economic system all businesses, including banks, are under pressure to extend their activities into any direction where they can make a profit without directly infringing the law. And certain controls which do not have a formal legal backing have quasi-statutory force.

Direct controls operate by placing limits on the banks' freedom to undertake certain activities. They are usually adopted because it is feared that other methods of influencing bank activity will not work sufficiently quickly or else will cause unacceptable consequences in other directions. If, for example, it is desired to check quickly the growth in the outstanding volume of bank lending, the straightforward economists' prescription is that the rate of interest should rise so that marginal borrowers are discouraged and only those who most need funds (as evidenced by their ability to pay a higher rate of interest) continue to be accommodated. The trouble is that borrowers may not respond immediately to a modest rise in the rate of interest. If this is true, it may require a very large rise in the rate of interest to secure quickly the desired reduction in borrowing; because this will cause the prices of fixed interest securities to fall markedly, and because it may be unpopular amongst politically influential groups (e.g., house buyers), direct controls may be resorted to.

Two of the commonest types of control are ceilings on lending by banks, which have a considerable history both in the UK and in several other countries of Western Europe; and ceilings on interest rates which banks may pay, common in the USA in the shape of 'Regulation Q'. Lending ceilings are usually introduced so as to hold back that component of banks' activities which is considered to be most inflationary—namely the granting of credit to the private sector. It is usually hoped that banks will ration credit under the ceiling, rather than allow interest rates to rise to balance supply and demand. In this way the authorities hope to hold down the growth of credit, without a politically embarrassing rise in interest rates. Ceilings on interest rates are designed to restrict the ability of banks to compete for deposits and so shield the politically sensitive area of non-bank savings and loan institutions which traditionally play a major role in financing the housing sector.

The trouble with direct controls is that, if retained for any length of time, they are likely to have the result of misallocating resources. If a ceiling on bank credit reduces borrowing without increasing the rate of interest, credit must be rationed other than by price. Under these circumstances there must be a presumption that some more worthy projects will be denied funds which are absorbed by less worthy projects. If banks continue to allocate credit within the ceiling on the basis of price (i.e., they allow rates to rise to their natural level) there will be a tendency for borrowers and lenders to bypass the banking system and lend direct or go through other intermediaries (which will probably be less efficient than the banks).

Nevertheless, it may be the case that the Government is prepared to accept some minor misallocation of resources in the short term, in order to have the benefit of a quick-acting monetary policy without the disadvantage of violent oscillations in interest rates. In these circumstances, which are strictly limited, direct controls have a role to play. They can provide breathing space during which a longer-term policy can take effect. If they are allowed to *become* the long-term policy, however, they have the disadvantages just referred to.

A very widespread type of direct control is the control over payments to and from foreign countries (exchange control). In a world where there are large multinational companies, close banking and trading links between nations, and where central banks intervene to hold exchange rates steady, there are inevitably large flows of funds from one country to another. These inflows and outflows of funds are embarrassing in the consequences they have both for a country's reserve position, and for its attempts to control the level of credit in its domestic economy. If one country is trying to damp down inflationary tendencies by pursuing a policy of high interest rates to restrict the growth of credit, while other countries have low interest rates, the high interest rate country may find itself faced with an inflow of funds from abroad which tends to undermine its policy of restricting the growth of its money supply.

Many countries have reacted to this dilemma by introducing exchange controls. The study of exchange control is a subject in itself, but in broad outline it involves restricting the freedom of individuals and companies to convert foreign currency into domestic currency and vice versa. The controls can be applied either to restrict an inflow of funds or an outflow. (Sometimes, as in the case of the UK in 1971, there are controls in inward and outward movements at the same time.) They can be more or less comprehensive, being applied only to residents, or also to non-residents; and being applied to a restricted range of transactions, or to all transactions. The disadvantage is that interference with the free movement of capital is liable to create a misallocation of resources between countries. In many circumstances, however, this degree of misallocation has been judged an acceptable price to pay for the (assumed greater) advantages of preserving the existing structure of exchange rates and a greater measure of autonomy in domestic monetary policy.

Further reading

Aschheim, Joseph, *Techniques of Monetary Control*, Baltimore, Johns Hopkins, 1961.

Bain, Andrew, *The Control of the Money Supply*, Harmondsworth, Penguin, 1970.

Bank of England, The operation of monetary policy since Radcliffe, in Croome, D. and Johnson, H. G. (eds), *Money in Britain*, London, Oxford University Press, 1970.

Dorrance, Graeme S., *The Instruments of Monetary Policy*, IMF Staff Papers, July 1965.

Federal Reserve Bank of Boston, *Controlling Monetary Aggregates*, 1969.

Fousek, Peter G., *Foreign Central Banking: The Instruments of Monetary Policy*, New York, Federal Reserve Bank of New York, 1957.

Radcliffe Report, op. cit., Chapter 7.

Tobin, James, An essay on the principles of debt management, in *Fiscal and Debt Management Policies*, published for the Commission on Money and Credit by Prentice-Hall, Englewood Cliffs, N.J., 1963.

Questions for discussion

1 In what ways are the consequences of the following policy actions likely to differ:
   (a) The sale of £100 million of long-dated gilt edged;
   (b) A call for £100 million of special deposits.

2 In what circumstances are direct controls over the banking system likely to be preferable to central bank operations in the money markets?

3 Can an increase in discount rate by itself be effective in restraining the economy?

4 'Speak softly and carry a big stick'. Is this a fair description of moral suasion as an instrument of monetary policy?

7

Financing the public sector

The previous chapter has underlined the importance of debt management in monetary policy. The operations which a central bank undertakes to finance government deficits or to change the structure of the government's outstanding debt can have profound effects on the structure of interest rates and the rate of growth of the money supply. The present chapter begins with a brief review of the growth of the public sector in the economy as a whole, and examines the broad considerations which determine the shape of the government's budget. It goes on to consider the question of the so-called 'burden' of the National Debt. Against the background of government financial operations in a particular year, we consider finally the specific methods by which the government obtains finance, and the impact of official debt management operations on financial conditions in other markets.

The role of the public sector in the economy

In the 20th century, the public sector has occupied a large and growing position in the economies of most countries. There are several reasons for this. National defence requirements, which in the 19th century were quite small, have grown both in size and complexity. Although the trend in recent years has been for defence expenditures to be stabilised, they still absorb a substantial proportion of the national product. Next, there has been increasing recognition of a need for the government to provide basic social services. This includes unemployment and sickness compensation, health services, education, and so on. Finally, the government has accepted an obligation for the general economic health of the country, which has led it to intervene, generally and specifically, in the organisation of industry. In the United Kingdom, for example, many basic industries are publicly owned. This is partly because of a desire to avoid a private monopoly in circumstances where economies of scale dictate a small number of concerns;

partly because of a need to rescue industries which are economically important but are unable to remain solvent, or to raise the necessary capital for expansion; and partly out of a desire to make the 'commanding heights' of the economy more publicly accountable than would be possible under private ownership.

The public sector in the United Kingdom can be divided into three broad categories: central government, local government, and the nationalised industries. There are important links between these three arms, however, and in particular the central government accepts the responsibility for controlling the overall spending of the other two parts of the public sector, and to some extent also of financing them.

The sheer size of the public sector gives it importance in several ways. In the first place, since the government controls some two-fifths of national spending, it can directly affect total incomes and the level of employment through its expenditure policies. Of more interest in connection with monetary policy, however, government spending can have an indirect effect on economic activity through the manner in which it is financed. It may be financed either through taxation or through borrowing, or more likely through some combination of the two. To the extent that the government is financed through borrowing, there are a variety of different kinds of debt instrument that may be used.

The manner in which the government satisfies its financial needs will affect the quantities of different financial instruments in existence, which, with a given demand for each, will cause their relative prices to vary. (This is simply another way of saying that interest rates will be affected.) This in turn will affect peoples' willingness to borrow and lend, both directly and through the intermediation of the banking system.

The budget

The government's annual budget is the starting point for any analysis of the impact of public finance on the economy at large. The budget is the centrepiece of the government's short-term economic strategy, and deserves attention in some detail.

Although the budget brings together in a single document the two aspects of expenditure and revenue, the considerations which govern each are to some extent separable. The determination of expenditure involves weighing the needs for the various types of public services against the total volume of resources the economy is capable of producing. At base, the allocation of resources between public and private uses is a political question to which an economist can make only a partial contribution. It is worth noting, however, that most programmes of public spending can only be expanded or cut back within fairly narrow limits in the short-term, if economic dislocation is to be avoided. For example, there is clearly a continuing need for the services of doctors, teachers, policemen, etc.; to suddenly reduce spending on them would create needless unemployment, while an attempt to increase spending could not be immediately successful because of the need to attract and train new recruits. Even capital spending programmes are hard to stop and start to fit in with short-term economic needs.

The principal way in which the budget mechanism is used as a flexible instrument of economic regulation thus tends to be through variations in revenue-raising, i.e., cutting and raising taxes. There are several factors governing the determination of taxation levels. First, there is the political question of social equity in the raising of revenue. This is a question of the distribution of a given tax burden. Second, there is the problem of the impact taxes may have on the efficiency of the economic system. This is an important matter, but its significance is more for the long-term growth of the economy than for cyclical regulation. Finally, there is the question of the impact of taxation on the level of demand in the short-term.

Very broadly, we may say that cutting taxes tends to increase disposable incomes and thus to stimulate spending, while increasing taxes reduces disposable incomes and therefore discourages spending. The need for tax changes will therefore depend largely on whether the economy is running above, below, or at the desired full-employment level.

This, however, is only part of the picture. The fact that, in the UK, government expenditure and tax receipts are to some extent separately determined in the short run means that there is not likely to be any fixed relationship between them. In other words, there will normally be a surplus or deficit in the government's accounts, which will be of varying size. It is in financing this deficit or surplus that the budget will have a monetary impact.

The finance of a deficit involves the government in issuing new liabilities which then form part of the assets of the private sector. Financing a surplus normally involves redeeming public sector debt held by the private sector, but it could in principle involve the acquisition by the government of private sector liabilities.

The impact of these financing operations on the real economy depends not on the ability of the government to obtain finance but on the manner in which the finance is obtained. The reason why there is no problem in obtaining *some sort* of finance for a government deficit derives from the role of the central bank. The central bank's liabilities are legal tender so that, to take the UK as an example, it is always possible for the government to borrow indefinitely at the Bank of England. This is what is meant by using the printing press to pay for deficits. Naturally, however, the consequences of this kind of finance are likely to be severe. The recipients of money created in this way are not likely to want to hold it, and will presumably try to spend their unwanted excess cash. The government's deficit will not therefore be matched by the willing saving of the private sector, and inflation will be the result. The successful financing of the government involves, broadly speaking, attracting sufficient willing savers to cover the government's deficit when there is full, but not overfull, employment of resources.

The size and burden of the national debt

What has been said in the previous paragraph about financing the government's deficit (or surplus) during a given accounting period applies also to the management of the outstanding stock of debt at a particular point in time. Even if the budget results in no net need for the government to borrow or to repay debt, it is still important from the point of view of monetary policy for the right balance to be struck between the demand of the public to hold government debt and the available supply of debt instruments.

If supply and demand conditions alter such that holders of government debt are no longer willing to hold the outstanding quantity of debt at prevailing rates of interest, they will attempt to sell and switch into other assets. To the extent that these movements involve switches, directly or indirectly, into goods and services, expenditure will be stimulated. An important role of debt management, therefore, is to influence the demand for and supply of government securities so that the effect of changes in private sector holdings of government debt on spending decisions complements and reinforces other measures taken to restrain or stimulate the overall level of demand for real goods and services.

Before turning to the methods by which the monetary authorities seek to achieve these objectives, and in particular the way in which the Bank of England manages the markets in government securities, it is worth spending some time looking at the size and structure of the national debt. For the effectiveness of an active debt management policy depends essentially on the nature of the response of debt-holders to official market operations.

In size, the UK national debt is larger, as a proportion of national income, than that of any other industrial country. The first substantial increase in the debt occurred as a result of borrowing undertaken to finance the First World War. Immediately after this war, the out-standing debt was in the region of £7,000 million, against national income of about £5,000 million. The Second World War saw a further large increase in the debt, and this was supplemented in the early post-war years by heavy borrowing to finance the nationalisation of certain major industries. By 1950, the national debt was about £20,000 million, against national income of some £12,000 million.

Since the heavy nationalisation programme of the late 1940s, the debt has continued to grow, as the government has, by and large, incurred deficits. The counterpart of these deficits, however, has been a large investment programme by local authorities and nationali-sed industries. As a result, an increasing proportion of the central government's debt has been 'backed' by interest-bearing loans to local authorities and nationalised industries, which are themselves 'backed' by investment in real plant and equipment (schools, roads, hospitals, factories, etc.).

From the point of view of monetary management, however, it is the gross size of the national debt that is more significant. This has been diminishing in relative terms in recent years. The economy has grown considerably faster than the national debt, with the result that the size of debt has declined from being almost twice the size of national income in 1950 to only two-thirds the size of national income in 1970.

It is sometimes suggested that the national debt constitutes a 'burden' on future generations. There is a grain of truth in this assertion, but it is largely fallacy. We have already seen that the national debt is the counterpart of substantial holdings of real assets. But even if it were not, to the extent that it is owned within the domestic economy, it represents merely a liability for one group of individuals to make payments to another group. If this results in an inequitable distribution of wealth, such a consequence can, in principle, be offset through the taxation system. There will be no net burden on the economy as a whole. If part of the national debt is owned by foreigners, then obviously some burden is passed on to a future generation. Except to this extent, however, the existence of a large national debt does not impose a *direct* resource cost on the economy.

Despite this, the national debt may nevertheless be a handicap to the economy if it imposes constraints on the conduct of policy. There is some debate in this connection about whether a large national debt is a help or a hindrance for monetary policy. On the one hand, it is clearly desirable that there should be a large and efficient market in the various categories of debt, so that it can respond flexibly to official operations. On the other hand, the larger the debt, the greater, other things being equal, will be the continuing flow of maturities. The need to continuously refinance maturing debt may induce the central bank to support the market for government securities on a more or less continuous basis to make it receptive to funding operations. Finally, if there is a substantial speculative element in the holding of the debt, small price movements may be accentuated by a sort of bandwagon effect. Economic theory does not really provide a conclusive answer to the question of whether a large national debt is a benefit or not; there is little doubt, however, that the Bank of England believes it to have been a hindrance in practice in its monetary policy operations.

Other characteristics of the national debt which are relevant to this question are the nature of holders of the debt, and the maturity structure of the debt. The UK national debt is quite widely held (there are over 2 million separate accounts), which would seem to indicate that security prices should be fairly resilient to sales of stock. However, holdings tend to be concentrated in large blocks, and these holders tend to be sensitive to expectational factors. Since there is no large class of 'captive' holders (who hold government securities by law or custom) this makes holdings rather volatile and has in practice increased the Bank of England's nervousness about permitting fluctuations in prices.

The average maturity of the UK national debt is some 12 years, and has been of this order over much of the post-war period. This relatively long life has reduced the problem of maturities (as compared, say, with the United States, where the average life of debt is much shorter). On the other hand, the Bank of England's willingness to support the price of longer-dated stocks by intervening to buy stocks in the market has increased the liquidity of holdings.

The mechanics of debt management

In practice, the financing of a given deficit during a particular accounting period cannot be separated from debt management operations involving the existing stock of outstanding debt. In what follows, the mechanics of debt management in the UK are described, using the figures for the fiscal year 1971–72. The fact that these figures represent *flows* of funds during the year must not be taken to imply, however, that the flows result solely from the finance of that year's deficit. They reflect also changes in the form in which existing debt is held.

For ease of reference, the following discussion will be conducted in terms of Table 7.1, based on figures in the Bank of England Quarterly Bulletin.

TABLE 7·1

Central Government Financing Operations, 1971/72

Borrowing requirement from domestic budgetary operations		*£ million*
Consolidated fund surplus		1,383
Loans to local authorities and nationalised industries		− 1,919
Other		54
	Total	− 482
External transactions		
Change in reserves (− = increase)		− 2,312
Overseas holdings of government debt		+ 262
Government debt total		− 2,050
		= 2,532
Domestic borrowing requirement financed by		
Bank of England		− 284
Notes and coins		166
Net sales of non-marketable debt		486
Net sales of stocks		2,043
Net sales of treasury bills		121
	Total	2,532

(+ = receipt of funds; − = payment of funds)

The two main ingredients of the central government's borrowing requirement are the Consolidated Fund balance which is, broadly speaking, the surplus or deficit of tax receipts above or below current expenditure (including grants); and the National Loans Fund, which makes loans to nationalised industries and local authorities to undertake capital investment.

In addition to the borrowing requirement which emerges from the government's domestic expenditure and tax-raising operations, there will be a need to finance the country's foreign exchange position. When the Bank of England intervenes in the exchange market to prevent the price of sterling fluctuating outside certain limits, it does so by buying and selling foreign exchange for sterling. If, for example, the pound is weak and the Bank is supporting the exchange rate, it will be selling foreign exchange and buying sterling. The sterling thus obtained can be used to finance a government deficit and thus reduce the need to borrow from domestic sources. On the other hand, when the reserves are rising, the Bank of England will be purchasing foreign exchange with sterling. The sterling needed for this purpose adds to the borrowing requirement.

It would, of course, be possible for the Bank of England to refrain from intervention in the foreign exchange market, so that there was no impact on the government's borrowing requirement from foreign exchange transactions. This policy has been employed at several times by Canada and by the UK.[1] The relative merits of intervention versus freedom in exchange rates is a wide topic, which is dealt with in more depth in Chapter 14. Here we need only note that most official opinion favours some intervention to stabilise exchange rates under normal circumstances. So long as this is the case, there will be movements in reserves which affect the government's borrowing requirement.

To some extent, changes in reserves are self-financing. If an overseas resident buys sterling in order to acquire a British government security, there will be no net effect on the amount of finance the government needs from the domestic economy. In terms of Table 7.1, the overseas resident's sale of foreign exchange will bring about an increase in the reserves, and therefore increase the government's borrowing requirement in sterling. However, his purchase of a government security automatically provides the government with the equivalent amount in sterling.

It is the combined total of the budget balance and external transactions that is most significant for the Bank of England's overall debt management objectives, and for changes in the money supply. In part, this 'domestic borrowing requirement' can be met by sales of non-marketable debt. This includes items such as Premium Savings Bonds, Save-as-you-Earn Contracts, National Savings Bonds, etc. The

---

[1] There have also been other occasions on which currencies have 'floated', but where central banks have continued to intervene in exchange markets.

terms of these savings media are usually kept unchanged over quite long periods and not varied simply for reasons of short-term monetary policy.

Increases in the total of notes and coin in circulation also provide finance to the government. Since the economy is growing year by year, the necessary circulating currency to finance transactions is also increasing. The method by which money is put into circulation is described in the next chapter, but we may note here that bank notes are economically equivalent to interest-free bearer bonds issued by the government. Although an increase in the note circulation provides the government with finance, however, the size of the increase is largely determined by the transactions needs of the general public and is not the object of deliberate control by the central bank.

We come finally to marketable debt. This is necessarily something of a residual since neither the domestic borrowing requirement nor receipts from sales of non-marketable debt can be easily manipulated in the short term. Despite this, it is the manner in which the Bank of England conducts its operations in marketable debt that determines the general thrust of monetary policy.

The two main markets in which the government borrows are the gilt-edged (or long-term bond) market, and the Treasury bill market. The gilt-edged market is important since the rates established there are communicated to other markets for long-term borrowing. They thus influence industrial borrowing costs and have a significant effect on economic activity. Furthermore, certain administrative rates, such as rates on national savings and the rate at which the central government lends to local authorities and nationalised industries are determined with reference to yields in the bond market. From the point of view of the banking system, the market for government bonds is important because the banks are substantial holders of short-dated bonds.

Stock is normally sold 'through the tap'. The Bank of England issues new stocks in large *tranches* of several hundred million pounds at a time. The price is usually pitched slightly over market levels and the bulk of an issue is taken up by the Bank itself and official agencies which temporarily have liquid funds available for investment. The Bank of England then fixes a 'tap' price at which it is prepared to sell stock as and when there is a demand for it. A similar procedure is used for the redemption of stocks. When stocks come within one year of maturity, the Bank starts to buy in outstanding holdings in the market. The objective of this gradual method of effecting both issues and redemptions is to avoid unsettling the market by sales and purchases of large tranches of stock.

In its management of the gilt-edged market, the Bank of England has several objectives, which sometimes come into conflict. It endeavours to preserve a healthy and active market, so as to facilitate the refinancing of the heavy burden of maturities which are continually falling in. It attempts to borrow on terms which, over the longer run, are as advantageous as possible to the government. It attempts to influence interest rates in the manner dictated by the needs of short-term demand-management policy. And it attempts to have an impact on the money supply that is also in line with conjunctural requirements. Perhaps the main point of conflict amongst these objectives is the goal of an appropriate rate of growth of the money supply and the objectives of preserving the health of the market through avoiding fluctuations in interest rates.

Although it would be possible in principle to aim at selling a given quantity of gilt-edged each day or week, the Bank of England does not operate that way. In its judgment, a given quantitative target for sales could only be adhered to at the cost of wider swings in prices than would be conducive to the efficient functioning of the market. Although, as we will see later, the Bank now places much more emphasis on achieving quantitative targets than it used to, it is still true that its day-to-day intervention is dictated by the willingness of the market to buy stock at existing price levels.

Given this policy, there will be a fluctuating residual need for finance to be met by sales of Treasury bills. Treasury bills are short-term negotiable securities, the interest on which is represented by the 'discount' at which they are sold. In Britain they are issued in two ways, at a weekly tender and through the tap. The Treasury bill tender takes place every Friday, when the Bank of England offers for sale an amount of 3-month bills related to the government's financing need in the following week. Bidders offer to take up bills at a specified price on a day in the following week—the actual day of the take-up and the denominations of the bills being a matter for the choice of the purchaser. Bills are allotted first to the highest bidders and then at successively lower prices until the total offering is exhausted. At the lowest price at which tenders are accepted, any remaining bills are allotted on a pro-rata basis to applicants.

Although the Bank of England relates its offering of bills to the anticipated financial needs of the Exchequer, it cannot arrange for the quantity of bills issued to be exactly right, since it does not know the exact pattern of government spending and receipts, and the financing requirement resulting from dealings in bonds and foreign exchange. And, of course, since the choice of day on which bills are taken up remains with the purchaser, the Bank cannot control day-to-day fluctuations in the government's cash position. As a result of this, shortages or surpluses may emerge, which are compensated for by purchase or sales of bills by the Bank of England. Sales are usually made by 'tapping' for bills, i.e. creating new bills in the Bank of England's portfolio, and then selling them. 'Tap' sales are also made to foreign central banks, and for certain other purposes—such as to employ funds received from commercial banks as special deposits—but these bills do not leak out into the market. 'Tap' bills, it should be noted, may be of any maturity.

All banks and discount houses and certain other brokers are entitled to tender for bills, either for themselves or on behalf of their customers. In point of fact, however, it is the discount houses who participate most actively and acquire most of the bills. Indeed, they undertake, collectively, to underwrite the tender by bidding for the whole offering. Some of the bills they acquire are sold to the banks, and there is a small amount of two-way dealing in bills between the houses; for the most part, however, bills are retained in the houses' portfolio against the need to sell them to the Bank of England on a day when money is short. In fact the 'market' in Treasury bills is dominated by dealings between the Bank of England and the discount houses. The Bank's operations are usually based on rates established at the Friday tender, although dealing does take place at other rates, usually when the Bank wishes to influence yields. Dealing is mainly with the discount houses, although the Bank may on occasion buy and sell bills with the main banks. Official operations are conducted through one of the discount houses themselves, Seccombe, Marshall and Campion.

The Bank influences rates in the bill market in a variety of ways. It may change the quantity of bills on offer at the weekly tender, which, other things being equal, will have an effect on the minimum price at which bills are allotted. It can force the discount market to borrow at the Bank of England on penal terms, thus pushing up the houses' cost of funds and reducing their willingness to hold bills at prevailing rates. It can vary the rate at which it deals in bills in its day-to-day operations. Finally it can give informal signals of its wishes, which can cause the houses to change the rates at which they bid for bills without the need for any official intervention to take place.

The impact of official debt management on other markets

The mere fact that the rate of interest on certain forms of government indebtedness changes as a result of the central bank's activities does not, in itself, have much direct impact on spending on goods and services. The central government's own expenditure is not significantly affected by the rate of interest it has to pay to borrow. Rates of interest established in the markets for government securities, however, can have an important influence on rates paid on the generality of debt instruments.

In order for this influence to be spread, government debt must be a substitute for private sector debt. The better a substitute it is, the more closely changes in rates of interest on government securities will be reflected in those on private sector securities. At the limit, if a government security was a *perfect* substitute, then clearly there could be no disparity between yields on public and private sector debt. Since the Bank of England's intervention is primarily in the Treasury bill market and gilt-edged market, the questions we wish to ask, therefore, are: how good a substitute are Treasury bills for other short-term instruments? And how good a substitute are gilt-edged securities for other long-term instruments?

As far as the non-financial sector and the banks themselves are concerned, there is very little point of contact with the Treasury bill market. The non-financial sector holds virtually no Treasury bills, and the banks hold only a very small quantity. The reason for this appears to be that the yield on Treasury bills has for some time been significantly below that on assets of comparable maturity, such as interbank lending, certificates of deposit, etc. What this means is that small changes in the yield on Treasury bills do not have a direct effect on interest rates through causing direct substitution of holdings between Treasury bills and other assets.

There is, however, an indirect route through which the effect is felt. It is through the intermediation of the discount market. The discount market is the primary holder of Treasury bills and, in addition, has a substantial portfolio of commercial bills, certificates of deposit, and short-dated gilt-edged securities.

The discount market, by convention, tenders for the entire allotment of Treasury bills. Other things being equal, a larger offering of bills will result in a lower price (i.e., higher interest rate). In order to cover their larger allotments of bills, the discount houses will have to bid more for the money they borrow from the banking system, and the fact that they are getting a higher running yield on the Treasury bills will enable them to do so.

The rates which the discount houses offer to borrow funds therefore fluctuates with Treasury bill rates. And money lent to the discount houses is, for the banks, a substitute for other short-term assets. It is not a perfect substitute, to be sure. For money lent at call to the discount market ranks as a reserve asset towards the required minimum $12\frac{1}{2}\%$ ratio, while most alternatives, such as interbank loans, certificates of deposit and, beyond a certain amount, commercial bills, do not. Nevertheless, once banks have the minimum $12\frac{1}{2}\%$ of reserve assets, the degree of substitutability between call money with the discount market and other liquid instruments, is reasonably close.

Perhaps the most important of these secondary liquid instruments are interbank loans, loans to finance houses, certificates of deposit, and loans to local authorities.

The *interbank market* is a market in unsecured, predominantly short-term loans between banks and discount houses. The market is made by a group of brokers who pass names of clients and quote rates for money at various terms, collecting commission on completed deals. They do not act as principals. A certain amount of business, however, is done by direct negotiation between banks. The largest amount of dealing is for overnight funds, but rates are quoted for all maturities up to a year. The market is particularly attractive to merchant banks and overseas banks because of the way in which they do business. They deal with large customers and like to be in a position to clinch a proposition, then finance it by bidding for the necessary funds in the market. They can tempt the necessary funds away from the discount market by bidding, if necessary, rather more than the going call-money rate. The interbank market is used by participants for three main purposes: to even out fluctuations in the flow of receipts and payments; to take a view on the future path of interest rates; and as a means for first class banks to finance less good names by taking an interbank deposit in their own name and passing it on at a turn. Some people consider the market to be a prime example of banks taking in each other's washing; nevertheless, the market has grown very rapidly, and by the end of 1972, accounted for about 15% of the banking system's total assets and liabilities in sterling.

Despite the large size of some of them, *finance houses* do not in general have a well-developed branch network. Even those that do, concentrate more on lending, finding that the taking of deposits through branches is usually more costly than bidding for funds in the parallel money markets. The bulk of finance house funds comes from fixed-term deposits by banks and other large lenders, provided through brokers. In general, finance houses have to pay a margin over interbank rates for the funds they need. This reflects the somewhat lesser security thought to be offered by a finance house—though some of the larger ones are more solid and safer than some banks. The usual practice is for the finance houses to finance day-to-day changes in their needs through bank overdrafts and then to fund this by bidding for term deposits in their own name. They are partly in a position of competing with the banks for the large deposits of big companies and partly takers of funds from the banks themselves.

Certificates of Deposit are bearer securities entitling the holder to payment of a given sum, with interest, on a particular day. It is an instrument that was developed in the US in the early 1960s, and introduced in sterling form to the UK in October 1968. Its great advantage over an ordinary bank deposit is that it is negotiable. This means that it is more liquid to the holder than an ordinary fixed-term deposit, but no more subject to withdrawal from the point of view of the bank. At the time of writing (January 1973) Certificates of Deposit may be issued by banks obtaining permission from the Bank of England, in round amounts of £50,000 and up, and for maturities of from three months to five years.

Since the attraction of CDs lies in their bearer nature, it is important that there should be a secondary market where they can be readily negotiated. This has been provided by the discount market, which quotes two-way prices in all the main maturities (and even for 'forward' CDs, not yet issued!). There are three main categories of holder of CDs. First come banks themselves, who prefer CDs to interbank loans for the longer maturities because of their negotiability and their greater anonymity—a borrower on CDs does not know who is lending to him by holding his CD. Discount houses are important holders in fulfilment of their function to make a secondary market. Finally, non-bank companies hold CDs where they want to combine the yield advantage of a term deposit, coupled with the ability to liquidate their holding if the need arises.

The market for CDs grew particularly rapidly in 1971 and 1972, reaching nearly 20% of the banking system's gross deposits in sterling by the end of 1972. Of this total, however, two thirds represented funds lent within the banking system, so that the *net* attraction of funds into CDs from outside sources was considerably less.

The *local authority market* is not one market but several. It grew up after 1955, when the government ended the automatic access of local authorities to central government funds, forcing them to borrow in their own name. By the end of 1972, the local authorities had nearly £10,000 million of debt outstanding in their own names. The three main forms in which they borrow are by the issue of bonds, bills, and temporary deposit receipts. Local authority temporary deposits can be of any maturity from two days up to about a year or so. The vast majority, however, are very short term—less than one week —so that they are a highly liquid investment. At the peak of their importance, temporary deposits with LAs constituted about 10% of the total sterling assets of the banking system.

Local authority bonds are mostly short-dated, one year being a popular maturity. During much of the 1960s, the banks were subject to restrictions on their lending to the private sector, and the local authorities found it relatively easy to make bond issues. They are subject, however, to a ceiling imposed by the Treasury on the total size of their outstanding negotiable bonds.

Local authority bills are a more recent development, and grew to prominence in the years 1969–71, when most authorities which were large enough to make issues took the necessary legal powers to do so. Even so, bills represent only a very small proportion of local authorities' outstanding debt.

All these short-term markets are influenced, to a greater or lesser extent, by official operations in Treasury bills. The price of funds in these markets governs the interest rate at which the banks and other financial institutions are prepared to lend to the private sector. And this in turn affects the willingness of the private sector to finance expenditure out of borrowing.

Turning to a longer-term debt, there is a more direct pattern of substitution between government and private sector securities. Since longer-dated government stocks are not reserve assets either for the banks or for the discount houses, the main difference from the point of view of institutions holding such assets is the greater security offered by a public sector stock (plus the fact, at the time of writing, that gilt-edged stocks are exempt from capital gains tax, while other stocks are not). In addition, because of the greater depth of the government securities market, there is normally a readier market for sales in large amounts. Because of these advantages, the yield on longer-dated government securities is usually a steady $\frac{1}{2}\%-1\%$ below the yield on comparably dated private sector debt. Any tendency for the margin to widen or narrow can be expected to promote substitution of private debt for gilt-edged in portfolios, and thus to bring the margin back to customary size.

Further reading

Bank of England, *An Introduction to Flow of Funds Accounting:* 1952-70 Bank of England, 1972.

Radcliffe Report, op. cit., Chapters 3 and 6.

Hicks, J. R., *The Social Framework*, 4th edition, London, Oxford University Press, 1971, Part V.

Sayers, R. S., op. cit., Chapter 10.

Tobin, James, An essay on the principles of debt management, op. cit.

Questions for discussion

1 Does a large national debt help or hinder the operation of monetary policy?

2 What conditions are necessary for the central bank's operations in government debt to have an effect on economic activity?

3 What effect would an increase in the reserves have on the level of credit in the economy?

4 Under what circumstances would it be fair to talk of the 'burden of the national debt'?

Part 3
Institutions

Part 3
Institutions

Introduction

Monetary policy, as we have examined it in earlier chapters, does not operate in a vacuum. It operates in a framework of institutions and markets which have, largely speaking, grown up to meet needs other than those of economic control. The financial system can change of course, both in relation to changing financial needs of private industry, and in response to the needs of the government in regulating the economy as a whole. This process of evolution takes time, however, and in the short-run, policy must work within a given institutional framework. In the next four chapters, therefore, we concentrate on a fairly detailed description of the network of banks and other financial institutions in the UK and the markets in which they deal.

The Bank of England is, both geographically and metaphorically, at the heart of the financial scene. It stands in the centre of the City's 'Square Mile', which contains all but a handful of the main British offices of banks operating in the UK. The Bank is the representative and spokesman for City interests, channelling City views and opinions to the government and interpreting government policy to the financial community. It is the guardian of an informal code of good order and conduct amongst financial institutions. It is responsible for regulating and controlling the banking system. Finally, and perhaps most importantly, it is the principal financial arm of government, responsible for raising loans and managing the national debt, and for operating official financial policy in all its aspects. It is appropriate, therefore, to begin a review of the institutional setting of the monetary system with the Bank of England.

In the private financial system, there are nearly three hundred separate banks, as well as a large number of non-bank financial intermediaries which are more or less close in nature to banks. The London financial scene is more diverse than that of any other major centre, and it would be impossible to deal with such a heterogeneous collection of institutions in a single chapter. The deposit banks, as the largest institutions, merit separate treatment, and are covered in Chapter 9. Chapter 10 deals with the rest of the banking system in the categories: merchant banks; British overseas banks; foreign banks, and discount houses. Chapter 11 casts its net somewhat wider, providing a survey of those financial institutions which fall outside the official definition of banks.

8

The Bank of England

Although the Bank of England has now become very much the government's arm in the City, this was not always the case. When the Bank was chartered in 1694, there was little thought of its being other than an ordinary private bank—though perhaps on a larger scale than its rivals. The ostensible purpose in establishing it was to raise funds for the government—actually in order to prosecute the war in the low countries. A group of 1,268 subscribers, including most leading merchants in the City of London, were incorporated as the 'Governor and Company of the Bank of England.'[1] In exchange for a loan of £1,200,000 (equivalent as a proportion of national income to several hundred millions today) the Bank was granted a Royal Charter entitling it to operate as a joint stock bank with limited liability.

From its inception, the Bank of England had substantial advantages over its rivals. Its role as the government's bank, besides bringing it the custom of the Exchequer, lent it considerable prestige, and this was enhanced by the number and standing of its shareholders. Finally, the joint stock structure permitted it under the Royal Charter enabled it to become much larger than its competitors. When banknotes replaced coins for most major transactions, it was inevitable that the most acceptable, and therefore the most widely used notes, should be those of the largest and most prestigious financial institution. During the eighteenth century, Bank of England notes became the principal circulating paper currency in London (though not in the provinces).

The general acceptability of Bank of England notes led to the growth of the Bank's role as banker to other banks. Since Bank of England notes were in demand, other banks found it necessary to keep an account at the Bank of England in order to draw out notes when

[1] The perplexing official custom of referring to the Bank of England in the plural is perhaps due to this.

needed by their customers. As paper currency and bank accounts replaced gold coin, other banks tended to cut down their holdings of gold, which were in any event costly to store and guard. Gold reserves were therefore centralised in the Bank of England, which in effect assumed the ultimate responsibility for the convertibility of paper money into gold. By 1777, Adam Smith was able to say of it 'it acts, not only as an ordinary bank, but as a great engine of state'.

The Napoleonic war period underlined the Bank's role as principal financer of the government, both directly through the loans it granted to the Exchequer, and indirectly as the issuing-house for government stocks. In addition, the Government seemed implicitly to involve itself with the affairs of the Bank when it made an Order in Council suspending conversions of the Bank's notes into cash.

In the years following the Napoleonic wars, the question of the government's role in managing the currency and the position of the Bank of England was the subject of lively controversy, culminating in the Bank Charter Act of 1844. In addition to coping with the real problems caused by the over-issue of notes by provincial banks, this act espoused the mistaken belief that the volume of currency in circulation was of critical importance to the health of the economy. As a result, it prohibited any further growth in the note-issues of provincial banks and provided for the separation of the note-issuing and ordinary banking functions of the Bank of England. This separation was accompanied by a strict limit on the quantity of bank notes that could be issued without being backed by gold. Gradually, the issuing powers of the provincial banks lapsed as a result of amalgamations, and the note issue came to be entirely concentrated in the hands of the Bank of England.

The role of the Bank of England as central note-issuing authority was thus formally recognised as early as 1844. At much the same time, the Bank was becoming aware of its duty to underwrite the basic stability of the financial system. In 1825 and again in 1837 there had been financial crises caused in part by individual bad management, but mainly by a cumulative crisis of confidence that led to unforeseeably large withdrawals of funds from banks, and thus to illiquidity. The Bank of England being the largest and most powerful financial institution in London, it was subject to considerable criticism for its failure to avert the crashes and ensuing losses. As a result, the Bank began, tentatively at first and later with more confidence, to extend assistance to the banking system at times of pressure by purchasing 'first class banking instruments' from certain institutions that found themselves in liquidity difficulties. 'First class banking instruments'

were defined as negotiable securities covering self-liquidating transactions and bearing two good British names—in practice bills of exchange. The idea was that the Bank of England should tide the banking
system over a difficult patch by acquiring assets that would be perfectly
sound in the absence of a widespread crash but which, because of a
cumulative crisis of confidence, had become temporarily unsaleable.
By providing assistance in this way, the Bank of England was generally
able to avert a crisis at no cost to itself since, in the absence of a
crash, the bills it acquired were paid at maturity in the normal course.

Thus the Bank had by the middle of the nineteenth century assumed
the role of 'lender of last resort' to the banking system. As a result,
however, it found itself in a position to influence interest rates in a
much more direct and substantial way than previously. Because of its
position of lender of last resort, other banking institutions paid close
regard in their operations to the rate at which assistance would be
available if needed. Changes in bank rate thus came to have a rapid
and pervasive effect on short-term rates in London. And in the heyday of the gold standard, when a change in the gold value of the
pound was virtually unthinkable, movements in interest rates had the
effect of directing gold flows to the financial centre with the highest
rates. Thus the Bank found that it could easily maintain its obligation
to convert paper money into gold by the 'delicate mechanism' of
adjustments in bank rate. Any tendency for gold to flow out of
reserves could be simply offset by an appropriate increase in bank rate.

By 1870, the main central banking functions of the Bank of England
were already being exercised, though they were seen more as the responsible actions of a large private bank than as conscious manipulation of
the monetary system in the national interest. The turning point in the
recognition of the Bank's role was the publication of Bagehot's
'Lombard Street', which enunciated the main principles of central
banking. The Central Bank was the note-issuing authority, it was
the protector of the nation's gold reserves, and it manipulated interest
rates with the general objective of maintaining the value of money.

Although the important national role of the Bank of England was
accepted in the nineteenth century, the anomaly in the Bank's continuing status as a private institution was not as great as might be thought.
Given the prevailing climate of economic laissez-faire, and the general
acceptance of the importance of maintaining the convertibility of
sterling into gold, the Bank's role was largely a technical rather than a
policy-making one. It was not until the interwar period that the
government accepted an increasing responsibility to intervene in
economic affairs in pursuit of objectives such as full employment

and balance of payments equilibrium. Once this responsibility was acknowledged, it was not really possible to divorce technical questions, which could be left to a private institution, from matters of national policy, which could properly be decided only by the government. Montagu Norman, Governor from 1922–44 defined the Bank's role in policy-making as 'the unique right to offer advice, and to press such advice even to the point of nagging; but always, of course, subject to the supreme authority of the government.'

The final recognition of the Bank of England's role as a Central Bank could be said to have been completed by the nationalisation of the Bank in 1946. In practice, this changed little since, as we have seen, the Bank had already acknowledged the overriding authority of the Treasury even before the latter assumed ownership.

Constitution

In form, the Bank of England is a nationalised corporation, with the right to manage independently its internal affairs. Since its most important responsibility, however, is the execution of monetary policy on behalf of the Government, this has given rise to a certain amount of speculation as to how much real independence the Bank enjoys, and how much it ought to enjoy. In the nineteenth century it used to be argued that the independence of the central bank was a necessary safeguard to prevent irresponsible governments financing themselves by resort to the printing press. This, however, was in the days when the preservation of the value of the currency was the primary financial aim, and before governments accepted responsibility for other economic goals. Now it is much more widely agreed that central banks should, in the last resort, be subordinate to political authority. (Though certain central banks, notably the US Federal Reserve System and the German Bundesbank, have a very substantial measure of independence.)

The subordinate status of the Bank of England is written into the 1946 Bank of England Act:

> The Treasury may from time to time give such directions to the Bank as, after consultation with the Governor of the Bank, they think necessary in the public interest.

In practice, however, the Bank is in a position of cooperating with the Treasury in the formulation of policy, and the need for formal direction does not arise. If its advice is sound and persuasive—and here it has the advantage of a much more intimate knowledge and understanding of the financial markets than is possible to obtain from Whitehall—then it will be influential and policy will reflect, at least in part, the Bank's views.

As far as the Bank's formal power over the rest of the banking system is concerned, this too is written into the 1946 Act:

> The Bank, if they think it necessary in the public interest, may request information from and make recommendations to bankers, and may, if so authorised by the Treasury, issue directions to any banker for the purpose of securing that effect is given to any such request or recommendation . . .

As with the Treasury's right to direct the Bank, the Bank's power to issue directives has never been used. The Bank feels that these would be unlikely to operate flexibly, and might produce unfortunate overtones of 'confrontation' in its relations with the banking system.

Turning to the organisation of the Bank, it is run by a Court of Directors which consists of the Governor, Deputy Governor, four Executive Directors and twelve part-time directors. The Governor and his deputy are appointed for five-year terms, the other directors for four years. All are Crown appointments, which is to say they are made by the Prime Minister on the recommendation of the Chancellor of the Exchequer. The Governor has frequently been brought in from outside the Bank, though Lord O'Brien, Governor from 1966 to 1973, was a career Bank official. The Deputy Governor and the four executive directors are usually officials with many years service in the Bank.

The part-time directors are in the main prominent industrialists and bankers, though with the occasional trade unionist and ex-civil servant. Since they cannot be let in to the full details of policy discussions, for fear of placing them in an embarrassing conflict-of-interest situation, their contribution to policy formation is bound to be somewhat limited. In the main, the usefulness of the part-time directors from a policy point of view lies in their ability to convey the views of industry and finance on the general development of the economy, rather than in their ability to comment on specific questions of policy. In addition, they provide useful expertise in matters of administrative policy in the internal running of the Bank.

An important role in the formulation of policy is played by the officials and advisers of the Bank's various departments.[2] These

---

[2] These departments are organised on functional lines. The historical division into Issue and Banking departments is preserved only for accounting purposes and has no economic significance.

departments, currently ten in number, give some indications of the wide-ranging aspects of the Bank's work. The most important is undoubtedly the *Cashier's department* which handles all the Bank's financial transactions and intervenes in markets both to finance the government and in furtherance of official monetary policy. Largest in size, however, is the *Printing works*, which employs nearly 2,000 people in the printing, examination and destruction of nearly 2,000 million banknotes a year. *The Accountants department* is responsible for keeping stock registers of all gilt-edged securities, and also some Commonwealth and local government loans. *The Exchange Control department*, as its name implies, administers exchange control on behalf of the Treasury. The *Overseas department* contributes advice on overseas financial developments both to the government and to other departments within the Bank. The *Economic Intelligence department* is responsible for the collection of statistics from the banking system, and for providing analysis and advice on developments in the domestic economy. It is in the Overseas and Economic Intelligence departments that most of the Bank's 30 or so specialist advisers work. The other four departments—*Audit, Secretary's, Establishments* and *Management Services*—are small departments concerned mainly with the internal running of the Bank.

The work of the bank

To fully appreciate the significance of the Bank's work, it is necessary to look behind the organisational structure to the economic functions. In the following sections, we consider these functions under three heads: the banking role, the monetary policy role and the regulatory role. To some extent, of course, these overlap: in providing finance to the exchequer, for example, the Bank of England is acting as the government's banker, but the manner in which finance is raised will have important implications for monetary policy.

The banking role

The Bank of England has four types of customer. First, and least important from the point of view of its role as a central bank, it still has a small residue of private customers, including members of its own staff. These accounts are kept on, partly for the sake of tradition, but partly also because involvement in ordinary commercial banking is thought to give the Bank some 'feel' for the kind of problems facing the institutions over which it exercises controls.

Secondly, the Bank is banker to other banks in the financial system. Any bank of the necessary reputation and standing may have an account with the Bank of England, and quite a large number do, but there are two types of financial institution which *must* have an account. The clearing banks use their balances at the Bank of England as the means of settling residual indebtedness resulting from an excess of debits over credits in transactions between their customers.[3] And the discount houses must have accounts to enable them to borrow from the Bank. It is through the discount market that the Bank of England extends the 'lender of last resort' help mentioned earlier.

Thirdly, the Bank is banker to almost a hundred overseas central banks and monetary institutions. For some of these, it simply holds working balances sufficient to enable the daily settlement of international indebtedness resulting from official interventions in foreign exchange markets. For others, notably those in the old sterling area, the Bank invests sums at short term in Treasury bills or similar instruments, and may provide investment advice on the placement of longer-term funds in gilt-edged securities. The Bank also holds special accounts for certain overseas central banks to facilitate short-term loan transactions (the swap network described on page 245–6).

Fourthly, and probably most importantly, the Bank is banker to the central government. This does not mean that every cheque of every government department comes through the Bank of England. The great majority use the facilities of the clearing banks, with their large branch networks, for this purpose. But the daily surpluses and deficits of departments are centralised in the Bank, and it is to the Bank that the responsibility falls for making sure that finance is available to cover a deficit, or for using any surplus to repay debt.

In the purely accounting sense, there is always finance to cover a deficit. The government can make payments to individuals and firms in the private sector by drawing on its account at the Bank of England; if funds are not available in this account, the Bank automatically extends a loan to the Exchequer. This loan will be covered by higher bankers deposits, since the money which, when it was paid out, created the deficit will have caused bankers deposits at the Bank of England to be higher. However, the finance of the government is more than simply a technical question of ensuring that funds are available to make payments to the government's creditors. Debt management is,

---

[3] These balances are the largest single item in the Banking Department's balance sheet and as such provide a substantial proportion of the Bank's independent income.

as we have seen in the previous two chapters, an important arm of monetary policy in its own right.

In addition to its other banking functions, the Bank of England is the central note-issuing authority for the UK. All transactions relating to the issue of notes are separated, for accounting purposes, in the 'Issue Department' while other transactions come under the 'Banking Department', this separation being a legacy of the Bank Charter Act of 1844. The profits of note issue are paid over *in toto* to the Exchequer.

These profits arise from the fact that the note liabilities are backed by holdings of government and other interest bearing securities. To a large extent, of course, the profit is on paper only, since the government pays the interest on most of the securities the Issue Department holds. Nevertheless, the fact that the money paid over for notes by banks and the general public is invested in government debt provides the exchequer with a sizeable, interest-free source of finance.[4]

Nowadays, the management of the note issue is an administrative and not a policy matter. Although under the 1844 Act the size of the fiduciary issue has to be authorised through Parliament, changes in its size are in fact made more or less automatically to meet seasonal and other fluctuations in the public's demand. The mechanism by which this is achieved is as follows: The Banking Department will usually hold a 'float' of notes among its assets. These will be drawn on by banks in exactly the same way as an ordinary person would draw money out of his account, i.e., through a compensating change in the bank's balance with the Bank of England. When the 'float' gets too high or too low, a change in the fiduciary issue is authorised and the Banking Department buys notes from, or sells notes to, the Issue Department. In exchange for the issue of a 'new' liability, the Issue Department receives payment in the form of securities formerly held by the Banking Department. The Issue Department holds a store of new but unissued (and therefore technically valueless) notes which it can bring out of store and issue to the Banking Department. Thus a change in the fiduciary issue can be achieved by a stroke of the pen in the Bank's ledgers and the redesignation of a stock of notes into the assets of the Banking Department.

As we have already noted, the note issue is no longer a matter of much economic significance, although as a practical matter it is the

---

[4] In Scotland and N. Ireland, local notes circulate which are the liabilities of commercial banks. These are, apart from a token amount, fully backed by Bank of England notes set aside in the Bank's vaults in London.

largest single task the Bank undertakes in terms of staff. It is worth noting, however, that the securities held as backing for the note issue provide a financial *masse de manoeuvre* which is important for the Bank's operations in financial markets.

The monetary policy role

To a large extent, the Bank's role in the field of monetary policy springs from its role as banker to government. Because of the sheer size of the national debt, operations to raise finance for government to fund or to repay debt are bound to have a substantial effect on financial conditions.

We can divide the Bank's work as an operator of monetary policy into several types. In the first place it intervenes in markets, buying and selling securities; secondly, it administers direct controls on behalf of the Treasury; thirdly, it uses its influence and prestige in the City to induce compliance with policies deemed to be in the national interest; fourthly, it undertakes research and analysis in order to be able to advise government on possible changes in policy.

The three markets in which the Bank operates are the bill market, the gilt-edged market and the foreign exchange market. In the first two markets, the Bank operates by buying and selling securities from its own portfolio (usually the Issue Department's but occasionally the Banking Department's). It operates through brokers, a procedure which it values as enabling it to keep at 'arm's length' from dealers in the market. In the bill market, the broker is the discount house of Seccombe, Marshall and Campion; in the bond market, the stock-broking firm of Mullens and Co. In the foreign exchange market the Bank deals directly, and here it is acting as agent for the Exchange Equalisation Account which is a Treasury account and does not form part of the Bank's own portfolio.

The principal form of direct control which the Bank administers is the Exchange Control, which regulates the payments that UK residents may make in foreign currencies and transactions in sterling involving non-residents. The legal authority for these restrictions is the Exchange Control Act, 1947, which operates on the principle of banning virtually all transactions and then granting administrative exemptions to certain categories. Up till the early 1960s there had been a strong trend away from the use of exchange control and towards liberalisation of payments, but since then this trend has gone into reverse as a result of currency crises. Consequently, the staff of Exchange Control, having dwindled to a low point of about 100, had by the early 1970s swelled to three or four times that figure.

Apart from legal types of restriction, such as Exchange Control, the Bank can and has used its prestige to secure the agreement of the banking system to observe voluntary restrictions on their activities. Ceiling controls on bank advances were a case in point: the Governor wrote to the various banking associations requesting that their members should observe a given degree of restraint on the expansion of certain types of lending. Other examples of the Bank's use of 'moral suasion' were the voluntary programme of restraint on investment in the developed countries of the sterling area; and the guidance given to banks on priorities to be observed in lending under successive credit squeezes. More recently, the Bank was able to use its influence to secure voluntary agreement to the new system of credit control introduced in September 1971. How far all these examples represent genuinely voluntary agreement is difficult to judge. All banks must be aware that the Bank has powers to issue directives to banking institutions and that if this device proved insufficient it would have to be equipped with legal powers.

Finally, in the realm of monetary policy, the Bank is the principal adviser to the Treasury. Since the Radcliffe Report, the Bank has increased the range of the statistics it collects and devoted more resources to their analysis. The Bank now has a fairly large staff of economists whose responsibilities range from monitoring statistics of banking activity as they become available, to providing econometric analysis with sophisticated computerised models. The objective of all this is to increase understanding of how financial and real variables interact, and thus provide policy-makers with a firmer basis for decisions.

The regulatory role

The Governor of the Bank of England is often thought of as 'first citizen' of the financial community. In this capacity he, and through him the Bank of England, has three distinct responsibilities. In the first place, he has a responsibility to represent the views of the City to the government of the day and vice versa. Secondly, he has a responsibility to ensure the good order and conduct of all City institutions and practices. Thirdly, he has a more specific responsibility for the health of the banking system.

In representing the views of the City to the government, the Bank covers a much wider scope than just the banking system. The stock exchange, insurance firms and commodity traders all look, at least in some measure, to the Bank for help and protection. Before each budget, the Governor normally writes to the representatives of these interests to ask whether there are any questions to which they would particularly like him to draw the Chancellor's attention. The flow of views is, of course, two ways. The government usually looks to the Bank of England to interpret its policies to the financial community.

The Bank's responsibility for the good order of City practices is again an informal one, and one that rests upon the traditional status of the Bank as the most important institution in the City, on whose Court are represented the various interests of the Square Mile. Because there exists in the UK no regulatory authority comparable to, say, the Securities and Exchange Commission in the US, the City has had to police itself. Although the Bank has no direct central banking interest in the conduct of, for example, the Stock Exchange or the Commodity markets, it has on numerous occasions used its influence as a catalyst to get various interests to agree on common codes of practice or methods of self-regulation. Perhaps the best example of this in recent years was the Bank's role in the establishment of the City Code on Takeovers and Mergers. After a number of spectacular takeovers had attracted a good deal of adverse publicity in the middle 1960s, there was much talk of an official regulatory authority. Various city interests were against this, feeling it would introduce an undesirable amount of rigidity into accepted practices and that the promulgation of a legal framework would simply create work for lawyers finding and plugging loopholes. Nevertheless, some kind of control was clearly needed. It was left to the Governor to propose the takeover code and the Panel that was to police it. The Bank also provided the finance necessary to pay the Panel's secretariat.

The Bank has a more direct responsibility for the health of the banking system. In most other countries, this responsibility is specifically entrusted to the central bank or to a banking commission. In the UK it is done strictly informally, through the Discount Office of the Bank of England. There are two aspects to this work. In the first place, the Bank is anxious to keep itself informed of the general development of the business of established banks. This is not always possible from published balance sheet information, since banks are allowed, under Schedule 8 of the Companies Act, to keep hidden reserves which enable them to conceal their true profits. The true figures must, however, be revealed to the Discount Office, which reserves the right to make representations if it does not like what it finds. Secondly, the Bank is concerned in advising government departments on granting of various banking recognitions to companies which have not yet acquired full banking status. The Bank is fairly cautious in recommending the granting of these recognitions, its general aim being to ensure that full banking status is only granted to those institutions which have proved their ability by a fairly long and arduous apprenticeship. The Bank has been criticised here for operating a kind of closed shop in banking, though its motives are not to protect existing banks so much as to prevent the establishment of incompetent or fraudulent concerns.

The various hurdles which aspiring banks must clear on the road to full authorised status are described in the Appendix to this Chapter.

Appendix

The legal framework of banking in the UK

In most countries outside the UK and Commonwealth, the activity of banking is legally defined, and certain companies are licensed, or chartered, to carry on this activity. Legislation defines the rights and obligations of banks and gives government departments and central banks duties of regulation and control.

In Britain, there is no general statute covering the activities of banks. There is not even a legal definition of what a bank is, beyond the classic 'a body of persons, whether incorporated or not, carrying on the business of banking'. In fact, anyone can establish himself as a bank and perform the basic banking functions of taking deposits and investing money. There are, however, a number of banking functions which may not be undertaken, and a number of rights which the intending banker will not possess, until he acquires certain official 'recognitions' of his banking status. In this section, therefore, we consider some of the legal restraints on 'bodies of persons carrying on the business of banking'.

The first restraint will be in the choice of a company name. The Department of Trade and Industry will not allow a company to use the words 'Bank' or 'Banking' in its title unless it has an established reputation as a bank in the financial community. In practice, this means that aspiring banks have to serve a lengthy apprenticeship using some other name. Overseas registered banks, which are not incorporated in the UK but which operate through branches instead, are able to use their own name, so that the UK authorities are dependent here on the surveillance of the monetary authority in the foreign country.

Companies which are not recognised by the Courts as 'bona fide carrying on the business of banking' are subject to the Moneylenders Act if they advance money. If they do not apply for moneylenders licences—something which aspiring banks are loath to do—they would be treated as 'unlicensed moneylenders' when they make a loan, thus placing themselves in breach of the law and absolving the debtor of any legal liability to repay.

There are basically two ways in which companies can get exemption from the provisions of the Moneylenders Acts. One is under section 6(e) of the 1927 Act. This empowers the Board of Trade (now the Department of Trade and Industry) to exempt companies that undertake not to charge a rate of interest of more than $12\frac{1}{2}\%$ p.a. on loans. The second, and more important, way is to get a Certificate from the DTI to the effect that the company is 'bona fide carrying on the business of banking' (a Section 123 certificate). Usually a Section 123 certificate will be issued to a company that fulfils the following criteria:

a Capital of at least £100,000.
b A significant current account business.
c Competent management.
d Satisfactory banking experience.

Banks which are well-established have no need of a Section 123 certificate, since there is no doubt that the courts would uphold their claim to be 'bona fide carrying on the business of banking'. Thus, the majority of foreign banks do not bother to apply for this recognition; those that do would usually obtain recognition straight away.

Recognition as a bank for the purpose of the Moneylenders Act is usually accompanied by recognition by the Inland Revenue for tax purposes. This entitles the bank concerned to pay and receive interest without deduction of tax. Generally speaking, this entitlement follows shortly after recognition by the Department of Trade and Industry for Moneylenders Act purposes. Usually the principals of the company would be expected to visit the Bank of England, to enable officials there to hear their intentions and to form a judgment of the management's abilities. Since 1969, the Inland Revenue recognition has, however, been of less importance to banks, since interest on the great majority of bank loans is no longer eligible for tax relief.

A much more important step is involved in advancing to the status of an authorised dealer in foreign exchange. This is an appointment made (by the Treasury on the recommendation of the Bank of England) for the purpose of administering the Exchange Control Act. Only authorised banks are allowed to deal freely in foreign exchange and hold accounts for non-residents. The prime consideration in making this appointment is that the bank is adequately staffed, particularly at the higher level, with people experienced in exchange dealing and exchange control work. It usually takes a newly established bank a considerable time, sometimes many years, to achieve the standing in the banking community which is expected of an authorised dealer. (The rather cautious policy of the Bank of England in this regard is due to the fact that considerable statutory powers in the administration of Exchange Control regulations are delegated to authorised dealers—hence the Bank prefers to wait until absolutely certain that appointment as an authorised dealer is fully merited.)

Before granting full authorised status, however, the Bank of England will normally grant a bank certain interim permissions *ad hoc*, which will enable it to build up experience and demonstrate its competence. Foreign banks which already have a substantial international reputation could normally expect their branches in London to become authorised after serving a nominal apprenticeship period—perhaps three months or so. British banks, however, who are establishing a reputation *de novo*, would be unlikely to receive authorised status for a number of years.

The ultimate statutory recognition for a bank or discount house is inclusion in the list of companies exempted from certain provisions of Schedule 8 to the Companies Act 1948—the select bank of companies (in 1972, 77 in number) which may maintain hidden reserves and conceal their true profits or losses. The criteria for banks to gain this privilege do not differ markedly from those for authorised dealer status, but since there has been criticism of the accounting privileges entailed, no bank has been added to the Schedule 8 list for several years.

The Protection of Depositors Act was superimposed on the existing structure of recognitions in 1963. This Act prescribes the conditions under which companies may advertise for deposits from the general public. Exemption from the provisions of this Act is granted to any bank or discount company enjoying Schedule 8 exemption, and to other banks designated by the Board of Trade. Generally this recognition—which may be said to have superseded Schedule 8 as the ultimate banking accolade—is not granted until a bank has been operating as an authorised dealer for a number of years.

All the recognitions listed above are granted by departments (the DTI, the Treasury, and the Inland Revenue). The Bank of England has no statutory role, but it does, of course, give advice and frequently its advice may well be the over-riding factor.

All the recognitions are granted administratively: that it to say there are no statutory criteria, and no rights of appeal for unsuccessful applicants. Nevertheless, an attempt is made to apply consistent criteria, and banks who are turned down are normally told the basis for rejection. Economic need for the services of a new bank is not a consideration in any of the recognitions—unlike the procedure in many other countries.

The Bank of England keeps a list of banks which defines the banking sector for the purposes of collecting information and collating figures of advances, money supply, etc. There is also a slightly different list of banks which have to observe assets ratios for purpose of monetary control. Generally speaking, banks are added to this list when they become authorised dealers, or when this status appears imminent. Branches of foreign banks which set up in London, however, are usually added directly to the list, even though they may not acquire authorised status for some time after their arrival.

Further reading

Artis, M. J., *Foundations of British Monetary Policy*, Oxford, Basil Blackwell, 1965.

Bagehot, Walter, *Lombard Street*, London, J. Murray, 1924, Chapter 7.

Bank of England, Organisation and functions of the Bank of England, *Bank of England Quarterly Bulletin*, September 1966.

Bank of England, The work of the cashier's department, *Bank of England Quarterly Bulletin*, September 1970.

Radcliffe Report, op. cit., Chapters 5 and 9.

Select Committee on Nationalised Industries Report, *The Bank of England*, 1970.

Sayers, R. S., *Modern Banking*, op. cit., Chapters 3, 4 and 5.

Sayers, R. S., *Central Banking after Bagehot*, Oxford, Clarendon Press, 1957.

Sykes Memorial Lectures, *The Bank of England Today*, London, Institute of Bankers, 1964.

Questions for discussion

1 What are the advantages and disadvantages of having a central bank independent from the government?

2 In what way do the Bank of England's functions as banker to the government overlap with its rôle in monetary policy?

3 What are the advantages and disadvantages of the Bank of England's method of regulating the private banking system?

9

Deposit banks

Deposit banks are those whose main function is taking deposits from the general public, providing account-keeping and money transmission services, and granting lending facilities. By far the largest and most important of the deposit banks are those which are members of the centralised clearing system, either in London or Scotland, and known as the clearing banks. There are a few smaller deposit banks (e.g., the Co-op bank) but, apart from remembering that they exist, they need not detain us here. On almost every count, the clearing banks dominate the British banking system. There are six English clearing banks and three Scottish, and between them they have about 12,000 branches in Great Britain, 95% of the banking offices in the country. Their sterling deposits at the end of 1972 amounted to about 55% of the total for the banking sector, and their share of total lending to about 60%. The relative sizes can be seen from Table 9.1.

TABLE 9·1

Gross Deposits of Clearing Banks

English:	December 1972 (£ millions)
Barclays	4,277
National Westminster	4,706
Midland	4,288
Lloyds	2,583
Williams and Glyns	706
Coutts	183
*Scottish:**	
Bank of Scotland	
Royal Bank of Scotland	1,581
Clydesdale	

* Individual figures not available for Scottish banks.

In fact, these nine banks belong to five groups, four large and one small. Coutts is a subsidiary of the National Westminster Bank;

Williams and Glyns and the Royal Bank of Scotland are both sub-sidiaries of the same holding company, the National and Commercial Banking Group; Clydesdale is a subsidiary of Midland, and the Bank of Scotland is part-owned by Barclays.

The first question to be asked about the structure of British banking is why there should have been such a strong tendency towards concentration in a small number of large groups. This tendency, in point of fact, is not confined to the UK but is apparent in all countries, except those—such as the US—where there are legal restraints on branching. The answer lies, simply enough, in the economies of scale that exist in banking.

These economies of scale were evident even in the early days of banking. Large banks were much more able to withstand financial crises than small ones. They were likely to have a larger number of depositors so that no single depositor could embarrass the bank by withdrawing his funds. In addition, if a bank had a number of branches, it would have a geographical spread of risks that would make it better able to withstand a slump in one particular industry or region. Besides the tangible benefits of bigness, of course, large organisations naturally engendered more confidence among potential depositors.

Another advantage of a large bank is that it is better able to economise on low-yielding assets. Instead of tying up a lot of its funds in liquid assets to meet the possibility of withdrawals, it can use balances taken at one branch to meet withdrawals at another. This is particularly useful when branches in one part of the country have a different seasonal flow of funds to their customers from branches elsewhere.

A large bank is better able to offer specialist services than a smaller unit. Once a bank reaches a size where it can have separate departments for documentary credits, foreign exchange, money market management, and so on, it can afford to recruit or train specialists with expertise in these areas. It can also have a research department which can provide credit analysis of particular customers and markets. Only a large bank is able to offer a 'package deal' to large industrial companies. As the scale of industry has grown over the years, so has its financial requirements. A small bank could not fully meet the needs of a major industrial company without upsetting the balance of its business.

A final impetus towards centralisation has been provided by electronic data-processing. Computer installations are costly and complicated, and are proportionately cheaper the larger the size of the bank concerned. Economies in the use of computer facilities were important arguments advanced to justify the merger in 1968 between National Provincial and Westminster Banks, and the proposed merger between Barclays, Lloyds and Martins Banks in the same year (though in the latter case, the Monopolies Commission considered that the disadvantages of monopoly tendencies more than outweighed the economies of scale, from the point of view of the public interest).

The logic of concentration has reduced the number of domestic banks gradually over the years. At the peak period for 'unit' banks, around the beginning of the nineteenth century, there were almost certainly well over 500 separate domestic banks in the UK although no precise records are available. Their numbers contracted gradually during the middle years of the nineteenth century, and after about 1870 the amalgamation movement gathered pace. By 1920, the number of London clearing banks had been reduced to eleven, at which time authorities made it clear that at that time they did not favour any further contraction in numbers. The situation changed over the next fifty years, however, and in the latter part of the 1960s there was a further wave of amalgamations reducing the numbers of London clearing banks from eleven to six, and Scottish clearing banks from five to three.

The work of the clearing banks is most easily discussed in terms of the main items on the two sides of the balance sheet—liabilities and assets. We must beware, however, of gaining the impression that we can discuss the two sides of the balance sheet in isolation from one another. Banks are in business to make profits. There is no benefit in taking a deposit if it cannot be profitably employed. The bank's management will attempt to increase deposits of various types to the point where the marginal cost of attracting an additional pound by one means is the same as by any other and is equal to the marginal yield obtained by employing the money.

Deposits

The clearing banks attract deposits from the public in three main forms: current accounts, ordinary deposit accounts, and large term deposits. Each of these categories is sufficiently distinct to warrant separate treatment.

Current accounts arise from the banks' traditional function of providing a money-transmission mechanism for the economy at large. Since individuals and companies are not in a position to synchronise perfectly their receipts and payments, they will need to maintain a credit balance at most times if they are to avoid becoming overdrawn when payments exceed receipts. Since current account balances traditionally bear no interest, we may assume that current account holders only hold these accounts to cover their normal flow of transactions; nevertheless, it may be seen from Table 9.2 that the clearing banks derive almost half their resources from current accounts.

TABLE 9·2

Clearing Banks Deposits, December 1972*

Current accounts	7,198
Deposit accounts	8,946
Other†	598
Gross deposits	16,742
Less Cheques in course of collection and items in transit	−754
Net deposits	15,988

* N.B. London Clearing Banks only.
† Mainly suspense accounts and credits in course of transmission.

Since the clearing banks have by far the largest branch network, and the most highly developed system of cheque clearing, it is not surprising that they hold over 90% of current accounts. They pay no interest on these accounts, although they are not, as in the US prevented by law from doing so, and some of the non-clearing banks—notably the Co-op Bank—do offer a small return on current accounts. In fact, however, the vast majority of current accounts cost more to operate than they produce in investment income, and the banks have to seek additional remuneration through direct charges. Banks do, however, allow balances held on current account to establish a notional 'credit' to offset against bank charges. Thus current accounts do earn a form of return, and one which, incidentally, is not taxable.

Competition for current accounts was until 1971 restricted by the cartel arrangements of the clearing banks. Such competition as there was, was in the form of additional branches, advertising, and other services. As a result of the 1971 changes, this competition will probably move into new areas. Also the Giro, the Trustee Savings Banks and some of the 'fringe' banks are competing more actively for current account money. Despite this, competition among the clearing banks is likely to remain in the area of service rather than rate, as they take the view that the cost of paying interest on all their deposits would be disproportionate compared with the value of the business such a move would bring.

Ordinary *deposit accounts* cannot be drawn on by cheque and bear interest. Normally they can be withdrawn at once with only a modest loss of interest, if any, so that they form a highly liquid asset which can be turned into purchasing power quickly and without difficulty. In principle, deposit accounts should be competing with other interest bearing liquid savings media, such as the Building Societies and Trustee Savings Banks. But under the cartel arrangements the interest rate offered by clearing bank deposit accounts was a poor one, and it is hard to believe that there were many interest-sensitive savers invested in bank deposit accounts. The banks relied on a combination of inertia, convenience for those who held current accounts with the same institutions, and legal requirements which provide that certain categories of funds (e.g., trustee funds) must be placed with banks. Despite the lack of attractiveness of deposit accounts they represented about half of clearing banks' resources. Since 1971, banks have been much more free to compete on rates in attracting funds from small savers. After a cautious beginning, it became apparent that competition would result in much more competitive yields being offered on banks' deposit accounts.

Investors in *large term deposits* tend to be much more interest sensitive, and banks have to offer more competitive rates. Unlike current and deposit accounts, there is a true 'market' for large term deposits in which prices change from week to week and day to day in response to supply and demand conditions. The large banks circulate their branches every day with the rates that they may offer for deposits of a certain size or a certain maturity. Really large deposits will merit a separate quotation.

In addition to ordinary term deposits, most banks offer 'Certificates of Deposit'. These are essentially deposits that are fixed-term as far as the bank is concerned, but which can be sold by the depositor if he needs funds unexpectedly. Thus they are the only element of banks deposits which are 'marketable' in the technical sense. Because of this additional attraction to the depositor, certificates of deposit tend to command lower rates than ordinary deposits of equivalent length and seem likely to grow at the expense of large non-marketable deposits.

Large depositors usually have the option of placing their funds directly in the money market, and many do choose to cut out the banks in this way. The banks cannot usually offer such attractive rates, since they themselves are investing in these markets and have to take a turn. They can offer somewhat greater flexibility, however, and they can add the security of their banking name, a service for which many borrowers are prepared to accept a modest cut in interest.

Banks find it more economic to meet fluctuations in their needs for funds by varying the rate they pay to these large, interest-sensitive investors. Any clearing bank could attract a large volume of funds by raising the rate it paid on CDs say $\frac{1}{8}\%$ over the going rate. A similar change, applied to ordinary deposit accounts, or used to reduce bank charges would have, in all probability, a negligible result, but would be costly in terms of the bank's profits since the concession would apply across the board to existing as well as to new customers.

Assets

On the assets side of the balance sheet, the portfolio decision facing bankers can be most simply expressed in terms of competing needs for income and liquidity. As profit-seeking organisations, banks naturally benefit from lending at the highest rates of interest available. But since their funds are invested on behalf of depositors who are entitled to seek repayment either immediately or at short notice, they also need to keep a substantial proportion of their assets in readily realisable form. Quite apart from the need to have liquidity available to meet withdrawals, banks will wish to have short-dated assets to reduce the risk of loss in the event of a rise in interest rates (which will affect the market price of longer-dated assets proportionately more than shorter-dated assets).

In addition to these purely commercial considerations determining the distribution of their asset portfolios, the banks face constraints imposed, largely for reasons of monetary policy, by the authorities. In the UK, this constraint is a requirement to hold $12\frac{1}{2}\%$ of deposits in certain designated 'reserve' assets.

At December 1972, the London clearing banks' principal assets were as shown in Table 9.3.

Cash at the Bank of England is the float held by the London clearing banks to meet unforeseen fluctuations in their day-to-day deposits. Experience has shown that these fluctuations can be as much as 1% of total deposits; accordingly the Bank of England has agreed with the six clearing banks that they will have 'target' balances equal to $1\frac{1}{2}\%$ of deposits (or, to be precise, of eligible liabilities). This is sufficient to ensure that the possibility of a bank being overdrawn at the Bank of England is remote.

Cash in tills is an essential part of the banks' role in providing basic money transmission services to the public. It is a non-earning

TABLE 9·3

Clearing Banks Main Assets, December 1972

	£ millions
Cash in tills and at the Bank of England	911
Bills discounted	801
Money at call	1,089
Interbank loans and Certificates of Deposit	1,946
Loans to local authorities	210
Special deposits	—
British Government stock	1,245
Advances	10,157
Total	16,359
Other assets	190

asset, and therefore the banks try to economise on currency floats as much as possible. But since they dare not take the risk of running out of cash, and since the Bank of England has only seven provincial note-distribution centres, there is an effective minimum cash holding for a retail bank of about 4% to 5% of deposits. Because this cash holding is part of the normal stock-in-trade of branch banking, and plays a much smaller role for other banks, it has been excluded from reserve assets by the authorities. (The reserve ratio is discussed in more detail in Chapter 13.)

Money at call with the discount market, Government stock with less than a year to go to redemption and certain categories of *bills discounted*[1], comprise those assets which, in addition to balances with the Bank of England, are regarded by the monetary authorities as 'reserve assets', of which the banks must hold a minimum 12½% of deposits. They are, in fact, those assets which the authorities will turn into cash, directly or through the mechanism of the discount market, more or less on demand. The banks are free to determine the composition of their reserve assets themselves (with the exception of the 1½% target cash balance, and a maximum of 2% in commercial bills). In practice, a large part of the clearing banks' reserve assets is held with the discount market. This is because of the extreme convenience and liquidity of the call-money instrument, and because

[1] The definition here is rather complex. Treasury bills and local authority bills are reserve assets without limit. Commercial bills are divided into two categories; those accepted by 'eligible' banks qualify as a reserve asset to a maximum of 2%, while others are not reserve assets.

the houses are often able to offer a better rate than that obtainable in Treasury bills.

In addition to the basic $12\frac{1}{2}\%$ reserve ratio, banks normally hold a 'cushion' of highly liquid instruments to guard against fluctuations in their deposits which might suddenly reduce their reserve assets. Some of this will be in surplus reserve assets, and some in other money-market instruments such as *inter-bank loans, certificates of deposit, temporary loans to local authorities* and non-eligible bills.

Special deposits may be called by the Bank of England when there is a need to restrict the capacity of banks to extend credit. These deposits, which were described in more detail in Chapter 6, are 'frozen accounts' at the Bank of England, which bear interest at the Treasury bill rate. They are called uniformly from all banks, in amounts expressed as a percentage of deposits subject to reserve requirements.

'*Investments*', for the clearing banks, means exclusively British Government and government-guaranteed securities. These are attractive to banks because they normally bear a higher yield than reserve assets and yet they are readily marketable. On the other hand, with an average life of 4–5 years, their price is more subject to fluctuations, due to changes in interest rates which make them less attractive as a liquid asset. It is perhaps best to think of them as second-line liquidity, to be called on to meet a prolonged increase in loan demand from customers. (To some extent, however, banks are now becoming more active in their portfolio management, and are looking also for dealing profits.)

Finally, comprising more than half of banks' assets, come *loans and advances*. These are the most profitable of a bank's assets, but also the most risky (in terms of the possibility of default) and, in practice, the least liquid. The vast bulk of lending by clearing banks in the UK is still done by means of the overdraft. A customer negotiates with his banker a limit up to which he may write cheques without having funds in his account. He is charged interest on the extent to which the account is overdrawn. The advantage of this system to the customer is its flexibility. He is not tied to any fixed repayment schedule, and he is only charged interest on the extent to which the facility is used, not on its total amount. For the banker, it has the advantage that the overdraft bears a rate of interest which may be changed with changes in the general level of interest rates, and it is, theoretically at any rate, repayable on demand through withdrawal of the facility. The whole system is based on understandings not legal contracts, however, and one of the unwritten understandings is that the banker will not recall overdrafts without reasonable notice.

Rates payable are a matter for negotiation. Most lenders, including the main clearing banks who handle the vast bulk of the business, quote a 'base rate' and grant overdrafts at a fixed margin over this rate. Banks do compete with each other but, since most large borrowers tend to be rate sensitive, it is unusual for there to be a difference in base rates that lasts for any length of time. The competition in the market to make loans tends to be mainly in the area of general service—the bank which can offer the most attractive all-round package getting the business.

The overdraft system, as well as the advantages we have just noted, has several major drawbacks as well. For the banks it introduces difficulty into the forecasting of loan commitments. Overdraft facilities are generally arranged for a larger amount than is on average outstanding over a period. This means that at any point in time, there is likely to be a sizeable volume of unused overdraft facilities. Studies have indicated that in the late 1960s unused facilities were probably half as much again as actual lending. Although banks are legally entitled to refuse to honour these agreed limits, for obvious reasons they virtually never do so. The result is that the total size of their lending is, at least in the short term, outside their immediate control.

There is also the point that, when a customer is not tied to a fixed repayment schedule for a loan, the financial discipline on him is looser. If he is not required to amortise a loan, the argument goes, he will not make provision for repayment, and his overdraft will become built-in, virtually part of his capital. In such cases, it becomes practically impossible to cut back an overdraft facility, despite its supposed liquidity.

As a result of an increasing awareness of these disadvantages, there has been some move towards 'term lending' as a means of extending bank finance (this is the typical method in the US). Under a term loan a fixed amount is credited to a customer's account and a fixed repayment schedule agreed. Interest payable is also fixed, so that there is no benefit to the customer if the loan is not fully utilised (though there may be a break clause with suitable penalties). This type of loan encourages stricter financial planning and control on the part of the customer. He will try to arrange the minimum loan he needs, and gear it to a planned repayment schedule.

Although overdraft finance was still overwhelmingly predominant in 1972, the deposit banks are beginning to offer customers a range of different facilities, including term lending at fixed rates, term lending at variable rates, fixed date repayment and phased repayments. The lengths of loans can be similarly adjusted to meet customers' particular needs and preferences.

It is perhaps worth ending the chapter on a cautionary note. In 1972, the structure and practices of the clearing banks were in the middle of a process of change and adaptation. This followed the major reform by the Bank of England of its methods of controlling the banking system introduced in 1971. Until 1971, the London clearing banks observed rather different ratios from those introduced at that time. There was a cash ratio of 8%, cash being defined as the combined total of balances at the Bank of England and till money; and a liquidity ratio (30% until 1963, thereafter 28%) which included bills, money market lending, and certain other short-term assets. To encourage the banks to extend credit for exports, they were allowed to include certain types of longer-term export paper in the liquid ratio so that their 'true' liquidity had, by 1971, become considerably less than reported liquidity.

The most striking change in banks' balance sheets since the war, however, has been in the relative proportions of investments and advances. During the war and in its aftermath, the government had a very great need of finance, but private industry was by and large self-financing. As late as 1955, investments made up 30% of banks' assets, while loans were only 20%. In the 1958–59 boom, however, and again in 1963–64 advances expanded very rapidly and, by 1964, accounted for over 50% of banks' assets. At this level, they are probably closer to the long-run desired proportion which the banks aim at.

Further reading

Day, A. C. L., *Outline of Monetary Economics*, op. cit., Part III.

Grant, A. T. K., *The Machinery of Finance and the Management of Sterling*, Macmillan, 1967, Chapters 4 and 5.

Hanson, J. L., *Monetary Theory and Practice*, op. cit., Chapter 2.

Nevin, E. and Davis, E., *The London Clearing Banks*, London, Elek Books, 1970.

Radcliffe Report, op. cit., Chapter 4.

Sayers, R. S., *Modern Banking*, op. cit., Chapter 2.

Questions for discussion

1 Why should there be only a handful of clearing banks in the UK, compared with over 10,000 in the US?

2 'Commercial banking must be a very lucrative business, since a large portion of bank's deposits are interest-free'. Comment.

3 What are the advantages and disadvantages of the overdraft method of making loans ?

4 What considerations govern the portfolio structure of a commercial bank's balance sheet ?

10

The rest of the banking system

Merchant banks

A large number of institutions style themselves 'Merchant Banks' though, in the case of some of the smaller ones, the designation reflects hopeful ambition rather than an accurate description of what they do. The principal merchant banks are members of the Accepting Houses Committee and in 1972 were seventeen in number, including some of the most prestigious names in British banking, such as Rothschilds, Hambros, Barings, and so on. Merchant banks which are not members of the AHC are usually smaller institutions, although they include some quite large names which have remained outside because they do not provide the complete range of merchant banking services. In what follows, we concentrate mainly on the business of the accepting houses.

The typical accepting house is very much smaller than a clearing bank, having perhaps five hundred employees against thirty thousand for a large clearer. It is, however, much more top-heavy in its staff structure, relying on specialist skills to attract business rather than the sheer weight of funds. The main functions of a merchant bank can be grouped under the following five heads:

a acceptance business.
b financial advice to companies.
c new issues.
d portfolio management.
e dealing in secondary markets.

Merchant banking had its origins in acceptance business and, as we have just noted, the principal merchant banks still like to be called accepting houses. The bank acceptance, or 'Bill on London', began to increase in importance around the middle of the nineteenth century, and was in its heyday in the three or four decades before World War I. It was a means of giving credit during the period of shipment of goods, and as such it helped to finance the growth of world trade in these years. In 1972, there were an average of perhaps £1,000 million bank acceptances in circulation, of which about half were accepted by members of the Accepting Houses Committee. Some of these they hold in their own portfolio, but the vast majority they sell on to the discount houses, taking a commission fixed by agreement at 1%. Acceptance business suits the merchant banks because they can provide the necessary expertise in arranging a credit and assessing potential risks, but they are not called upon to provide the finance for more than a very limited period. They are essentially selling their 'name'.

Financial advice to companies is the activity which brings merchant banks most publicity, when they find themselves acting for the parties in a takeover bid. In fact, however, their advice can be sought on any aspect of a company's financial requirements. They will provide advice about how much to borrow, and how and when to borrow it. And, of course, they will advise on the terms of loans and dates of repayment. They will advise on dividend policy, on how to structure a company so as to take best advantage of fiscal grants and allowances. They will also advise expanding companies on how to set about a takeover bid; and they will advise companies which are being bid for how best to resist the takeover. In the foreign field, they will have contacts and correspondents abroad which can advise companies planning to sell or invest abroad. In short, the merchant banks aim to provide comprehensive financial expertise of a kind that the clearing banks, with their more rigid structure, are less able to give.

In addition to advice, the merchant banks can give more tangible help in floating new issues. When the decision to borrow has been taken, a company will have the choice of equity, fixed interest or convertible stock, and the choice of a public offer for sale or a placing. As well as advising on the method of raising cash, the merchant bank will usually perform the task of floating the issue. If it is a public issue, the bank will draw up a prospectus, which under stock exchange rules has to be a very detailed and comprehensive document; it will decide on the offer price, arrange underwriting, receive bids, make allotments, and possibly keep a register of holdings. For a house which is active in this field, new issue work can be an important activity and, for that reason, many merchant banks are also referred to as issuing houses and belong to the Issuing Houses Association.

Where an offer of shares for sale is not appropriate, the merchant bank will usually try and put a financial package together for its customer. If, for example, a large export contract requires finance for the period until payments start to be made, the merchant bank (which is unlikely to be able to raise all the funds needed from its own resources) will usually approach other banks to form a syndicate, each member of which will take a percentage of the loan. In order to be able to 'lead' a syndicate like this, a bank will normally have to have contributed to other syndicates as a subsidiary partner.

Because of their close involvement with companies, and because their directors are usually experts in a variety of different financial fields, merchant banks are in a particularly favoured position to give advice in matters of portfolio management. The banks will rarely hold ordinary shares amongst their banking assets because it is traditionally regarded as imprudent in the UK for banks to lend in this way. They will, however, manage portfolios for clients, and many of them have established investment and unit trusts, which they manage in return for fees.

TABLE 10·1

Accepting Houses—balance sheet, 31 December 1972

		£ millions
*Deposits**	*Sterling*	*Other currencies*
UK banks	353	613
Other UK residents	1,152	167
Overseas residents	143	1,261
Certificates of deposit	501	137
	2,149	2,178
*Financial assets**		
Cash and balances with Bank of England	1	—
Interbank lending	450	315
Money at call	177	—
Sterling bills	37	—
Special deposits	11	—
Local Authority temporary debt	334	—
Certificates of Deposit	497	—†
British Government stock	13	—
Advances	745	1,597
Other Assets	166	295
	2,441	2,207
Acceptances‡	[453]	

* Financial assets do not necessarily equal deposits because of the existence of non-financial assets and non-deposit liabilities, e.g., fixed assets and shareholders funds.

† Non-£ CDs included in other assets.

‡ These are a contingent liability and therefore not in the main balance sheet.

Finally, the merchant banks have an ordinary banking business, taking funds on deposit, and investing these funds in a wide range of marketable and non-marketable assets. Although in this very general sense the merchant banks resemble the deposit banks, the nature of their banking assets and liabilities is rather different. On the deposit side, most merchant banks have very few demand deposits, and very few small deposits. They are in the market for large blocks of interest-sensitive funds, and they have no automatic reservoir of branch deposits, as do the clearing banks. As a result they operate much more on the basis of 'matching' liabilities and assets. If they have a lending proposal which offers a margin over the cost of borrowing, they will take it on and then bid for the necessary funds in the open market. They are therefore very active dealers in the secondary market, both as takers and lenders of funds. Since the development of the euro-currency markets, they have also participated actively in this area.

It will be seen that foreign currency business is as large, in quantitative terms, as sterling business. However, since margins are very much smaller than on sterling business, it would not be true to say that foreign currency business provides half the profits.

Loans to local authorities, which have also become very large, are convenient assets for the banks, since they are wholly secure and highly liquid—the bulk having a maturity of less than a week. They had the added advantage during the period of credit ceilings of being public sector debt and exempt from ceiling requirements. Temporary loans are attractive to the local authorities when the latter do not want to borrow at longer term from the Public Works Loan Board.

The British overseas banks

These are British registered banks, with head offices in London, but whose principal area of activity is overseas. Most of them were formed during the nineteenth century, when London bankers provided the initiative and expertise for the establishment of branch banking systems in the colonies. Some of the banks have a particular geographical flavour, such as National and Grindlays, whose main operations are in the Indian sub-continent, and the British Bank of the Middle East, which has branches throughout the Arab World. Others such as Barclays International (formerly Barclays DCO) are more widespread, with branches in almost all countries, though predominantly in the Commonwealth.

There are now fewer overseas banks with head offices in London than there used to be. Many Australian and Canadian banks used to have London head offices but, as their domestic economies have

developed and they have become economically and politically auto-
nomous, it has been recognised as more sensible to be incorporated in
the country where most business is carried on. Thus the former
London head offices have become ordinary branches, like those maintained by other foreign banks. In time, this may well happen to some
of the remaining British overseas banks as well.

Although there is undeniably a logic in shifting the seat of power
in a bank to the country where most of its branches are, there were,
and in some cases still are, strong reasons for having a head office
in London. In many cases where there is a widely diversified branch
network, communications with London are easier than with any local

TABLE 10.2

British Overseas and Commonwealth Banks—Balance Sheet, 31 December
1972

		£ millions
*Deposits**	*Sterling*	*Other currencies*
UK banks	652	1,508
Other UK residents	564	95
Overseas residents	869	4,270
Certificates of Deposit	735	624
	2,820	6,497
*Financial Assets**		
Cash and balances with Bank of England	3	—
Interbank lending	826	1,664
Money at call	186	—
Sterling bills	136	—
Special deposits	17	—
Local Authority temporary debt	505	—
Certificates of Deposit	444	—†
British Government stock	268	—
Advances	766	4,665
Other assets	115	397
	3,266	6,726
Acceptances‡	[166]	

* Financial assets do not necessarily equal deposits because of the existence of
non-financial assets and non-deposit liabilities, e.g., fixed assets and shareholders funds.
† Non-£ CDs included in other assets.
‡ These are a contingent liability and therefore not in the main balance sheet.

centre. Also, since the head office of a large branch network will be expected to hold liquid reserves, to deal in financial markets and provide skilled financial advice, there is obvious advantage in being in a well-established financial centre such as London. There is much more scope for investing funds and recruiting skilled manpower than is the case in the countries where the branches are located.

Because they act as the central point of large branch networks, the head offices of the British overseas banks tend to have slightly different balance sheet structures than is the case with other banks in London. They are more heavily weighted towards liquidity because they are carrying liquid reserves on behalf of their branches as well as for head office use. Also, because the investment opportunities in the less developed countries in which they have a large part of their operations are often less than in the UK, they normally hold a rather greater proportion of their portfolio in the form of government securities. Finally, again because of their role at the centre of large branch networks, the British overseas banks in London tend to maintain a greater administrative staff, in relation to the size of their balance sheet, than other banks.

Unfortunately, it is not possible to show statistics for the British overseas banks separately, as they are included in the statistics along with Commonwealth-registered banks and also some overseas-owned banks registered in London (e.g., the Moscow Narodny Bank!). However, the composite figures for this grouping, given in Table 10.2, do give some indication of the spread of business of the overseas banks.

Foreign banks

The foreign banks are perhaps the most diverse category, ranging from the First National City Bank, the largest international bank in the world, which has a large London office providing full facilities, down to small branches with a handful of employees. Although the most obvious difference between the various foreign banks lies in their countries of origin, there are also differences in the reasons for which they came to London. Those banks with long-established branches in the City, say since before the war, were primarily interested in a UK office to service the needs of their domestic customers with interests in the UK. There was relatively more emphasis on personal travel and later, as international investment began to grow, banks sought the custom of the foreign subsidiaries of domestic clients.

In the last ten years or so, however, many banks have been attracted to London by the phenomenal growth of the euro-currency markets in that period. This has been particularly the case with the American banks, whose numbers have increased from 8 in 1960 to 37 at the end of 1971. Several reasons have contributed to this large influx. Firstly, the size of the euro-dollar market; by end–1972, the total of foreign currency deposits with London banks was the equivalent of $80,000 million. Secondly, the fact that at times of credit squeeze in the US, American banks may be effectively prohibited under Regulation Q for competing for deposits at home, means that they are forced to borrow abroad in order to maintain their lending. Thirdly, there is the bandwagon effect, based partly on real and partly on psychological factors. On the real side, the more banks there are in London, the greater the size and depth of the markets. On the psychological side, there is at least a suspicion that a London branch has become an essential status symbol for a large US bank.

TABLE 10·3

American banks in London—balance sheet 31 December 1972

		£ millions
Deposits*	*Sterling*	*Other currencies*
UK Banks	989	3,312
Other UK residents	510	359
Overseas residents	240	10,494
Certificates of deposit	845	1,510
	2,584	15,675
Financial Assets*		
Cash and balances with Bank of England	1	—
Interbank lending	683	4,092
Money at call	189	—
Sterling bills	68	—
Special deposits	16	—
Local Authority temporary debt	263	—
Certificates of Deposit	441	—†
British Government stock	12	—
Advances	987	11,430
Other assets	3	130
	2,663	15,662
Acceptances‡	[118]	

* Financial assets do not necessarily equal deposits because of the existence of non-financial assets and non-deposit liabilities, e.g., fixed assets and head office funds.

† Non-£ CDs included in other assets.

‡ These are a contingent liability and therefore not in the main balance sheet.

It is naturally not possible to say that any bank comes to London for *only* one of the above reasons, or that it is likely to confine itself to one function. Many American banks, for example, may have been attracted by the prospect of participation in the euro-dollar market, but they were also keen to serve the European needs of their domestic clients and, once established in London, to participate in the sterling money markets.

Table 10.3 illustrates the dominance of the euro-dollar market in the operations of the American banks. It also shows the extent to which euro-dollar business is an entrepot trade, with most of the borrowing and lending done with non-residents. The euro-dollar market plays such a large role in the business of the foreign banks in London that it is worth pausing to consider its nature in rather more depth.

The Euro-dollar market

A euro-dollar was originally a deposit with a bank in Europe denominated in dollars. The market was first established in London in the early 1960s, and London dollar deposits are still the bulk of the market; but the term 'euro-dollar market' is used loosely to describe transactions in all foreign currencies, and in centres as far apart as Singapore and the Caribbean.

Originally euro-dollars were created when the owner of a deposit with an American bank transferred the title to that deposit to a bank based, say, in London. He then had a dollar claim on the London bank, and the London bank had a dollar claim on a New York bank. At this stage a euro-dollar was simply an indirect way of holding a deposit with a US bank. When the London bank started lending its euro-dollar assets, however, the situation changed. If the dollars lent by the London bank were redeposited in London, then euro-dollar liabilities in London would no longer be fully matched by claims in New York.

Let us take a simple case where a London bank takes a deposit of $100 in the form of a claim on a New York bank. Its balance sheet is as follows:

Liabilities	*Assets*	
Deposits $100	Balance with New York bank	$100
——		——
100		100

Now assume that it lends the $100 to a UK resident, who spends it on acquiring goods. The seller of goods now has the $100. Should he

decide to keep this on deposit with the London bank, its balance
sheet would be as follows:

Liabilities	Assets	
Deposits $200	Balance with New York bank	$100
	Loan to UK resident	100
200		200

The important aspect of the above transaction is that, by making
loans, and taking deposits, banks in London can create euro-dollars in
excess of the extent to which they hold deposits in New York. *Somewhere* in the system there must be deposits in New York, for it is by
shifting the title to funds in New York that transfers of funds are
made. But these deposits need not be very large for the market to
function efficiently.

From fairly simple beginnings, the euro-dollar market has grown,
mainly in London, to become virtually a complete financial system
in its own right. The basic unit for dealing is $1 million, and funds
are both taken and lent for periods ranging from overnight to upwards
of five years. In sheer size of total deposits, the euro-dollar market
in London is larger than the market in banks' sterling funds. This
gives a slightly misleading impression of size, however, since quite a
large proportion of these funds are shifted around within the banking
system, and are in a sense being double-counted.

Why has the euro-dollar market grown so rapidly, and why has
London emerged as its centre? It is sometimes stated that the
American balance of payments deficit is the main reason, since it has
placed dollars in the hands of Europeans. However, as we have
pointed out, it is quite possible for banks in Europe to generate
euro-dollar liabilities and claims without any change in the overall
indebtedness of the United States to other countries. In 1972, in
point of fact, the bulk of the euro-dollar market consisted of claims
on non-US residents, so that the market was to only a small extent
the direct result of the US deficit. Anyway, the mere fact that Europeans were receiving dollars did not compel them to hold bank
deposits in this form. They could easily, if they had wished, have
exchanged the dollars they were receiving as a result of their trade
with the US into their own domestic currencies.

The reason for the growth in the market lies in the usefulness of
balances denominated in dollars as working balances for financial
and commercial use. One cause of this is the increasing proportion of
world trade invoiced and settled in dollars. The holding of dollar

balances reduces transaction costs of dealing in foreign exchange, and eliminates the risk of fluctuations in exchange rates. Even where payments have to be made in non-dollar currencies, dollars may have to be used as the vehicle for effecting an exchange between third currencies, making it advantageous to hold them as working balances.

There are thus good reasons for firms to hold balances in dollars, but why in Europe rather than the United States? For firms based in Europe the reasons are obvious. Local banks can provide a more intimate and immediate service, without the expense of long-distance telephone calls and cables and the inconvenience of a five or six hour time differential. Another advantage is that deposits placed outside the US escape certain Federal Reserve requirements. Perhaps the most important of these from the point of view of the development of the euro-dollar market is Regulation Q, which sets maximum rates which banks may pay for deposits in the US. When domestic interest rates in the US rise above the Regulation Q level, banks can no longer increase their resources by bidding more in their own markets. But since Regulation Q does not apply outside the US, they can offer more in London. At such times, therefore, large multinational corporations tend to invest their surplus funds in London, from where they are lent back by the branches of American banks to their head offices in the US. The euro-dollar market is thus used by US banks to mitigate the worst effects of a credit squeeze.

London has emerged as the centre of the euro-dollar market largely by a band-wagon process. In the early 1960s London had the greatest concentration of international banks because of its traditional role as a centre for the finance of trade. Since a large element of euro-dollar business involves borrowing from and lending to other banks, and arranging participations in syndicate loans, it was obviously more attractive to deal in a centre where there was already an established network of banks. And when others wanted to get into the market, it was natural that they should come where the market seemed to be the largest. In 1971, London probably had comfortably over half the total outstanding euro-dollar business with Frankfurt in second place and Paris and Zurich some way behind. Despite its concentration in London, however, the market is highly international. Something like two-thirds of the assets and liabilities of London banks in euro-currencies were transactions with non-residents.

There are virtually no restrictions on the international aspects of the market, although exchange control restrictions limit participation by UK residents other than authorised banks. Central bankers have occasionally expressed reservations about the role of the market in facilitating flows of hot money between centres. However, few people doubt that these flows would take place anyway, and it is clear that euro-dollar centres derive considerable earnings from the business; so it seems unlikely that there will be any concerted attempt to control the market. The US authorities have introduced some measures to curb the extent to which American banks can channel funds taken in the euro-dollar market back to the US, thus avoiding the full effect of a credit squeeze. As a result the proportion of euro-dollars lent back to the US fell from a maximum of 25% in 1969 to only about 5% in 1971. The euro-dollar market has therefore become largely separate from the US banking system.

The discount houses

The discount houses perform a rather different kind of function from other banks. They are in a sense bankers to the banks, in that they specialise in taking funds from banks, that may be withdrawn on demand or at very short notice, and investing them in slightly less liquid form. In 1972 the London Discount Market Association consisted of eleven houses. There were also three smaller firms doing a similar kind of business, though on a smaller scale, known as discount brokers. In addition there was a group of six banks which had a money-trading department. After the introduction of the Bank of England's new system of credit control in 1971, these banks separated the accounts of their money departments which were then run as largely separate businesses. Finally, there were six 'money-brokers', members of the stock exchange who specialise in lending funds to stock exchange firms to enable them to 'carry' their portfolios of stocks. Thus there were, at mid–1972, a total of twenty-six money market firms in the London money market.

The history of the discount market goes back to the early nineteenth century, when the typical bank in England was a small country bank, usually without branches and with a fairly small number of customers. Most lending at this time was done by way of bills of exchange. A bill of exchange can be thought of as a post-dated cheque. The drawer of the bill gives an instruction to the acceptor (to whom he may have supplied goods) to pay a fixed sum of money on a certain date, and signs the bill to this effect. This certificate of indebtedness, once accepted, then becomes title to payment of a fixed sum at a future date and is a marketable security. It would normally be sold at a discount (hence the term 'discounted' meaning bought or sold) with the discount representing the interest received by the holder of the bill. Generally speaking the seller of goods would draw a bill on the buyer, and the buyer would 'accept' the responsibility of making payment at the due date. Since the whole purpose of the transaction is to provide credit, however, the bill would usually be sold, immediately or almost immediately, to a bank.

In the early years of the industrial revolution, the number of potential borrowers wishing to discount bills was greater in industrial areas than in agricultural areas. Some mechanism was needed to bring together the surplus lending of the agricultural areas and the surplus borrowing of the industrial areas. The mechanism was the London bill market. As this market grew, the need became apparent for brokers who could grade bills according to risk, date, etc., and arrange them into convenient parcels for the purchasing banks. This was not handled by the London banks, partly because of a reluctance on the part of the banks to deal directly with their competitors, and partly because the necessary skills for bill-broking were not at that time available within the banks.

In the early stages, the brokers simply sold bills on commission without tying up their own funds. After about 1825, however, they began to deal as principals, and fairly quickly gave up the broking aspect of their business. (Confusingly, however, the discount houses refer to themselves as bill-brokers to this day.) The reasons for the change were twofold: firstly, the brokers wanted to use their skills in dealing, which offered greater prospects of profit, rather than simply in broking; secondly, after the financial crash of 1825, banks were looking for a secure outlet for their liquid funds. The discount market offered such an investment, and the houses were able to borrow funds from the banks in order to finance their own books.

The banks were interested in absolute safety, having previously been caught out by a financial crash. A feature of the discount market to the present day is that the majority of the funds it takes from banks are secured (i.e., the discount houses pledge assets against the borrowing) and are subject to a margin of security in excess of the value of the borrowing. This margin protects the lending bank against any decrease in the value of the security and, since the margin has to be provided out of the houses' own resources, places a limitation on the imprudent expansion of business.

A necessary parallel development to the growth of a 'call money' market was the gradual acceptance by the Bank of England of the role of lender of last resort. In order to protect the discount houses against an inability to repay the banks on demand (and thus, indirectly, to protect the entire banking system) the Bank of England gradually undertook the responsibility of standing ready to buy the houses' assets if the need arose. The Bank would only provide this support on penal terms, but nevertheless the knowledge that it was prepared to use its power to prevent a crisis added considerably to the stability of the London financial scene. It also added immeasurably to the status of the discount market, for the houses alone had access to the Bank's facilities.

By the 1870s, when the Bank of England's crucial role was firmly established, the structural pattern of the discount market was set. The later years of the nineteenth century saw a decline in the inland bill of exchange, and a parallel growth in the use of bills for financing overseas trade. Overseas trade bills suffered an eclipse in their turn when, in the inter-war period, there was a catastrophic decline in world trade. Again, however, the decline of one instrument was offset by the growth of another—the Treasury bill. The discount market showed its adaptability once more by turning its hand to dealing in this new form of exchequer finance.

The recession of the 1930s almost put the discount houses out of business, as deflation pushed interest rates down to levels where the banks were unwilling to lend to the market. Times were hard for the banks, too, and the result was the establishment of various agreements (known collectively as 'the cartel') among the banks, and between the banks and the discount houses. The cartel had the effect of limiting competition amongst the banks, but it also effectively underwrote the continued existence of the discount market. The banks agreed not to compete with the houses in tendering for Treasury bills and to hold a certain proportion of their assets in prescribed liquid forms, of which money at call with the discount market was one. The houses agreed to cover the weekly Treasury bill tender at a collectively agreed (or 'syndicate') price. The syndicate prescribed a margin between the buying and selling price for bills which provided the houses with a reasonable and reliable, if not particularly lucrative, source of income.

The cartel and the syndicate survived largely unchanged until 1971. It may be asked why the banks and the Bank of England permitted a situation to endure which was so apparently beneficial to the discount houses. The Bank of England probably acquiesced in the arrangements because it felt it would be easier to exercise the desired degree of control over short-term interest rates through the discount houses than through the banks. There were fewer houses, which facilitated communication; the Bank traditionally gave its lender of last resort facilities to the market, and the existence of their quasi-monopoly position in the tender meant that the houses felt a responsibility to cover the tender at a reasonable price even when they were not very anxious to take up bills. The banks agreed to the system, partly as a *quid pro quo* for the houses' agreement not to compete directly in the field of ordinary banking, and partly because the market could offer them a genuinely liquid asset at very little cost in terms of loss of yield.

The Second World War increased if anything the market's dependence on the Treasury bill. From the middle–1950s, however, a number of new short-term instruments were developed which posed both a threat and an opportunity to the discount market. Short-term loans to local authorities became an important liquid asset to non-clearing banks, and the discount houses formed or took over broking firms to enter this kind of business. The market in unsecured inter-bank loans (usually referred to simply as the interbank market) grew up soon afterwards, and the houses are active in this market, both as principals and as brokers. The commercial bill staged a revival in popularity almost immediately after the Radcliffe report dismissed this business as being of only 'vestigial' importance to the houses.

The houses also made a market in dollar certificates of deposit and, from their inception in October 1968, in sterling certificates of deposit too. By 1971, when the cartel and syndicate were abolished in the wake of the Bank of England's new proposals for credit control, the discount houses had already shown their traditional ability to adapt profitably to changing circumstances.

Under the new arrangements of 1971 the money market firms had their position officially recognised. The arrangements provided that all banks should hold $12\frac{1}{2}\%$ of their sterling resources in specially desig-nated 'reserve assets'. Broadly speaking, these assets consist of bills, short bonds and call money with the money market. Because the money market firms are able to invest money taken from banks in a wider range of assets then fall within the $12\frac{1}{2}\%$ ratio, including some which are rather higher-yielding, they have been able to attract the lion's share of banks' reserve assets.

It would clearly defeat the purpose of a reserve assets ratio if banks could lend to their customers indirectly by placing money at call with the money market which was then on-lent to the banks' customers by way of discounting commercial bills. The discount houses and other money market firms (except the money brokers) have therefore agreed to hold not less than 50% of their borrowed funds in certain specified categories of public sector debt, namely: public sector bills, public sector marketable bonds with less than five years to maturity, and tax reserve certificates. In addition, the Bank of England reserves the right to require a given proportion of the security it takes against last-resort facilities to be in the form of Treasury bills and, for prudential reasons, it asks money market firms to observe limits on the amount of borrowed funds taken as a multiple of capital and reserves.

Although the 1971 arrangements protect the continued existence of the money market as a whole, they by and large remove those aspects of the cartel which prevented competition among the discount houses. Thus, the syndicated Treasury bill tender has been abolished, and also the agreed buying and selling prices for various categories of bills. With twenty or so firms actively competing for the available business, there is now very little reason to believe that the arrangements work to the monopolistic advantage of the discount market as a whole.

Two features of the old system have been retained under the new arrangements. The Bank of England continues to confine to the discount market (including the discount brokers and money brokers, but not the money trading banks) its extension of last resort lending facilities. And, in return, the discount market continues to underwrite the weekly Treasury bill tender.

As far as the discount houses are concerned, the main changes which seem likely to result from the 1971 arrangements are a squeezing of their profit margins under the influence of greater competition, and a tendency for the source of their funds to switch away from the clearing banks to the mass of other banks which now have to observe ratios. The margin between the buying and selling price for bills has shrunk from an agreed $\frac{1}{8}\%$ to perhaps $\frac{1}{16}\%$ — the smallness of this margin reflecting the efficiency with which the houses are able to run their portfolios.

The abandonment by the Bank of England of its policy of deliberately stabilising prices of gilt-edged stocks has given the discount market a greater opportunity for dealing profits in the bond market. Several of the houses' chairmen have pointed to bond-market dealing as an area in which there will be greater profit opportunities in the 1970s. So long as the houses are relatively successful, the authorities will probably welcome this development. Successful jobbing in bonds will mean that the houses are helping to stabilise price fluctuations by buying when prices fall and selling when they rise again.

The combined portfolios of the houses at December 1972, compared with the position in December 1970, is shown in Table 10.4.

Several features of the table are worthy of comment. In borrowed funds, there has been a reduction in the proportion of funds taken from the clearing banks, and an increase in the proportion coming from other banks. This reflects the fact that under the old liquidity ratio, the clearers were obliged to hold more liquid assets (a sizeable proportion of which were in the form of call money) than is necessary under the new reserve ratio rules. The non-clearing banks, on the other hand, have had to increase their call money in order to meet the prescribed ratio. (It is interesting to note, however, that even before the 1971 proposals were announced, the discount houses had succeeded in attracting as much as one-third of their borrowed funds from non-captive, i.e., non-clearing bank, sources.)

TABLE 10·4

Discount houses: combined balance sheet*

		£ millions
Borrowed funds:	*December 1970*	*December 1972*
Bank of England	—	—
London clearing banks	1,407	1,020
Scottish clearing banks	108	130
Other deposit banks	29	57
Accepting houses and overseas banks	510	936
Other sources	204	386
Total	2,259	2,529
Assets	*1970*	*1971*
Treasury bills	876	475
Other sterling bills	697	565
LA bonds	224	636
$CDs	39	153
£CDs	268	458
BGS	160	112
Other	88	219
Total	2,352	2,618

* Detailed figures for other money market firms are not available. However, at October 1972, the combined borrowed funds of the discount brokers and money trading banks were only £103 million. Figures for money brokers are not published.

It is not possible to detect what proportion of borrowed funds are secured. Certainly it is the vast majority, since only secured funds are eligible as reserve assets. Most dealing still takes place in the traditional way, i.e., by the representatives of money market firms, attired in the regulation top-hat, calling personally on the banks to fix the days money position (which may involve calling, placing fresh funds or no change) and the rate. Telephone dealing is on the increase, and in the interbank market virtually all deals are done by telephone.

Turning to the assets side of the balance sheet, the decade of the 1960s, and more particularly the last few years, has seen the discount houses change from being primarily dealers in Treasury bills and short bonds to having a comprehensive book in the whole range of short-term assets. The return from making a secondary market in CDs (in which all the houses deal) and dollar CDs (which are the province of a few specialists) is reflected in the growth in holdings of these assets. Commercial bills have grown from the 'vestigial' role noted by Radcliffe to a position where they have in recent years been as much as one-third of the market's combined portfolio. To some extent, however, the recent growth of the commercial bill has been fostered by the distorting influence of credit ceilings. Now that these have gone, the commercial bill may well decline in popularity as an instrument for borrowing.

The period of the 1960s has been one of considerable change and adaptation for the discount market. The market still acts, however, as the mechanism for smoothing out irregularities in the flow of money, and through which the authorities act to influence short-term interest rates. By virtue of its size, the discount market can have a profound effect on rates in all short-term markets. And, since individual houses can only survive and grow through successful dealing, it is likely to be even more true in the future that the market will tend to be a stabilising influence.

Further reading

Bank of England, The UK banking sector 1952-67, *Bank of England Quarterly Bulletin*, June 1969.

Central Office of Information, *British Banking System*, London, HMSO, 1968.

Day, A. C. L., *Outline of Monetary Economics*, op. cit., Part III.

Grant, A. T. K., op. cit., Chapters 4 and 5.

Radcliffe Report, op. cit., Chapter 4.

Revell, J. R. S., *Changes in British Banking*, London, Hill Samuel, 1968.

Rybczynski, R., The UK financial sector since Radcliffe—the non-clearing banks, in *Money in Britain*, Croome and Johnson (eds.), London, Oxford University Press, 1970.

Sayers, R. S., *Modern Banking*, op. cit. Chapter 3.

Scammell, W. M., *The London Discount Market*, London, Elek Books, 1968.

Swoboda, Alexander K., The Euro-dollar market—an interpretation. *Essays in International Finance* No. 64, Princeton University, Dept. of Economics, International Finance Section.

Questions for discussion

1 Why have specialised banking institutions continued to exist in London, when the clearing banks have been merging into large groups ?
2 What are the main reasons why so many foreign banks have established branches in London ?
3 To what extent has the development of the euro-dollar market resulted from the US balance of payments deficit ?
4 What special advantages does London derive from the existence of a discount market system ?

11

Non-bank financial intermediaries

If money was a unique asset, for which there were no close substitutes, then, from the point of view of the impact of monetary policy on aggregate demand, a study of financial institutions could safely be confined to those whose liabilities ranked as money. This is not to say that other financial intermediaries would not be important. They would play a vital role in securing the best allocation of resources by equating supply and demand in their various markets in the most efficient way. But they would have no different a role in this sense than a dealer in fruit or meat or anything else. In other words their activities would not affect the level of demand or the price level.

There is in fact considerable debate about whether money is sufficiently different from other assets to enable one to study it on its own. Monetarist economists would probably hold that it was—although they would not all agree where the dividing line between money and non-money should be drawn. On the other hand, there is a considerable body of economists, following in the tradition of the Radcliffe report, who believe that money should be seen as simply one financial asset amongst many, though with some special properties. In its most developed form, this is expressed in the 'New View' of financial intermediation, particularly associated with Yale University.

There are therefore three reasons why it is of interest to study the non-bank financial intermediaries. Firstly, they are important channels of credit in their own right, and their efficient functioning is essential to the smooth working of the financial system as a whole. Secondly, many of them issue liabilities which are virtually indistinguishable from the liabilities of banks. It can be claimed, therefore, that they may be regarded as subsidiary creators of money. Thirdly, even when their liabilities are clearly not 'money', they are sufficiently close to being money to make them substitutable for money balances if the yield on them is sufficiently attractive. It would be misleading to say that the total liquidity in the economy had not changed just because bank deposits were constant if, for example, there had been a rapid growth in the liabilities of savings banks and building societies.

In what follows, we start with those institutions whose liabilities are closest in their nature to bank deposits. These are the building societies and savings banks and the National Giro. We go on to discuss the role of finance houses and unit and investment trusts. Finally, we consider those financial intermediaries which are perhaps furthest from the creation of money-like liabilities, the insurance companies and pension funds. For completeness, the chapter is rounded off by looking at the activities of some specialised financial agencies that do not fall easily into any of the other categories.

The building societies

Building societies serve two main aims. They are an investment medium for small savers and they provide a source of finance for house purchase. In the early days of building societies, these two objectives were very closely linked, and the contributors to societies were the same people as the borrowers. Now, savers and borrowers are more separate, but many societies still give preference in their lending to those who have previously saved with the society.

Records of building societies go back as far as the eighteenth century, but it was in the Victorian period that they became firmly established, their emphasis on thrift and self-help appealing to Victorian morality and economics alike. They are non-profit organisations, and adjust their rates and charges so as to earn no more than is needed for normal additions to reserves. Their depositors are their shareholders.

In 1972, there were almost 500 building societies, though this number is tending to diminish as a result of mergers between smaller societies. By the end of 1972, total deposits had grown to some £13,000 million. At this level, they are as great as the sterling deposits of the London clearing banks and, since their trend rate of growth has been much higher, the building societies in the 1970s seem destined to become larger (in sheer volume of funds) than the clearing banks.[1] This is a dramatic reversal in status from what earlier prevailed. At the outbreak of the First World War, it is estimated that building society resources, at some £70 million, were less than one-tenth of those of the banks. By 1939, they had grown to

[1] Though the ending in 1971 of the cartel arrangements among the clearing banks (see Chapter 9) may enable the banks to compete more effectively with building societies.

nearly £800 million when they were one quarter the resources of the banks. As late as 1963, the societies' resources were barely half as great as the clearing banks'.

The societies obtain their funds by accepting shares and deposits. The only material differences between these two are that shares rank behind deposits in the event of liquidation; and shares carry voting rights. But for the investor, the difference is largely semantic, since there is little danger of a building society failing, and the method of investing and withdrawing funds is the same. Deposits usually carry a rate of interest lower by $\frac{1}{4}\%$ than shares, and as a result, only a tiny proportion of building societies' funds are taken in this form. For the rest of this section, we will use the term 'deposits' to include shares.

In principle, most building societies reserve the right to require notice for withdrawals, but in practice moderate withdrawals are permitted on demand, and it is only for large sums that notice is demanded (often not even then). Generally there is no loss of interest for sums withdrawn on demand. It can be seen, therefore, that building society deposits have considerable attractions for the saver. Deposit and withdrawal arrangements are simple, and an account may often give priority in obtaining mortgage advances. Interest rates are attractive, and are paid net of income tax.[2]

In 1971, there were over 10 million building society accounts, against twice that number of bank accounts. Clearly many of these are genuinely savings accounts, not in practice subject to rapid withdrawals. But the evidence is that building society accounts are being treated more and more like bank accounts. Withdrawals as a proportion of gross receipts have tended to increase, and the number of transactions per account also appears to be rising. As yet building societies do not offer cheque facilities, and they have fewer branches than do the banks, but it nevertheless seems likely that some of their expansion in recent years will have been at the expense of the banks.

On the assets side of their balance sheet, building societies' business is overwhelmingly concentrated in mortgage lending, predominantly for residential purposes. The societies dominate the residential mortgage market, accounting in 1972 for some three quarters of outstanding private debt for house purchase. Generally speaking, a little over 80% of their assets at any given time are in mortgages. The remaining 15% or so are in liquid assets. These are liquid in the sense of being

[2] The societies have an arrangement with the Inland Revenue authorities to deduct an average, or 'composite', rate of tax from interest payments, and this is somewhat less than the standard rate of tax.

readily marketable, but not necessarily in the sense of being short-term. If a society's 'liquid' assets ratio is less than $7\frac{1}{2}\%$, gilt-edged securities may only be taken up if they have a maturity of less than five years; any excess between $7\frac{1}{2}\%$ and 15% may be invested in medium-dated government stocks of up to 15 years maturity, and beyond 15% the societies may hold government bonds of up to 25 years maturity.

As far as interest rates are concerned, building societies attach considerable importance to maintaining a stable rate structure. One way of achieving this would be to lend at fixed rates of interest. This practice, however, has considerable disadvantages, and is not widely used. Since mortgage loans usually have a life of twenty years or so, while deposits are repayable at very short notice, fixed-rate lending poses problems at times when interest rates are rising. If the societies do not increase the rates they offer on deposits, they lose funds to competing institutions; but if they do raise their rates, they incur losses, since the rates on their loans are fixed. (This problem has plagued the building societies' counterparts in the USA, savings and loan associations, who do lend at fixed rates. It is partly in order to protect them from competition from the banks that the Federal Reserve has, from time to time, imposed an interest rate ceiling on the banks under Regulation Q.)

In the UK, however, building society loans are made on the basis that mortgage rates can be changed for existing borrowers, and this has the advantage that societies are not 'locked-in' to low yielding assets in times of rising rates. Changes in rates, however, are costly to administer and inconvenient to the borrower (though he is usually offered the option of a longer repayment period as an alternative to higher repayments). As a result building societies tend to respond to a change in the general level of interest rates only after a lag. Because of their slowness to adjust rates it follows that societies generally gain funds when other interest rates are falling and lose them when they are rising. This often leads to temporary rationing of advances, and occasionally there is rationing in the acceptance of deposits.

Because of their nature and size, the building societies may well play a role in allowing a given quantity of bank deposits to finance a higher level of economic activity than might otherwise be possible. The convenience and yield of building society deposits presumably encourages people to economise on bank balances in order to hold liquid savings with the societies. And their dominant role in the mortgage market has almost completely prevented the banks from becoming active in this area. Should building societies become more active in the future in attracting more volatile funds, and employing them in a broader range of lending, it is to be expected that they will slice further into the banks' business.

Savings banks

The savings banks fall into two categories: the National Savings Bank and the Trustee Savings Banks. Their similarities are probably more important than their differences, but it is of interest to chart their different historical origins. The Trustee Savings Banks are the older, the earliest ones dating from the beginning of the nineteenth century. They are managed by boards of honorary trustees, but their activities are under close government supervision. The Post Office Savings Bank was established in 1861, partly in order to provide a greater spread of offices for the purpose of accepting savings. Its name was changed to the National Savings Bank when the Post Office became a public corporation (instead of a government department) in 1969. The NSB is now operated by the Post Office on behalf of the Department for National Savings.

Both the NSB and the TSBs maintain ordinary accounts providing deposit facilities for small savers in amounts up to £10,000 (in practice the average deposit is very much smaller than this). The banks do not, however, have control over the employment of these deposits, or the interest paid on them. All deposits are paid into funds managed by the national debt commissioners,[3] and withdrawals and interest payments are met by drawings from these funds. The interest paid on accounts remained static at $2\frac{1}{2}\%$ from 1888 until 1970, when it was raised to $3\frac{1}{2}\%$. The national debt commissioners invest the money they receive in government stocks, but this is merely a book-keeping transaction: they have no legal obligation to break even or make a profit and any surplus or deficit at the end of each accounting period is used (or made good) by a transfer to or from the government's general revenue account.

From the foregoing, it can be seen that neither the NSB nor the TSBs are run according to commercial banking principles. Nevertheless, deposits with them do have certain attractions and savings banks are undoubtedly used by some people for much the same purposes as others use commercial banks. Although the rate of interest on deposits is low, the first £15 of interest is tax free, so that the real yield is comparable to that obtainable through a deposit

[3] In the case of the NSB, this is the National Savings Bank fund; for the TSB, it is the Fund of the Banks for Savings.

account at a clearing bank. The NSB has the advantage of being represented in post offices, which means that it is open in more locations and for longer hours than is the case with banks. Small amounts, up to £20, can be withdrawn on demand and larger amounts at short notice, without loss of interest.

The Trustee Savings Banks are less widely spread. (There are about 80 TSBs with some 2,000 branches.) However, most of them provide current account facilities, with cheque books, to depositors who have £50 in an ordinary account or who have been customers for a given minimum period. The principal difference between a current account with a TSB and one with a clearing bank is the fact that TSBs offer a more restricted range of services, and do not at the present time (1972) offer overdraft facilities. However, their costs are lower, and their services are attractive to personal customers who do not require full banking facilities. It would be hard to argue that the current account liabilities of the TSBs lacked many of the 'money-like' qualities of clearing bank accounts.

In addition to their 'ordinary' deposit and current accounts, most of the Trustee Savings Banks have 'special investment departments,' which do not have to place all their funds with the national debt commissioners and can, in consequence, pursue a rather more independent policy with regard to the investments they make and the interest rates they pay. Some 70 banks with 1,500 branches offer this service, though it is restricted to depositors with a balance of at least £50 on an ordinary account. Deposits at one-month, three-month and six-months' notice are taken, and the proceeds are mainly invested in local authority bonds and mortgages. Interest is paid to depositors without deduction of tax and is usually somewhat higher than the net-of-tax yield offered by building societies. These deposits are therefore an attractive investment to those who pay less than the standard rate of income tax.

The counterpart in the NSB of these special investment departments are investment accounts, which were introduced in 1966. Like the special investment departments, these are only open to depositors already holding £50 in an ordinary account, and are also subject to a maximum deposit of £10,000. Their funds are invested by the national debt commissioners, with the largest proportion going into government stocks. Interest rates offered are comparable to those of the special investment departments.

The total funds invested in the savings banks were some £5,000 million in 1972, with TSBs accounting for rather more than the NSB. This figure represents the equivalent of rather over one third of clearing bank deposits and building society deposits. The number of accounts, however, at 15 million, is very large, and it is clear that many people with modest financial needs use the savings banks as a store of surplus liquidity and as a means of effecting money transfers. The average number of transactions across NSB ordinary accounts, for example, is estimated to be more than one per week.

The savings banks, like the building societies are providing services that compete at least with the fringes of the clearing banks' business. This need not hinder analysis unduly if the relative sizes remain fairly static. But to the extent that the savings banks encroach on ordinary banking business, by offering cheque facilities, by bidding for term deposits and possibly ultimately by providing lending facilities, it will become difficult to interpret the significance of secular trends in the money supply as conventionally defined. The same sort of difficulty would be presented, of course, if the banks used their new freedom to encroach on the business of the non-bank financial intermediaries. Indeed, in Canada, where the banks were freed from restraints on competition, they quickly expanded their position at the expense of building societies. The result was an increase in the stock of money, as recorded, that was disproportionate to any real change in inflationary pressure.

This does not necessarily mean that the money supply is unimportant; conceptually it is extremely important, and for practical purposes it may be the best instrument available. It would, however, be wise to use it with caution and realise that the precision with which it can be defined in theory is not matched by equal precision in practice.

The National Giro

Although the National Giro is not usually thought of as a bank, it is defined for statistical purposes as being part of the banking system, and its liabilities are classified as money. It is the smallest component part of the banking system, with assets in 1972 amounting to less than $\frac{1}{2}\%$ of those of the banking system as a whole. 'Giro' is a term borrowed from continental systems of money transmission operated through post offices. In essence the National Giro offers current account banking facilities to its customers without any of the services or frills provided by the full service banks. It is primarily attractive to the individual or company with a large number of payments or receipts and little need for borrowing or financial advice facilities. To encourage the spread of the system, money transfers to other account-holders within the Giro system are usually performed free, with a charge being levied only for withdrawals from the system.

The Giro has two advantages over banks. It operates through post offices which gives it the convenience of making its services readily available and, by concentrating on money transmission and cutting down expenses on other aspects of banking, it is able to offer a cheaper service. On the other hand, it is unable to offer a financial package deal in the same way that banks can. It therefore tends to attract the smaller and relatively less profitable customer.

The National Giro was established in 1967, and since that date, it has tried to broaden its appeal by offering companies attractive terms for wage payment, and by offering its depositors access to borrowing facilities through a finance house. Thus far, it has not been entirely successful in meeting its growth objectives, largely because the banking system in the UK probably provides a more highly developed money transmission service than is the case in countries where the Giro plays a larger role.

Finance houses

Finance houses are those institutions which have traditionally specialised in hire purchase and other instalment credit, either to consumers or to business firms. It is the specialised nature of their lending that has in the past been considered to distinguish them from banks. But they are very similar to banks in certain essential respects. They take deposits from the general public and employ them in loans. This similarity is reflected in the fact that nearly all finance houses have recognition from the Department of Trade and Industry as banks for the purposes of the Money-lenders Act. It now seems likely that finance houses will increasingly make straightforward loans which are not formally related to the purchase of specified goods, thus making them even more like banks. Indeed in January 1972, the largest five houses were requested by the Bank of England to start contributing figures to the official banking statistics.[4]

A large part of the finance houses' funds comes from the banking system, either through the discounting of finance houses' bills, or through direct lending at fixed term. The houses generally find it cheaper to borrow from banks than to mobilise funds themselves through an expensive network of branches. However, they do also borrow substantial blocks of funds both from companies and from the

[4] This followed their recognition as banks for the purposes of the protection of depositors act.

general public. Funds placed by companies are usually term deposits, three months being a typical maturity; while the bulk of personal accounts are conducted by mail with minimum notice requirements for withdrawals. Depositors with finance houses tend to be relatively interest sensitive, so that the houses reckon to put their rates up or down quite frequently to keep their inflow of funds in line with their lending business.

On the lending side, the bulk of finance house assets are hire purchase loans and other forms of instalment credit. Since 1965, however, when the Hire Purchase Act restricted lenders' rights of repossession, an increasing proportion of their business has been done by means of ordinary loans, which may or may not be intended to finance a particular purchase. These changes have tended to make the lending business of the houses more like that of the banks; and if the recent recommendations of a Royal Commission for simplifications in the laws relating to consumer credit are adopted, the differences will become smaller still.

Because they specialise in relatively small loans to consumers, administrative costs are higher, and default risks are greater than is the case with most forms of bank lending. As a result, interest rates are high (often 20% or more), and loans are normally secured. An increasingly popular form of security is the unmortgaged element of owner-occupied property; lending against this kind of collateral is known as second-mortgage lending.

It may be asked why the banks have not taken a larger share in hire purchase business, especially when it is remembered that it is largely bank money which goes to finance the houses' lending activities. The reason for the banks' initial reluctance probably lay in an unwillingness to be associated with the selling methods (and in particular, the repossession methods) of some of the early hire purchase operators. However, as hire purchase business grew in size and respectability during the 1950s, the banks responded to the challenge of the new institutions by taking stakes in some of the large houses, or establishing subsidiaries of their own. More recently the clearing banks have started developing direct forms of personal credit themselves, but they will probably continue actively to try and expand the business of their finance house subsidiaries. Some of these have now become so well established that they have acquired full recognition as banks in their own right.

Because of the role of finance houses as important deposit-taking and lending institutions at the fringe of the banking system proper, the monetary authorities have tried to extend their controls to them.

Throughout the 1950s and 1960s, the government used its power to regulate the terms of hire purchase contracts as an active weapon of economic management. Experience showed that sudden changes in the required down-payment for consumer durables had a rapid and size-able effect on the demand for them. From May 1965, the Bank of England used its influence to persuade the larger finance houses not to evade this control by lending in the form of personal loans on easier terms. And at the same time, the Bank asked the members of the Finance Houses Association to observe quantitative ceilings on their lending.

When the new arrangements for credit control were introduced in 1971, the importance of the houses' deposit-taking role was recognised. Under the scheme that was then introduced, houses with total deposits from the public of over £5 million will have to observe a reserve ratio of 10%. Some of the largest houses have in fact chosen to become banks and observe a $12\frac{1}{2}\%$ ratio, so that there are only a handful of finance houses in the separate scheme.

In total, the finance houses had assets of over £1,000 million in 1972. Their deposits are less than one tenth those of the banking system, though they account for perhaps a quarter of consumer credit. Despite their relatively small size, however, they are important because they operate in an area where depositors appear to be sensi-tive to changes in interest rates and borrowers to changes in the terms on which they can borrow.

Unit trusts and investment trusts

Unit and investment trusts both aim to serve the needs of small investors wishing to participate in the stock market. A holding in a trust is basically a share in a portfolio of securities, the difference between the two types of trust being that an investment trust is fixed in amount and often has a terminal liquidation date, while units in a unit trust can be bought or sold from the trust manager, and there is no terminal date. Investment trusts are 'closed-end' while unit trusts are open-ended.

At first sight, it would probably seem that holdings in these trusts are rather far removed in nature from bank deposits. And it is still generally true that unit and investment trusts tap a somewhat different source of funds than do the banks. But with the continuance of inflation and the increasing sophistication of wealth-owners, it seems likely that some medium-term funds that were previously held in bank deposits are being switched into unit trusts. The ease of investment in these media and the secular rise in stock market prices have together proved an increasingly popular magnet to small investors in recent years. As gross investment in unit trusts has grown, so have realisations; there are clearly, therefore, an increasing number of investors for whom their unit trust holdings represent second-line liquidity.

The attraction to the small investor of these kinds of indirect investment in the stock market are several. They enable him to spread risks more effectively than he could if he was investing directly; they enable him to benefit from professional management relatively cheaply; they reduce transactions costs and ease the complications of capital gains tax assessment.

Investment trusts have a longer history than unit trusts, and at the end of 1971 they had assets roughly three times as great as the unit trust—though the latter have grown more rapidly. Between 1963 and 1972, the total assets of investment trusts grew from £2,800 millions to over £6,000 millions, while unit trusts grew from £350 millions to £2,300 millions. Investment trusts raise capital in two ways, by equity issues and debenture issues. The amount of fixed interest finance is known as the 'gearing' or 'leverage', and the greater this is, the bigger the fluctuations in the value of the equity as share prices move up or down.

Unit trusts generally have a greater appeal to small savers than investment trusts. Members of the public buy a share in a unit trust by purchasing units. The managers of the trust fix a price for units based on strict procedures for valuing the trust's assets, and stand ready to buy and sell units at that price. Normally the selling price is 5% above the buying price, to cover costs and deter jobbing by unit holders. The managers of the trust are remunerated partly by the 5% initial charge and partly by an annual levy, commonly $\frac{3}{8}\%$, on the value of the portfolio they manage.

Pension and life assurance funds

Life insurance and pension funds are the two main forms of long-term contractual savings. As such, they do not compete directly with banks; but they do receive each year large sums of money in excess of the sums they have to pay out, and in the management of their very large resources they are a very significant force in financial markets. At the end of 1971, for example, life insurance companies managed funds totalling £15,000 million, while pension funds managed about £11,000 million.

In principle, there is very little difference between the two types of institutions, and indeed many pension funds are managed by insurance companies and are included in the life assurance statistics. Life funds tend to have more liabilities fixed in money terms, and for this reason tend to show a rather greater preference for fixed-interest assets. While life funds' investments divide roughly two-to-one in favour of fixed interest assets, the proportions are roughly reversed for pension funds.

Special finance agencies

Besides those financial institutions which have been noted above, there are a number of other financial agencies which do not fit neatly into any of the categories. For the sake of completeness, we note these here.

The *Crown Agents* are something of an anomaly, having no recognised legal form. They perform a variety of services of advice, procurement of materials, export promotion, etc., for their 'principals', who are almost all governments of former colonial territories. In addition, they act as an investment outlet for funds, amounting in 1971 to some £1,500 million, placed with them by their principals. In their employment of these funds, they act partly along banking lines, emphasizing prudence and liquidity, and also partly in pursuit of the best return for their principals.

The *Agricultural Mortgage Corporation* specialises in lending to farmers for the purchase and improvement of agricultural land. It is a governmental body, but it raises most of its finance through the issue of loan stocks on the London capital market. Its total lending outstanding in 1971 was £250 million.

The *Industrial and Commercial Finance Corporation* was established in the 1930s to fill what appeared to be a gap in the range of finance available to medium-sized companies. Its funds are provided by the banks, and it makes medium-term loans to companies that have outgrown ordinary overdraft finance, but are not yet big enough to utilise the capital market.

The *Finance Corporation for Industry* is a sister institution to the ICFC, designed to provide finance for industries of national importance that for one reason or another find it difficult to borrow, e.g., the steel industry before nationalisation. It too is financed directly by the banks.

The *Commonwealth Development Finance Company* provides funds for development, though on a commercial basis, to overseas countries, mainly in the Commonwealth.

These last three institutions may provide finance in any of several forms—by a straightforward loan, a convertible loan, direct equity participation, or leasing. Generally, the agencies try to avoid acquiring control of companies to whose finance they contribute.

Conclusion

The non-bank financial institutions control between them assets which are several times larger than the resources of the banks. They are very significant sources of finance for both public and private sectors. On the liabilities side, funds invested in the non-bank intermediaries are generally of a longer-term nature. There are nevertheless substantial investments of a liquid nature which possess at least some of the attributes of money.

It is sometimes said that it does not very much matter where one draws the line in defining the money supply, because the trend rate of growth of the various possible definitions is much the same. This is not really true. For example, the building societies have grown very much more rapidly than banks over the eight-year period 1963–71. If their liabilities were to be included in a definition of money, a very different picture of the trend rate of growth of the money stock would emerge.

Further reading

Aschheim, *Techniques of Monetary Control*, op. cit., Chapter 7.

Ball, R. J., *Inflation and the Theory of Money*, Allen and Unwin, 1964, Chapter 8.

Bank of England: The financial institutions, *Bank of England Quarterly Bulletin*, December 1971, March 1971, June 1971.

Gibson, N. J., *Financial Intermediaries and Monetary Policy*, London, Institute of Economic Affairs, Hobart Paper No. 39, 2nd edition, 1970.

Radcliffe Report, op. cit., Chapter 4.

Sayers, R. S., *Modern Banking*, op. cit., Chapter 7.

Questions for discussion

1 What distinguishes banks from other financial institutions?

2 Why should a monetary economist be interested in the activities of non-bank financial intermediaries?

3 If the money supply had been held constant, while the business of non-banking financial institutions was expanding rapidly, what conclusions would you draw for the operation of monetary policy?

4 Should the central bank attempt to control the non-bank financial institutions? If so, which aspects of their business should it seek to regulate?

5 What would be the effect on the money supply of depriving building societies and savings banks of their special tax privileges?

Part 4
The operation of policy in the UK

12

Monetary policy in the post-war period

The period since the second world war in the UK is a fascinating mosaic of monetary policy. Most of the main instruments of monetary control (with the exception of Regulation-Q type interest ceilings) have been tried at one time or another. These shifts in the emphasis of policy have stemmed from a variety of considerations. The problems facing the economy have changed, as fear of recession has given way to preoccupation with inflation; and concern with economic growth and the balance of payments has grown. There have been developments in theory too, notably after the middle–1960s when the revised version of the quantity theory began to gain adherents. Finally, experience with the use of particular policy instruments has shown up shortcomings in their operation, or the existence of adverse side-effects.

Because of its diverse nature, however, the post-war period cannot really be studied as a whole. It needs to be looked at in terms of sub-periods of recognisably different emphasis in monetary policy. This kind of arbitrary division is bound to impose a pattern of uniformity that does not exist in practice. There are elements of continuity between sub-periods, and there are diverse strands of thought within each sub-period. Nevertheless, signposts are certainly needed, and in this chapter the years since 1945 are divided into four main parts: cheap money and after; the revival of monetary policy; the Radcliffe era; and the rise of monetarism. In 1971 the Bank of England made proposals for the reform of methods of operating monetary policy in a consultative document entitled 'Competition and Credit Control'. This represented an attempt to synthesize the Radcliffe view with later refinements in theory, and to do this within a more competitive framework for the banking system. Because of the radical nature of the changes proposed, the new arrangements merit separate consideration, and a study of them is deferred until the next chapter.

Cheap money and after (1945-51)

By the time the Second World War was finished, economic theory had largely absorbed the immense upheaval that had been caused by Keynes' 'General Theory'. Policy-makers made a positive effort to use the lessons of Keynes' teaching to avoid the pitfalls into which economic management had fallen in the interwar years. It is worth pausing to try and put oneself in the intellectual climate of the time in order to fully understand the policies that were adopted.

In the first place, Keynes had demonstrated that unemployment could be more than a transient cyclical phenomenon caused by the existence of imperfections in the market mechanism. He had shown, to the satisfaction of an influential proportion of the economics profession, that unemployment could be long-lasting, without any necessary tendency to return to full employment. The conclusion to be drawn from this piece of theory was that the government ought to have an economic policy to deal with the *causes* of unemployment, rather than simply with its *consequences*. This conclusion had in fact been accepted by the Government's commitment in a White Paper on employment policy, published in 1943, to maintain a 'high and stable level of employment'.

The second lesson to be drawn from the General Theory, and the literature that stemmed from it, was that the way to deal with unemployment was to act directly on the level of demand through the budget. Indirect action through the rate of interest was less predictable, and therefore less useful as a policy instrument. This conclusion had been reinforced by an enquiry conducted by the Oxford Economists' Research Group, which appeared to show, on the basis of survey data, that businessmen's investment decisions were not particularly responsive to changes in the rate of interest. These studies have subsequently come in for a certain amount of methodological criticism, but in 1945 they were widely accepted.

Finally, there was the widespread belief in the immediate post-war years that the most pressing economic problem was likely to be deflation rather than inflation. This feeling was due partly to the recent experience of the 1930s and in part to an analogy with experience after the First World War when a short sharp boom was followed by an equally sharp, though more prolonged slump. Also encouraging expectations of deflation was the 'stagnation thesis', which was quite popular and held that investment opportunities were being used up, and that there was a declining willingness on the part of businessmen to undertake sufficient investment to generate full employment.

As far as monetary policy was concerned, the conclusion to be drawn from this view of the post-war world was that interest rates would probably not contribute very much to the attainment of the government's domestic economic objectives, but that they should be kept as low as possible so as at least to make a small contribution towards maintaining full employment. A cheap money policy had other advantages which commended it to a government with an ambitious social programme. It kept down the interest cost of servicing the government debt, and thus eased the financing problems presented by a heavy programme of nationalisation. In so far as the national debt was internally held, this represented a saving to taxpayers at the expense of rentiers which was probably not unwelcome to a Labour government. In so far as the debt was held overseas—and quite a substantial amount was—cheap money was a direct benefit to the balance of payments.

There was no technical difficulty in achieving a reduction in the cost of short-term borrowing. Since the Bank of England was continuously dealing in the bill market it was virtually impossible for market rates to depart from the rate at which the Bank was prepared to deal. This rate was reduced from 1% to $\frac{5}{8}\%$ shortly after the Labour Government took office in 1945.

The authorities' power to influence long-term rates, however, was much more limited. The Chancellor of the time, Dr Dalton, whose name is closely associated with the policy that was pursued, believed strongly that the long-term rate of interest was largely a psychological phenomenon. In so far as long-term rates are primarily determined by expectations of future rates, he was right. If people could be induced to believe that for the future rates would be held at low levels, this would encourage rates to fall, and make the expectation self-fulfilling. Dalton summed up his policy in the Budget speech of 1947: 'We have been gradually conditioning the capital market to a long-term rate of $2\frac{1}{2}\%$ for gilt-edged'.

To base a monetary policy on public relations, however, which is what Dalton's strategy amounted to, is essentially dangerous. Psychology which is used to induce a market reaction in one direction can backfire and have the opposite result. Early in 1947, the annual statements of the clearing bank chairmen opposed the continuation of the cheap money drive and this had a considerable effect on market sentiment. Later in the same year, the failure of the attempt to make sterling convertible cast more general doubt on the success of the government's policy. Financial commentators doubted the feasibility of holding rates at $2\frac{1}{2}\%$, and their opinions weighed just as heavily with the market as the Chancellor's earlier proselytising.

Furthermore, although expectations are an important part of the story, they cannot in themselves sustain a level of interest rates that is unrealistic in terms of real market forces. Even before the convertibility crisis, sustained inflationary pressure and acute bottlenecks in certain areas of production were making very low rates of interest difficult to maintain. When it became clear that the issue of $2\frac{1}{2}\%$ undated stock in October 1947 had met an unenthusiastic response, the active cheap money policy was quietly dropped.

After the end of cheap money, there was no very coherent framework for monetary policy until the return of the Conservative Government four years later. The authorities paid lip-service to the objective of low interest rates, partly to ease the government's burden of refinance, and partly in order to redistribute income away from the rentier classes. But monetary policy was not consciously used as a prime instrument of demand management, nor were there any deliberate attempts to control the level of long-term interest rates.

The most significant act of monetary policy in this period was the devaluation of September 1949. This was undertaken in order to move to an exchange rate in which it would be realistic to aim at a progressive liberalisation of external payments. Given the framework of controls within which the domestic economy was operating at that time, however, the devaluation, despite its large size (30%) did not have a very large impact on the level of internal demand.

The revival of monetary policy (1951-58)

1951 marked a revival of interest in monetary policy, for three main reasons. Perhaps the most important was increasing concern with the balance of payments situation. Although superficially the external position was not too bad, the inflationary conditions associated with the Korean War boom had reached their peak in 1951 and given rise to fears of a further devaluation. Secondly, it had always been widely accepted that tight credit was more effective in restraining excess demand than easy money was in stimulating the economy in a depression. The growing belief that inflation had come to stay prompted a reconsideration of the rôle of monetary policy. Thirdly, the return of a government of a new complexion, pledged to less direct intervention in the economy, introduced a renewed willingness to experiment with the more anonymous influence of monetary policy.

As far as external considerations were concerned, the monetary weapon which was traditionally most effective in controlling financial flows was bank rate. It was probably this to which Professor Robbins was referring when in a lecture on the balance of payments delivered in 1951 he referred to 'the delicate mechanism of financial control which the experience of ages was gradually fashioning'. The bank rate weapon had lain virtually unused from 1933 to 1951: in the next eight years bank rate was changed no fewer than 14 times.

Since most short-term rates in London were tied administratively or quasi-administratively to bank rate there was little difficulty in bringing about a change in yields on the kind of assets held by overseas investors in sterling. It was recognised, too, that bank rate had a psychological as well as a direct impact. Indeed, over the years, psychological considerations probably came to outweigh pure interest rate considerations. Increases in bank rate, by underlining the government's resolve to take a certain course of action, and its willingness to see a general upward movement in rates, were perceived to have an important effect on the climate of expectations, and in particular on confidence in the foreign exchange market.

The use of bank rate over most of the period since 1951 was, therefore, mainly dictated by external considerations. In this sense one could say that the authorities, consciously or unconsciously, were striving for a 'mix' of policy measures that would leave to fiscal policy the primary responsibility for regulating the level of demand, while monetary policy would concentrate on influencing inflows and outflows of funds.

Despite the primacy of budgetary policy in managing the level of activity in the domestic economy, a growing emphasis was placed after 1951 on the need for monetary policy to play an active supporting rôle. The policy that was adopted had the effect, in a rough and ready way, of controlling the growth of the money supply. The policy was not expressed in this way but this was what it amounted to. To discourage bank lending at the same time as trying to sell as much government debt as possible outside the banking system was bound, if successful, to slow the rate of growth of bank deposits, which were the major constituent of the money supply. To a large extent the policy was successful. Between 1952 and 1960, bank deposits rose by only 2% p.a. as against a growth of over 6% p.a. in the gross domestic product.

What were the means used to achieve this result? In the first place, the authorities sought to place pressure on the banks' portfolios by requiring (or encouraging the observance of) certain asset ratios. The old cash ratio was not believed to be particularly effective for the purpose in hand, since the authorities had for some time stood ready to convert, quasi-automatically, liquid money market instruments into cash. It would have been possible to change the market arrangements in London so that it was not so easy for the banking system to generate cash, but this was judged likely to produce unacceptable fluctuations in short-term interest rates, if a scramble for cash ever got out of hand. In any event, such a change would be unnecessary if, in place of the old-style cash ratio, a new ratio could be devised which would be set at a higher level and would incorporate all the near-cash assets.

This was the liquidity ratio, which was observed by the clearing banks until 1971. The ratio had its origin in prudential requirements which the banks agreed amongst themselves. Although it was always formally a ratio which the banks imposed on themselves, in the years after 1951 it quickly lost its voluntary nature and became in fact if not in law an official requirement.

Having activated the liquidity ratio as a weapon of monetary policy, the authorities had to make it bite. In 1951, the banks were excessively liquid, with something like 40% of their funds in assets which qualified for inclusion in the ratio, against a required minimum of only 30%. This excess threatened to hamper the operation of monetary policy, so the banks were required to convert a large part of it into a form which would no longer be regarded as liquid. This was achieved by the forced funding of £1,000 million of Treasury bills and Treasury deposit receipts (of which the banks' share was about half) into serial funding stock—reducing the banks' liquidity ratios at a stroke from a comfortable 39% to a barely adequate 32%.

In the years following 1951, the desire of the authorities to control the money stock by operating on the banks' liquid asset ratios came in conflict with another objective of policy at that time—to maintain orderly conditions in the market for government stock. In order to squeeze banks' liquid assets, it was necessary to reduce the proportion of floating government debt by selling more long-dated bonds. If additional bonds were pressed on an unwilling market, however, it was the Bank of England's judgment that investors would be demoralised at seeing the value of their holdings fall. This would have complicated the long-term problem of refinancing of the government's enormous volume of maturing debt, and would have increased the rate which the government would have had to pay to raise a given sum of money.

Nevertheless, despite misgivings about the consequences of falling gilt-edged prices, the authorities accepted a gradual rise in yields as the inevitable concomitant of a policy of restricting money supply growth. By 1960, the yield on 20 year stocks had climbed to about 6%, against about 3% a decade earlier.

The initial period following the revival of interest in monetary policy could be said to have come to an end with the appointment of the Radcliffe Committee in 1957. Some of the enthusiasts for monetary policy had hoped that monetary measures could shoulder a large part of the burden of demand management and thus avoid the need for unpopular taxation measures. The failure of monetary policy to contain the 1955 boom largely scotched these hopes, and was a contributory factor to the appointment of the Radcliffe Committee. Nevertheless, although opinion was already beginning to turn against active monetary policy to control domestic demand as early as 1955–56, it was not until Mr Thorneycroft left the Chancellorship in 1958 that control of the money supply ceased to be officially advocated.

The Radcliffe era (1958-68)

Many of the changes in emphasis in monetary policy that were noted in the Radcliffe Report had been introduced gradually over the preceding years. The philosophy of the report was to play down the rôle of the money supply as a crucial variable. In this sense it was a break from the policy which seemed to have been followed under Mr Butler's chancellorship in 1951–54, and later under Mr Thorneycroft. In place of control over the money supply, it was suggested that the monetary authorities should concentrate on influencing 'the general level of liquidity' in the economy. The reasoning behind this suggestion is worth setting forth in a more extended quote from the Report, in which the Committee justify their rejection of the money supply as a target variable in monetary management.

> If there is less money to go round in relation to other assets (both physical and financial) it will be held only by people willing to make a greater sacrifice in order to hold it: that is to say rates of interest will rise. But they will not, unaided, rise by much, because in a highly developed financial system, there are many highly liquid assets which are close substitutes for money, as good to hold and only inferior when the actual moment for a payment arrives. (Para. 392)

Unfortunately, the concept of liquidity defied precise definition, either by the members of the Committee itself or by the report's interpreters. Wrestling with an undefinable concept gave employment to economists, but proved singularly unfruitful for policy makers, and this notion did not play a large role in policy in the 1960s.

But when the Radcliffe concept was put in another way, it did seem to contain an implication for policy. The report placed emphasis on 'the ease or difficulty encountered by spenders in their efforts to raise money for the purpose of spending on goods and services'. It was noted that certain types of expenditure appeared to be particularly sensitive to the availability of credit. For example, the demand for cars had responded substantially and quickly to the stiffening of hire purchase controls in 1955 and 1956. As a result, the authorities were drawn increasingly to direct controls on credit to the personal sector as a more immediate and swift-acting policy than more generalised control over the money supply and rates of interest.

These controls were of two types. The first involved control over the terms (down-payment and period of repayment) under which hire-purchase contracts could be written; the second involved administrative restraints on the amounts banks lent. As well as being more effective than other means of influencing credit, direct controls had an additional advantage: if lending could be curbed by administrative methods, this would leave interest rate policy free to be used as a means of influencing inflows and outflows of funds.

Restraint on bank lending was escalated from very mild at the outset, to very severe later on. In 1952, when bank rate was raised to 4%, the Chancellor's request to the banks that they should observe restraint on the volume of their lending was largely incidental. In 1955 and 1957, the requests were expressed in semi-quantitative terms, but were still largely informal. By 1965, the Bank of England had taken to specifying precise lending ceilings and interviewing banks which contravened them. Over the following six years, apart from a brief interlude in 1967, the banking system operated continuously under a system of ceilings expressed in quantitative terms.

Although lending ceilings were thus frequently employed in the 1950s and 1960s, and although they were consistent with the principle of acting on the availability of credit, they were not really welcomed by the authorities. It was recognised that administrative controls would ultimately be avoided by the development of other forms of financial intermediation; and that in the meantime the economy would suffer by the throwing of grit into the financial mechanism. Nevertheless, in economic policy the needs of the long-term have to be balanced against those of the short-term; and the precarious balance of payments situation during much of the 1960s made it difficult to accept the short-run consequences of an abandonment of ceilings.

In a similar category were hire purchase terms controls. Experience seemed to show that it was a quick-acting method of reducing demand for consumer durables. As a result, changes in terms control often formed part of policy 'packages' despite the representations of the industries concerned about the harm being done to long-range prospects by these sudden fluctuations in demand.

Largely out of a desire to move away from lending ceilings, the Bank of England introduced in 1961 the device of special deposits. This was basically a means of varying the liquidity ratio of the banking system, with the presentational advantage that it did not violate the sacrosanct 30% (later 28%) basis for the liquidity calculation. If there was excess liquidity in the banking system, there was a danger of undesired expansion of bank advances unless the excess liquidity was either funded or frozen. Funding of a large amount in a short period of time was reckoned by the Bank of England to be, at times, virtually impossible without an unacceptable rise in interest rates. This technical difficulty could, however, be overcome by simply requiring the banking system to convert its excess liquidity into frozen 'special deposits' at the Bank of England.

The difficulty with ratio controls, however, is that, by limiting banks' freedom to lend, they tend to force interest rates upwards. If the authorities are not prepared to see sharp upward movements in rates because of the effects on confidence in the gilt-edged market, ratio controls will be rendered ineffective. The only way they could be made to work was by encouraging the banks to respond to a shortage of liquidity by rationing their lending, rather than increasing its cost. This meant that special deposits were used, not so much as a market weapon, but as a means of reinforcing official 'guidance' to the banks, and of expressing the authorities determination to be tough when it was necessary to impress foreign opinion.

As far as domestic monetary policy was concerned, there is no doubt that hire purchase controls and bank lending ceilings played the central rôle in the post-Radcliffe period. Little or no attempt was consciously made to control the money supply, and bank rate policy, as in the earlier period, was primarily directed towards influencing the external situation. (It is, however, interesting to note that the reductions in bank rate in 1967 were made for domestic reasons, despite continuing weakness in the balance of payments.)

The rise of monetarism

Around about 1968–69, there was an important change in the way many people thought about monetary policy. 'Monetarism', as a modern intellectual force, had its roots in the United States, but its impact on official thinking and on monetary policy was felt at about the same time on both sides of the Atlantic. For twenty years or so after the end of the Second World War, there had been fairly widespread agreement that monetary policy was less important, from the point of view of managing the domestic economy, than fiscal policy. This general consensus did not prevent the rôle of monetary policy being debated; it was thought that it should work with budgetary policy, that it could have some effect on the distribution of income, and that it might have an important influence on international capital movements. But it was rarely suggested that monetary policy could be the key to domestic economic management.

The change in thinking that came about in 1968–69 was due both to a feeling of frustration at the apparent ineffectiveness of the old, mainly fiscal, policy and to the apparently strong evidence for supposing that the monetary factors had been important in determining cyclical movements in income in the past. In the UK doubts were felt about the efficacy of fiscal policy when, in the aftermath of devaluation, a very tight budgetary policy appeared to have been unsuccessful in curbing demand and improving the balance of payments. In the United States, similar sentiments were felt when President Johnson's 1967 tax surcharge failed to have the desired effect in restraining inflationary pressures.

In these receptive circumstances, monetarist doctrines were quite readily accepted. As early as 1963, Professor Friedman had analysed statistical data spanning a century, and produced powerful evidence of the link between the quantity of money and the business cycle. There was considerable academic debate about how strong this link was, how predictable it was, and whether money caused changes in economic activity or vice versa. Nobody, however, disputed the link, and Friedman was a persuasive advocate of the view that the quantity of money had a direct causal impact on the level of economic activity. Since this conclusion was potentially highly valuable for policy-makers left in something of a vacuum by the comparative failure of fiscal policy, there was a tendency to ignore Friedman's other conclusion, which was that the causal connection was subject to lags and random fluctuations which made it impossible to use effectively as an instrument of counter-cyclical policy.

In the UK the intellectual impact of Friedman's advocacy of the importance of money was added to by the support of the International Monetary Fund. Since it had begun to consult with member countries in the early 1950s, the IMF had believed in the efficacy of monetary policy as an anti-inflationary weapon, and particularly in its usefulness in supporting the balance of payments adjustment process. The new rôle for monetary policy in the UK that began to emerge towards the end 1968 owed not a little to the influence of IMF advisers, who worked out some of the details of the new policy with the Treasury and Bank of England.

The new policy involved much greater emphasis on controlling the rate of growth of the money supply. In the policy advocated by the IMF, however, there was a novel twist. Because of the importance which was attached to the balance of payments, a device was sought which would provide some sort of self-correcting mechanism if the balance of payments went wrong. This was to be achieved by expressing the monetary target in terms of domestic credit expansion (DCE).

In a closed economy, domestic credit expansion would be broadly the same as changes in the money supply, since the two magnitudes would simply be measuring different sides of the balance sheet of the banking system. In an open economy, however, credit expansion could differ from changes in the money supply because of the balance of payments. For example, a high rate of credit expansion need not result in a rapid growth in the money supply if the newly created credit was leaking abroad in a payments deficit. The successful achievement of a given money supply target might be produced by an undesirably high rate of credit expansion being offset by a balance of payments deficit. (This had indeed happened in the UK in 1968.)

The adherence to a target expressed in terms of DCE, it was argued, would minimise the likelihood of following an inappropriate policy. If the monetary authorities pursued a set target for domestic credit expansion, then any unexpected deterioration in the balance of payments would result in a less-than-expected expansion of the money supply. This would in turn set up disinflationary pressures tending to improve the balance of payments. Similarly, an unexpected improvement in the balance of payments would cause the money supply to grow by more, thus stimulating demand and causing the balance of payments to deteriorate.

Domestic credit expansion, it is freely admitted, is of most use when the balance of payments is the prime concern of the economic authorities. As far as the domestic economy is concerned, the effect of a credit expansion target depends on whether departures from forecast in the balance of payments result from unexpected developments in the domestic economy or overseas. If, because of unforeseen developments in the domestic economy, the level of national income falls short of its expected value, the lower pressure of demand is likely to cause the balance of payments to turn out better than forecast. The consequent expansionary effect on the money supply from external sources will tend to mitigate the unexpected shortfall in national income.

If, on the other hand, the balance of payments departs from forecast for reasons unconnected with the domestic pressure of demand, the consequences will be less desirable. Adherence to a credit expansion target in these circumstances would require adjustments in the money supply that might not be in line with the needs of the domestic economy.

As far as the UK was concerned, however, an improvement in the balance of payments was the prime objective in the years following the 1967 devaluation. A credit expansion policy was pursued with reasonable seriousness for two years, 1969–71, though the Bank of England was careful to point out 'the stress at present laid on DCE is as a prompt shorthand supplement to, rather than a replacement for, the regular "real" and financial forecasts of the economy'. After the budget of 1971, however, there tended to be fewer references to DCE in official statements. This probably reflected some official doubts about the theoretical basis of the policy, but also the fact that by 1971 the balance of payments was no longer a problem.

However the monetary quantity is defined, a central bank is bound to experience considerable difficulty following even a very broadly defined target rate of growth for a monetary aggregate over some fixed period. In the first place there are substantial random fluctuations due to distortions in the figures on the day on which statistics are reported. Then the growth in bank lending may become quite large before the authorities can set policy moving in a direction to offset it. Finally, there is the difficulty of going against basic forces, such as the foreign exchange position and the government's budget deficit. If these are exerting a strong influence on the money supply from one direction, it may be virtually impossible for the central bank to offset this influence without pushing interest rates up to unacceptably high levels.

During the period 1968–71, the UK monetary authorities acknowledged quantitative monetary objectives at a time when they did not really have adequate tools to achieve these objectives at all precisely. In the gilt-edged market, the Bank of England was still following a a policy of 'leaning into the wind' to preserve the health of the market by preventing undue fluctuations in the price of gilt-edged stock. This policy may or may not have been necessary in the interests of the long-term future of the gilt-edged market. What is certain is that, in the short run it made it impossible to prevent investors turning gilt-edged stocks into cash when they wanted.

Because the authorities did not have full control over the amount of bonds taken up by the non-bank public, they could not control the extent to which the government had to have recourse to borrowing from the banking system. This meant that most of the weight of quantitative monetary policy had to be thrown on restraining bank lending to the private sector. This was attempted through an intensification of ceiling controls. It is not really possible to attempt a judgment about how successful monetary policy was in this period. The monetary instruments at first failed, and then succeeded in restraining the rate of growth of monetary aggregates. Their eventual success might be ascribed, however, not to diligent use of monetary techniques, but to the turn-round in the government's budgetary position and later the falling off in demand for bank loans. Policy also succeeded in halting the growth in demand and improving the balance of payments. Again, however, this result can be ascribed to devaluation and budgetary policy, with monetary restraint being more a consequence than a cause of the success. It is not really possible to draw any firm conclusions.

What had become clear by 1971, however, was that the existing monetary weapons were deficient in certain respects for controlling the growth of monetary aggregates and that the use of ceilings was having a harmful effect on banking efficiency. It was for these reasons that the new arrangements of 1971, described in the next chapter, were introduced.

Further reading

Dow, J. C. R., *The Management of the British Economy*, 1945-1960, London, Cambridge University Press, 1946.

Goodhart, C. A. E., British monetary policy—1957-1967, London School of Economics and Political Science.

Kareken, John H., Monetary policy in *Britain's Economic Prospects*. R. E. Caves (ed). London, Allen and Unwin, 1968.

Radcliffe Report, op. cit., Chapter 6.

Worswick G. D. N. and Ady, P., *The British Economy in the 1960s*, Oxford, Clarendon Press, 1962, Chapter 9.

Questions for discussion

1 What would be the consequence of a return to cheap money policies in the circumstances of the 1970s.

2 What are the advantages and disadvantages of direct controls as an instrument of monetary policy?

3 What did the Radcliffe Committee mean when it emphasized the importance of liquidity?

4 In what circumstances is DCE a better guide to the impact of monetary policy than the money supply?

13

Competition and credit control

The new arrangements for regulating the banking system which were introduced by the Bank of England in 1971 were certainly the most far-reaching reform of the post-war period. They were proposed in a consultative document, 'Competition and Credit Control,' and had two objectives: to remove impediments to competition in the banking system, and to establish a new pattern for official operations which would enable the authorities to influence effectively and speedily the rate of growth of the monetary aggregates.

The desire for a new scheme grew out of dissatisfaction with the existing instruments used for operating monetary policy. The dissatisfaction was voiced mainly by commercial banks, but the authorities themselves made it clear in their official pronouncements that they, too, were unhappy with the existing controls. Although these had been intended to disturb as little as possible the existing framework of banking institutions, the protracted use of such instruments as lending ceilings and special deposits had tended to distort competition without in the long run improving the effectiveness of monetary policy. There were three aspects of the pre-1971 arrangements which worked against free competition in the banking system: ceiling controls, the clearing banks' cartel, and the agreed cash and liquidity ratios of the clearing banks.

Ceiling controls on bank lending in sterling had been introduced because they had been seen as the most effective way of getting a quick reduction in credit creation without damaging disruptions to the banking system. It was of course recognized that the use of ceilings would impair competition, but so long as the ceilings were to be in force for only a short period, this was not thought to be a particularly serious consequence. By 1971, however, ceiling controls had been in existence for nearly six years, and their drawbacks had grown with the passage of time. In the first place, they tended to create a misallocation of resources within the banking industry, as efficient and innovative banks were prevented from expanding their sterling lending, and the less efficient were able to continue to exist on the basis of business the efficient were forced to turn away. The structure of sterling lending was thus 'frozen' at a point in time, and banks which were small at the base-date had virtually no scope to expand their business. Secondly, ceiling controls encouraged bankers to favour well-established 'safe' customers. Since they were only able to lend a fixed amount of money, there was little point in assuming the risks involved in making a loan to a new fast-growing company. These companies, however, might be the ones which needed finance most, and which could make the greatest contribution to economic growth.

The Clearing Bank Cartel, which had been in operation since the middle 1930s, was a voluntary agreement amongst the banks concerned which dictated the rates of interest to be paid on deposits and minimum charges to be levied on advances to customers. The Bank of England was not a direct party to the Cartel, and could not therefore dictate its abandonment. Nevertheless, the banks had previously indicated their willingness to terminate the agreements and the authorities were reasonably confident they could be persuaded to do so in the context of revised arrangements such as were eventually put forward.

The Clearing Bank Cartel did not have all the disadvantages, from a resource-allocation point of view, of traditional monopolies. As far as it is possible to judge, the banks appeared to follow what they believed was the public interest, and not simply to use their monopoly position to maximise their private profits. Nevertheless, the Cartel could still have the effect of misallocating resources. If the banks held down the rates of interest they charged borrowers, in order not to make excess profits, they would have to ration their available resources in some other way. In such circumstances, they were again likely to favour old-established and safer customers at the expense of possibly more dynamic and innovative newcomers.

The third impediment to competition under the old arrangements was the different requirements to hold cash and liquid assets as between clearing banks and other banks. Again these requirements were, strictly speaking, voluntary arrangements between the banks, but it is probably fair to say that the authorities had used their influence to preserve their existence. The London clearing banks held an average of 8% of their deposits in the form of cash in tills and balances at the Bank of England. These funds earned no interest and, since they were in excess of what the banks needed for purely commercial reasons, effectively constituted a tax on them. Similarly with their liquid assets, which were greater than their needs, and with special deposits, which were called from the clearing and Scottish banks only. All these arrangements tended to undermine the capacity of the clearing banks to compete against banks which were not subject to these asset ratios. (In fairness, however, it must be noted that the banks which were thus inhibited all set up subsidiary companies, not subject to ratios. Thus most of the disadvantages were overcome.)

In addition to militating against free competition in the banking system, the pre-1971 monetary instruments were less than fully effective in attaining the goal of credit control. There were two main reasons for this: the continued support of the gilt-edged market (i.e. reluctance to see sharp fluctuations in the prices of gilt-edged securities) meant that the authorities could find themselves buying in stock, and thus increasing the quantity of money, at times when, for purely monetary policy reasons, they would have preferred to see a reduction in the quantity of money.

The continuance of ceilings over a long period meant that financial channels not subject to ceilings (e.g., borrowing from 'fringe' banks or direct company-to-company lending) tended to be opened up and exploited. It was thus becoming increasingly difficult to gauge precisely what effect a given ceiling was actually having. Furthermore, by concentrating on 'credit' indicators, ceilings neglected to take full account of the consequences of expansionary monetary policy which was reflected in ways other than an increase of bank lending.

The new arrangements

Despite the far reaching nature of the reforms proposed by the Bank of England, the new arrangements were arrived at by voluntary agreement with the banks, and they have no legal backing. The fact that the scheme is voluntary cannot be taken to mean that all banks are equally happy about all aspects of it. Many of them expressed detailed reservations; but in the end they accepted it as the best compromise between their own desire for greater freedom and the need for the authorities to have some means of regulating the banking system. Having formally assented to the new arrangements, it is to be expected that the banks will operate within them as though they had the force of law.

The circumstances of 1971 were particularly propitious for a new initiative. The recently elected Government had a commitment to foster greater competition; there was a slackening in loan demand and so little risk that an easing in restrictions would lead to unmanageable growth in borrowing; there was temporarily no danger on the balance of payments front.

The first of the two objectives, the removal of impediments to competition, was the easier to fulfil. It involved primarily getting rid of restrictions which were generally recognised to be onerous or at any rate hard to justify on a long-term basis. The removal of ceiling controls had no opponents. The ending of the Cartel and the abolition of cash and liquid assets by the clearing banks was dependent only on satisfactory new arrangements being worked out.

It was not so much the abandonment of the existing arrangements that occasioned debate, but the proposed form of what was to replace them. There were three aspects to the proposals put forward in the paper published by the Bank of England in May 1971:

a A change in dealing tactics in the gilt-edged market.
b An across-the-board reserve ratio of $12\frac{1}{2}\%$ to be observed by all banks.
c The power to call special deposits.

The first of these three proposals was designed to limit the extent to which the Bank of England created money through its operations in the gilt-edged market; the other two were designed to increase the effectiveness and predictability with which the authorities' open market operations impinged on bank lending and the money supply.

Dealing tactics

The change in dealing tactics was clearly not something that could be debated with the banking system before its introduction—the uncertainty which would have been caused in markets would have been too great. It was therefore the one aspect of the 'Consultative Document' that was effective immediately and not subject to negotiation. The nature of this change has been the subject of much misunderstanding, and it would be expecting too much to hope that this could be cleared up here. Nevertheless, it is helpful to see the development over time of the Bank's gilt-edged tactics in a number of stages. This is because the 1971 change is not so much a brand-new policy but a reversion to roughly the situation of the 1950s.

Given the size of the national debt, it is inevitable that the Bank of England has to sell medium and longer-dated stocks on a substantial scale simply to maintain the average life of the debt constant. At the same time, the Bank has always rejected any attempt to sell debt when the market price of government securities was falling. It felt that it would only be possible to sell in such circumstances with grave consequences for the price, and therefore the future marketability of gilt-edged. Open-market sales of gilt-edged in the 1950s operated something like a man going up a down escalator. When circumstances were unfavourable, the authorities were largely out of the market, so that the passage of time tended to make the average life of the national debt get shorter. When circumstances became favourable again, however, and the market started to rise, the authorities began to sell to lengthen the debt, and like the man running up the down escalator, arrived back at their starting position.

Although no public statements can be found which suggest that the authorities were consciously pursuing a given quantitative target, the policy they adopted had a quantitative result. In fact, they were successful in restraining the rate of growth of the money supply below the rate of growth of the economy. In so doing the rate of interest on long-term bonds rose from about 3% in 1950 to twice that level in 1960.

In the early 1960s, however, the Bank of England began to adopt a policy of more active intervention in the market. It did this by buying stocks (instead of merely withdrawing from the market) at times when prices were falling. This tactic was employed to minimise what were thought to be unnecessary fluctuations in rates, and thus to increase the attractiveness of gilt-edged stocks to large institutional investors, who were thought to prefer price stability. This stabilising function is one which, in traditional economic theory, ought to be performed by private speculators, who will buy low and sell high, thus making a profit for themselves and performing a valuable economic service by ironing out price fluctuations.

The view was taken, however, that participants in the gilt-edged market had neither the resources nor the necessary knowledge to be fully effective in performing this function. But whatever the strength of stabilising forces from within the market before the Bank began its support, they tended to diminish afterwards. As the Chief Cashier put it in 1971, 'a market dominated by a dealer with resources far and away beyond those which any other single dealer could possibly command was not likely to be attractive to newcomers'.[1] By performing the function of stabilisation with its massive resources, the Bank left no rôle for the private speculator. The policy of active intervention therefore tended to widen beyond the shorter-dated stocks with which it began, to embrace stocks of all maturities.

1 Sykes Memorial Lecture, Reprinted in *Competition and Credit Control*, Bank of England, 1971.

This policy was not seriously questioned until control of the money supply became a live issue in about 1967–68. Its shortcomings in circumstances where the authorities were seeking to control monetary aggregates were obvious and, in 1968, the Bank of England modified its previous policy by marking down its prices much more rapidly when it was being offered a lot of stock. In the 1971 paper, the bull (or perhaps it should be the bear) was taken firmly by the horns and the Bank announced it would go back to the 1950s situation and no longer automatically intervene to support the market. In the Bank's own words, the new tatics were designed '... to limit, further than can be achieved solely by alterations in the Bank's dealing prices, fluctuations in the resources of the banking system arising from official operations in the gilt-edged market'. In announcing this change in policy publicly, and at a time when prices were strong rather than weak, the Bank hoped that operators would have time to safeguard themselves against the risks of a sudden fall in prices, and that new institutions would be encouraged to participate in the market as a result of the greater profit opportunities which a freer market presented.

It is important to realise what the new policy is *not*. It is not a purely quantitative policy where the authorities sell a fixed quantity of Government securities irrespective of consequences for yields. The Bank is still only a seller of stock when the market is strong and it is still prepared to buy stock under certain conditions, when this is desirable for reasons of monetary policy. At best, therefore, the Bank can only work towards a target of bond sales over a longish period. What has changed is that the Bank need no longer find itself pumping out substantial quantities of liquidity into the banking system at a time when it does not want to.

The new arrangements and the banking system

One of the main purposes of the proposals set forth in the Bank's paper on 'Competition and Credit Control' was to give the authorities greater powers to influence magnitudes such as the money supply. Since money is broadly speaking created by the banking system, it might be thought that it is those features of the scheme which directly affect banks—reserve ratios and special deposits—which are most important. This is not really the case. In a speech to the International Banking Conference in Munich in 1971,[2] the Governor of the Bank of England emphasised 'What we have in mind is a system under

[2] Reprinted in 'Competition and Credit Control', Bank of England, 1971.

which the *allocation of credit is primarily determined by its cost.*'
(Italics in the distributed version of the speech.) The centrepiece of
the system was, therefore, the Bank's assertion of its willingness to
allow, or encourage, interest rates to move to whatever level was
necessary to restrain or expand the money supply to the desired extent. In this context the weapons applied to the banking system—
reserve ratios and special deposits—should be seen primarily as ad-
juncts to the basic principle of the new proposals, which is the freedom
of interest rates to regulate and allocate credit.

The new instruments were, however, necessary, in the words of the
Chief Cashier, '... to ensure the responsiveness of [the banks and
finance houses] to modifications of policy. For this purpose it appeared
not possible for the authorities to rely on the voluntary observance of
ratios which banks and finance houses habitually maintain for reasons
of commercial prudence, for two reasons. First the dictates of commercial prudence are by no means immutable. A ratio that seemed
appropriate at one point in time could well change with circumstances and change appreciably.... Secondly, the composition of the
liquid assets held for reasons of commercial prudence might also
change ...'.

The principal instrument of control applied to the banking system
is the requirement to hold a minimum proportion of $12\frac{1}{2}\%$ of sterling
resources in reserve assets. Broadly speaking, sterling resources means
deposits, and reserve assets means those assets which the Bank of
England stands ready to convert into cash more or less on demand.
Nevertheless, it is helpful for the sake of completeness to know just
what is understood by the two magnitudes.

'Eligible liabilities' is the somewhat inelegant name by which the
quantity of resources against which reserves must be held is known.
Eligible liabilities comprise:

a all deposits in sterling, whether held by UK or overseas residents,
with an original term to maturity of two years or less,
b any funds taken in foreign currencies and switched into sterling,
irrespective of the maturity of the foreign currency deposit,

less

c funds lent in the inter-bank market and
d holdings of sterling certificates of deposit issued by banks.

The purpose of excluding liabilities with an original term to
maturity of over two years is to exclude sources of bank funds which
are more akin to loan finance than deposits. The two-year cut-off, it is

frankly admitted, is arbitrary. The objective of the netting procedure in **c** and **d** above is to avoid discouraging movements of funds within the banking system which do not add to total resources available to the system as a whole. The reserve holding liability falls on the ultimate user of the funds, rather than on the bank which borrows and on-lends to another bank.

Against these 'eligible liabilities' banks must hold not less than $12\frac{1}{2}\%$ in the form of reserve assets. These comprise:

   (i) Balances at the Bank of England
  (ii) British and N. Ireland Government Treasury bills
 (iii) Local Authority Bills
  (iv) Money at call with the London money market
   (v) Commercial bills (to a maximum of 2% of eligible liabilities)
  (vi) Gilt-edged securities with a life of up to one year
 (vii) Tax reserve certificates.

The reason for the choice of this somewhat heterogeneous collection of assets was that such a choice would upset least the Bank of England's existing mode of operation in the short-term money markets. In order for a reserve ratio to perform its function of increasing the speed and predictability with which the banking system responds to official operations, it is necessary for the authorities to have at least some control over the available quantity of reserve assets. If a new system had been constructed out of nothing, it might have made more sense to restrict reserves to those assets whose supply was completely within the control of the authorities—bank notes and Bank of England balances. But in order to make this control effective, it would have been necessary for the Bank to have abandoned its policy of dealing freely in Treasury bills. It was judged less disruptive to existing market practices to define 'reserve assets' as comprising those instruments which the Bank of England, directly or through the intermediation of the discount market, stood ready to convert into cash.[3] (Somewhat paradoxically, cash, in the form of notes and coin, was excluded, on the grounds that a minimum float of till money was an essential prerequisite for banking activity, and could not effectively be run down.)

Several commentators have expressed reservations about the details of the proposed ratio, but it is worth reiterating that it is not the

---

[3] Banks are only allowed to include commercial bill holdings as reserve assets up to 2% of eligible liabilities. This limitation does not affect the encashability of commercial bills in a crisis, but it is designed to limit the capacity of banks to generate liquidity through lending to customers by way of bills.

cornerstone of the proposed new method of credit control. It is essentially an adjunct to improve the response of the system to official action. Its precise definition is of less importance than the fact that it can, in a general way, bring pressure to bear quickly on banks' portfolios and stimulate them to adjustment.

Why $12\frac{1}{2}\%$? The choice appears to have been governed by a desire to upset as little as possible the existing pattern of holding of reserve assets. Given the logic of reserve ratios set out above, the important feature is not that they should be set at any particular level, but that they should be capable of being made effective quickly. It seems likely that $12\frac{1}{2}\%$ was chosen as being low enough to appeal to the banks as no more than a minor constraint on their freedom, and sufficiently close to existing practice that it could be made to bite without massive calls for special deposits.

Another question that may be asked is whether the imposition of a reserve ratio interferes with the objective of promoting freer competition in banking. To some extent, of course, any compulsory asset ratio represents a form of tax on banking activity. The question is whether a uniform ratio of the kind adopted distorts competition as between banks of different types. It has long been recognised that one of the great strengths of London as a financial centre has been its diversity. Banks have specialised in particular areas of business which impose widely varying needs from the point of view of balance-sheet structure. To impose the same portfolio constraint (i.e. $12\frac{1}{2}\%$ reserve assets) on dissimilar institutions, it may be argued, is just as inequitable as it would be to impose different ratios on similar banks.

Although this argument is easy to grasp conceptually, it is not easy to resolve. To impose differential reserve requirements would probably create more inequities than it would remove. For although banks have different specialities, there are considerable areas of overlap, and in these areas a bank with a low ratio would be at a completely unjustified advantage vis-à-vis banks with higher ratios. It was concluded by the Bank of England that, in the matter of sterling deposit-taking and sterling lending, the similarities amongst banks were more important than the dissimilarities. It was plausibly argued that, by setting the ratio at a low level, the distortions produced by adopting a uniform ratio would be reduced to acceptable proportions.

Two provisions in the new arrangements seem to work against the clearing banks. They are not allowed to count their substantial holdings of till money as a reserve asset, and they are required to hold an average balance of $1\frac{1}{2}\%$ at the Bank of England. On closer examination, however, these restraints on the clearing banks are not, perhaps, as serious as they appear at first sight. Till money holding is a necessary part of operating a retail banking service. If any other institution wished to challenge the clearing banks in their branch activities, it would find itself obliged to hold non-interest bearing till money in much the same way. And when the clearers expand the wholesale side of their business, with large fixed deposits, they do not have to increase their till money commensurately. It is therefore hard to argue that the exclusion of till money from reserve assets reduces the capacity of the clearers to compete with the other banks.

The requirement that clearing banks should hold $1\frac{1}{2}\%$ of their eligible liabilities, on average, on deposit with the Bank of England is an agreement between the banks concerned and the Bank of England. Starting from the principle that the banks should not overdraw at the Bank of England, the figure of $1\frac{1}{2}\%$ was arrived at as the minimum target balance which would be necessary to reduce the risks of overdraft to negligible proportions (i.e., the banks' balances do not fluctuate more than about $1\frac{1}{2}\%$ as a result of the unforeseen credits or debits in the clearing). This again is a tax on an *activity*, clearing, rather than a tax on an institution. If any other institution were to join the clearing house, it would presumably be subject to the same régime.

Special deposits

The third string to the authorities bow, besides open market operations and the $12\frac{1}{2}\%$ reserve requirement, is the right to call special deposits. These are deposits held in 'frozen' form at the Bank of England, bearing interest at Treasury bill rate, but not counting towards the $12\frac{1}{2}\%$ reserve ratio. Calls for special deposits are expressed as a percentage of eligible liabilities and are made across the banking system.

The special deposits mechanism has two main purposes: to support open market operations in bringing pressure to bear on banks' portfolios, and to provide a means of sterilising inflows of funds from abroad. Where the banking system has a comfortable margin of excess reserve assets, it would in principle be possible to operate a restrictive monetary policy by substantial sales of longer-term government debt aimed at reducing reserve assets to a level where banks begin to feel pressure on their portfolios. The disadvantage of such a policy is that it might take time to become effective, and it might have adverse consequential results (e.g., on long-term investor confidence). In such circumstances, it may be more effective and less disruptive to 'freeze' the excess by a call for special deposits.

The second purpose which it is envisaged special deposits might serve is to discriminate against overseas deposits.[4] The intention here would presumably be to sterilise an inflow of funds at a time when domestic monetary policy was intended to be restrictive. Deposits of overseas residents, and possibly also foreign currency funds switched into sterling, would be subject to a differential rate of special deposit call. There is a provision for this to be levied incrementally (i.e., only on deposits taken after a certain date) but no provision for a rate of interest other than the Treasury bill rate to be paid.

The role of the discount market

The discount market traditionally stands between the banks and the Bank of England. Money market firms take the banks' excess funds at call or short notice and invest them in short-term instruments such as bills, certificates of deposits and short-dated bonds. They are able to offer the banks perfect liquidity on their call money by virtue of the last resort facilities which they, and they alone, enjoy at the Bank of England.

To fit the discount market into a scheme in which reserve ratios played a part posed a tricky problem for the authorities. To exclude call money from reserves would have required a change in the existing traditional mechanisms. Since the essence of a reserve ratio is that the authorities should be able to influence the creation of reserve assets something would have had to be done to reduce the almost-perfect convertibility of money at call into cash. This would have required a considerable dimunition in the discount houses' ability to convert their assets into cash in dealings with the Bank of England; the corollary of which would have been a reduction in the liquidity which the houses could confidently offer the banks on their call money. Such changes would have drastically curtailed the scope of the discount market's activities.

This degree of change in the system would have been difficult to put through on a voluntary basis. The banks and the discount houses had found the existing arrangements convenient, and the Bank of England itself preferred to deal with a small number of discount houses rather than a large number of banks. It was therefore a change which the authorities were only prepared to make if the advantages were commensurate. As it was, with the reserve asset mechanism

---

[4] It would also be possible to discriminate in favour of overseas deposits by exempting them from a special deposit call. This, however, is not a likely use of the instrument.

cast in a supporting rôle, it was considered sufficient to have a somewhat looser definition of reserve assets, with less precise control for the authorities.

Defining reserve assets so as to include money at call with the discount market meant that the banking system could generate reserve assets internally by lending money to the discount market which the latter could in theory use to acquire assets from the banks. The scheme that was eventually devised does not make it impossible for this internal generation of reserve assets to take place; but it does hinder it. The discount houses are required to hold half their borrowed funds in certain categories of public sector debt, viz. Treasury bills, other public sector bills, British Government securities and local government bonds with up to five years to maturity.

Well over three-quarters of these assets are held outside the discount market, and all are traded freely. The requirement that the discount market must hold 50% of its borrowed funds in these assets is, therefore, clearly not an absolute constraint on the amount of call money the houses may take. In practice, however, it limits their ability to generate reserve assets when the Bank of England is trying to tighten credit. In particular, it limits the extent to which the houses can expand their books by buying commercial bills from the banks. And if rates are edging up, the houses are not likely to want to take large quantities of bonds from the banks. (Treasury bills are virtually all held by the discount market.)

To sum up: it does not seem to be intended that the reserve ratios (either for the banks or for the discount market) should be sufficiently watertight to achieve complete control over the creation of reserve assets. If this had been the intention, the authorities would presumably have devised a different scheme. Rather the intention seems to have been to create a loose portfolio constraint that would enable the authorities to put enough gentle pressure on the institutions concerned to induce them to sell non-reserve assets. To quote from the Governor's Munich speech again 'It is not expected that the mechanism of the minimum asset ratio and special deposits can be used to achieve some precise multiple contraction or expansion of bank assets. Rather the intention is to use our control over liquidity, which these instruments will reinforce, to influence the structure of interest rates'.

The problem of external flows

The proposals that were implemented during 1971 have given the Bank of England sufficient power to vary interest rates to the extent necessary to control the rate of growth of monetary aggregates *in a closed economy*. The rider is important, because there are a whole set of problems which exist in an open economy which have not been considered so far in this chapter. (By 'open' in this context is meant an economy where there are no controls on the movement of capital and where the economy concerned is a relatively small part of the world economy.)

It has for a long time been recognised that it is not strictly possible to pursue an independent monetary policy at the same time as having a fixed exchange rate and eschewing exchange controls. This is quite simply because, with fixed exchange rates, capital flows to the financial centre where interest rates are highest. If one country should wish to restrict credit by encouraging an upward movement in interest rates, the result will be an inflow of capital that will nullify the domestic policy measures.

There are three instruments available to the UK authorities to combat an unwelcome inflow of funds:

a exchange rate flexibility,
b exchange controls,
c differential special deposits.

Complete flexibility of exchange rates can give the authorities of a country freedom to pursue an independent monetary policy, unencumbered by unwelcome flows of funds into and out of the reserves. Sterling was, in fact, allowed to float between August and December 1971 and from June 1972 (although on both occasions the reasons for the float were not so much to give freedom to domestic monetary policy as to prevent large changes in the reserves).

Despite the attractions of floating for domestic monetary management there are important international considerations, described in more detail in Chapter 14, that make it unlikely that general floating will be a normal feature of the reformed international monetary system. Even where countries have a fixed par value for their currency, however, there will still be scope for the market rate of exchange to move in a band around the par value without the authorities needing to intervene. And forward rates can move outside this band. Since speculators normally cover their operations by hedging in the forward market, interest rates in one country can differ from those elsewhere by the cost of forward cover. This is a useful additional measure of freedom in the conduct of domestic monetary policy.

Exchange controls are another means by which the domestic economy may be shielded from international capital flows. In Britain, the usual reason for the imposition of exchange controls has been to prevent an outflow of funds, but in 1971 controls were used to prevent inflows as well. Everyone agrees in principle that exchange controls are a bad thing; they interfere with the freedom of individuals and companies to invest where they feel the returns are highest. Nevertheless, there have been numerous occasions where, in the absence of international agreement, individual countries have concluded that the use of exchange control, either to protect their reserves or to preserve their domestic freedom of action in monetary policy, is the lesser of two evils. The selective use of exchange control may thus give a second useful additional measure of freedom in policy.

The third weapon is the one introduced in the new arrangements— similar to a device used in West Germany for a number of years— differential special deposits. As they will be applied in the UK, differential special deposits will probably only have a marginal effect in keeping out unwanted funds from abroad. The banks are to be paid the Treasury bill rate on their special deposits, so that the reduction in the rate they are able to pay overseas depositors will probably not be very great, even if 100% special deposits are called. It seems unlikely that this slight interest penalty will do very much to dissuade speculators gambling on revaluation. Special deposits may not therefore do much to restrain the growth of sterling deposits—but they may effectively freeze the additions to the money supply. If, for example, additional overseas residents' deposits have to go 100% into locked deposits at the Bank of England, it is arguable that this will have little effect on the domestic economy. The money cannot be on-lent in the UK and currency speculators are not likely to use their bank deposits to fuel inflationary demand for real goods.

It seems likely that the UK authorities intend to use some combination of these three devices in the years ahead—they may thus regain some of the freedom to operate monetary policy that is bound to be lost by adherence to a fixed exchange rate régime. (However, the implementation of proposals for European monetary integration may revive these problems in a European context.)

Further reading

Bank of England, *Competition and Credit Control*, September 1971, Selected Articles from the Bank of England Quarterly Bulletin.
The Banker, June 1971, Symposium on *The New Bank Controls*.
The Bank of England proposals, *The Bankers Magazine*, June 1971, articles by A. B. Cramp, N. J. Gibson, and J. R. S. Revell.

Griffiths, Brian, Resource efficiency, monetary policy and the reform of the UK banking system, *Journal of Money, Credit and Banking*, February, 1973.

Questions for discussion

1 To what extent are competition and credit control conflicting objectives ?
2 Why was it necessary for the Bank of England to modify its tactics in the gilt-edged market in 1971 ?
3 How can special deposits be used in support of monetary policy under the new credit control arrangements ?
4 What is the principal means by which the Bank of England controls the money supply under the new arrangements introduced in 1971 ?

Part 5

International monetary relations

14

The theory of international exchange

International monetary theory is concerned with the efficient organisation of payments across national frontiers. The question may be asked where this theory differs from that of organising payments within the domestic economy. In each case a payment has to be made because a buyer has purchased goods or services from a seller, or because a lender has lent money to a borrower. In each case purchasing power has to be transferred from the purchaser or the lender to the seller or borrower. Why then should we regard a sale of English goods to a Frenchman as creating a different kind of problem from the sale of English goods to a Scotsman?

The answer, of course, lies in the fact that, in an international transaction, different currencies are involved. When an Englishman sells goods to a Scotsman, settlement can be simply made by the transfer of money balances from one account to another. When he sells goods to a Frenchman, he will expect to be paid in pounds, while the French buyer will expect to pay in francs. It is evident that an additional transaction is needed to complete the sale. There must be a market where the Frenchman can sell his francs for pounds in order to pay the Englishman. The central question in international monetary economics is how this market should be organised and regulated. The key issue that dominates debate on this subject is whether currencies should stand in fixed relation to each other, or whether their values should be allowed to fluctuate in response to pressures of supply and demand. We shall examine the two extreme theories first and then proceed to some of the numerous compromise proposals that have been made to try and secure the best of both worlds.

Fixed exchange rates

The principal virtue of rigidly fixed exchange rates is that they remove uncertainty from international trade and capital transactions. It is true that currencies still have to be exchanged in order for sales and loans to be made but, if the rate of exchange between currencies is fixed, this is a minor matter. Transactions across national boundaries are subject to no more uncertainty than internal transactions. Because uncertainty exposes businessmen and investors to unwelcome risks, it can be argued that fixed exchange rates tend to increase the volume of trade and productive international investment. This means that the allocation of the world's resources, as a whole, can be improved, since the presumption is that each country will export these goods which it can produce relatively efficiently in exchange for imports of those goods which it is relatively less efficient at making. And countries which have a greater desire to save can place resources at the disposal of countries where there is a relatively greater desire to undertake capital investment. The greater the certainty with which exchange rates are expected to remain fixed, the greater, obviously, are these advantages to welfare and economic growth.

Typically, a fixed exchange rate system involves the countries that adhere to it setting the value of their national currencies in terms of a common standard. The earliest examples in international payments were standards fixed in terms of commodity money, and usually gold. Under the gold standard, all countries fixed a value for their currency in gold, thereby fixing at the same time the 'cross rates' at which the various currencies exchanged for each other. The gold standard endured for much of the nineteenth century, and remains in vestigial form to the present day. It is also possible to have other standards, of course. Certain currencies were, for a time, tied to sterling; these links are much less strong now, but it is still unlikely that the Irish pound would depart from its fixed relationship with the pound sterling. In much of the post-war period, the world has been, effectively, on a dollar standard, with most countries quoting the values of their currencies in terms of dollars. (Until 1971 dollars were, in turn, exchangeable into gold, so that there was an indirect link with gold.) A rather more complex arrangement would be to value currencies in terms of some composite index of other currencies, or even a composite index of commodity values. The important point is that all national currencies should have a value fixed in terms of the common standard.

To maintain their currency at a fixed value, the monetary authorities of a country must stand ready to buy and sell the currency against the agreed standard at a fixed price. This means they must have large quantities of their own currency and of the monetary standard in order to meet any excess of demand or supply at the fixed price. It would be precisely the same if a merchant at Covent Garden wished to fix the value of apples. He would have to buy apples any time their price seemed like falling below the fixed value and sell apples any time the price seemed like rising. In order to be successful, he would need to have a large store of both apples and money in order to meet the possibilities of surplus or shortage.

An apple dealer would probably not be able to keep his price fixed for long in the face of a shift in the demand for apples relative to the costs of production. The same law holds good in the foreign exchange market. Therefore, if a fixed-exchange rate system is to survive, there must be some mechanism to ensure that the supply and demand for currencies do not get too far out of balance. This is simply another way of saying that there must be a means of correcting the balance of payments when it gets into surplus or deficit.

Under the old gold standard, theorists could point to an automatic mechanism which tended to correct balance of payments disequilibria. Consider the case where a country experiences a sudden increase in the demand for imports. The balance of payments will deteriorate, and more domestic currency will be offered for sale by the overseas exporters. The central bank will have to step in and buy the excess supply of its own currency. It will give in return gold from its reserves. In the process, the money supply in the domestic economy will have gone down, since foreigners will have received domestic currency from importers, which they will then have sold to the central bank in exchange for gold.

With domestic money harder to come by, people will be prepared to pay more to get hold of what there is. Interest rates will therefore rise, with two consequences. In the short term, higher rates will probably attract some capital from abroad, thus providing cash to partly offset the drain which is occurring through higher imports. In the longer run, the higher rates of interest may cause people to cut back expenditure, particularly on capital goods, thus lowering the pressure of demand and causing sellers of goods to reduce their prices in order to make sales. This reduction in prices will, of course, tend to make the country's domestic production cheaper, thus encouraging exports and discouraging imports. The wheel comes full circle when this process restores the balance of payments to full equilibrium, and the outflow of gold stops.

It is always possible, of course, for the monetary authorities of a country to offset the effects on the money supply of the balance of payments through open market operations or other domestic policies.

If the authorities are adopting a policy of managing their currency, there will be no automatic link between the balance of payments and the quantity of money. If this is the case, the automatic gold standard mechanism cannot be relied on to correct the balance of payments, and the authorities must take deliberate action to remove the source of disequilibrium if the fixed exchange rate is to be maintained. That action could either be in the field of monetary policy or budgetary policy or some combination of the two. In any event, the end result will be much the same as under the gold standard. If the problem is of a deficit in the balance of payments, a deflationary policy will cut back imports and reduce the level of domestic activity. In consequence, prices will be restrained, thus stimulating exports and, in an ideal world, restoring balance of payments equilibrium at full employment.

Unfortunately, things do not work quite so smoothly in practice. The foregoing analysis implies that wages and prices can respond quickly and flexibly to small changes in the pressure of demand. In fact, prices may be very slow to adjust, particularly in a downward direction, so that the process of adjustment, whereby a balance of payments deficit is eliminated by a reduction in the prices of a country's products, may be a long and painful one.

Some indication of the difficulties of securing wage and price adjustment through deflation may be gained by looking at the experience of regions within a single economy. The position of a separate region within a national economy is not dissimilar to the position of an independent country in a fixed exchange rate world. Within individual countries, it is possible to point to regions which have remained in a depressed state for very long periods without any apparent tendency for full employment to be restored. Examples are Northern Ireland, the Appalachian region of the United States, and the Mezzogiorno in Italy. Between different countries it is perhaps easier to have divergent movements in wages and prices, but even so it is far from certain that the process of adjustment could be relied on to take place fast enough to be acceptable to an independent government.

It can be argued that this feature of a fixed exchange rate system provides an element of necessary financial discipline on governments, which makes it more unlikely that balance of payments deficits will be allowed to develop in the first instance. There is some virtue in this argument. The need to defend a fixed exchange rate can sometimes be useful in mobilising political or administrative support for necessary but unpopular policies. On the other hand, the discipline of a fixed rate can impose wholly unnecessary burdens. In the first place, it means that the price level of traded goods in all countries will have to go up at a broadly similar rate. If one country sets a high store by full employment but is not much bothered by inflation, while another is determined to avoid inflation, even at the cost of some underemployment, they are unlikely to agree on a single, mutually acceptable rate of change in the price level.

There may also be structural changes in supply and demand conditions which make exchange rates inappropriate, despite an unchanged general price level. If, for example, world demand for a particular raw material drops because of the development of an artificial substitute, the countries producing that raw material will experience a deterioration in their balance of payments. The same thing can happen with manufactured products, when demand falls because of a change in tastes or the development of substitutes. It is scarcely equitable, in the name of financial discipline, to force additional deflation on a country which has already suffered from a structural change in demand.

Apart from the general requirement, under a fixed rate system, for countries to orient their domestic economic policies towards securing a balance of payments equilibrium, there is an even more specific constraint on the operation of monetary policy. If exchange rates are fixed and unchangeable, and there is free movement of capital between countries, then interest rates cannot vary internationally. Consequently, countries cannot have independent policies with respect to their money supply or interest rate levels.

Floating exchange rates

There is no reason, so the advocates of floating exchange rates claim, why countries should be forced by the discipline of a fixed parity to forgo an independent monetary policy, or to adopt demand-management policies which are not welcome on other grounds. They believe that the price of a nation's currency should be determined in the same way as the price of any other commodity, namely by the interaction of supply and demand in free markets. The supply of a currency would reflect a country's payments abroad for imports and lending to other countries; the demand would reflect exports and borrowing from abroad. The market would be made up of a very large number of relatively small and independent transactions, so that, in a technical sense, it would be virtually a perfect market.

Any change in supply or demand conditions would initiate a

movement in the exchange rate, which would proceed freely and easily to a level at which the amount of a currency being offered just equated the demand for it. Payments would be continuously in equilibrium, and there would be no such thing as a balance of payments problem.

This does *not* mean, it should be noted, that exports would always have to equal imports. If exports and imports have different seasonal or cyclical patterns, then to balance the current account at all times might produce violent oscillations in the price of the currency. This would make it profitable to buy the currency at the time of year, or point in the cycle, when it was cheap and sell when it was expensive. This activity, of buying a currency (or, indeed, any commodity) when it is cheap, in the hope of a rise in its value, is speculation. In economic jargon, speculation does not have the pejorative connotation of everyday usage; indeed successful speculation is recognised as potentially a beneficial activity. It has the effect of smoothing the price of a commodity by adding to demand when demand from other sources is low, and adding to supply when supply from other sources is low. The existence of successful speculators is essential to the efficient functioning of floating exchange rates. They ensure that movements in the exchange rate of a currency will call forth sufficient new buyers or sellers to balance supply and demand with only a small change in the rate. They thus safeguard the system against excessive oscillations in rates and enable traders to plan their operations with less uncertainty about future prices.

Advocates of floating exchange rates, therefore, claim that floating enables countries to balance their payments without having to adopt unwelcome domestic economic policies, and without producing undue fluctuations in exchange rates. To the extent that underlying supply and demand conditions change over time, it would, of course, be recognised that there will be a measure of uncertainty about future movements in exchange rates. But, they would argue, this may well be less than the degree of uncertainty resulting from the need of countries to adopt domestic demand management policies to defend a given exchange rate.

In any event, uncertainty about future exchange rates can be minimised by the development of forward markets. The mechanism of forward markets is quite simple. If a UK exporter enters into a contract to sell goods in France on six months' credit, he can assure himself of a certain sterling sum by entering into a contract to sell francs for pounds in six months' time at a rate to be determined today. The rate for the forward deal is determined by supply and demand in precisely the same way as an ordinary spot transaction. In normal conditions, it should be possible for forward deals to take place at reasonable cost, since French exporters to the UK will be wanting to buy the forward francs the British exporter wishes to sell.

The objections to floating exchange rates, like those to fixed rates, concern not so much the theoretical nature of the case as its failure to reflect practical realities. The first practical problem is that exchange rates are not left to the free play of market forces alone, since in the present state of political cooperation governments cannot be relied on to refrain from intervening in exchange markets to influence rates in one direction or another. Exchange rate changes inevitably have consequences for domestic employment, the cost of living and industrial profitability, and it is hard for governments not to be swayed by the pressure of politically powerful interest groups.

If there is no mutually agreed rate at which currencies are exchanged against each other, there is the risk that the views of governments will be incompatible, and the consequences for exchange markets anarchic. If, for example, the UK believes that, in the British national interest, the pound–dollar exchange rate should be $2.30 per £, while the US authorities believe it should be $2.60 per £, then the Bank of England and the Federal Reserve will exchange indefinite amounts of dollars and sterling until some sort of truce is reached.

In other words, the mere abandonment of fixed rates does not produce freely floating rates. There must also be an agreement that central banks refrain from intervention in foreign exchange markets and there must be machinery to enforce this agreement. Direct market intervention by central banks, however, is not the only way in which national monetary authorities can influence the exchange rate. Exchange controls, tariffs, quotas, subsidies, voluntary programmes, etc., are all means by which market forces can be prevented from establishing a market equilibrium price. A successful floating exchange rate regime would also require governments to agree to limit these other forms of 'dirty floating'.

The second major problem with floating rates is that the forward markets, which are essential to encourage longer-term trade and investment contracts, are not always capable of handling the enlarged role that floating brings. In part, this is because the intervention of governments in exchange markets makes scientific forecasting of future rates particularly hazardous. In part, it is because individual forward contracts are often of a very large size compared with the market in a particular currency as a whole. Where forward quotations exist, therefore, the cost of securing cover is often high and, in the case of minor currencies, there may be no effective forward market at all.

Thirdly, it is widely believed that speculators cannot be relied on to play the beneficent role assigned to them by proponents of floating rates. The essence of successful speculation is not so much knowledge of the underlying facts as knowledge of what other participants in the market believe those facts to be. It is a characteristic of many free markets, for example commodity markets and stock markets, that prices can fluctuate quite widely without any very great changes in underlying supply and demand conditions. If prices do fluctuate widely, then it will be difficult and costly for traders to get forward cover, and international trade may suffer.

Some compromises

Thus far we have examined only the two extremes of fixed and floating exchange rates. Either regime is perfectly defensible as a theoretical construction, but each relies for its successful operation on assumptions that are not likely to hold in practice. Not surprisingly, therefore, economists and politicians have sought compromise solutions which attempt to combine the advantages of the two regimes, without incurring the disadvantages. Here we consider a few of the more important of the compromises.

The adjustable peg

This is the system by which the world monetary system has been operated for most of the period since the Second World War. The essence of this system is that countries should adopt fixed par values for their currencies which they endeavour to maintain through the adoption of appropriate domestic policies. Countries undertake, therefore, to maintain an exchange equalisation fund, and to use it to prevent the market value of their currency moving outside a certain specified range. In addition, they can borrow from the International Monetary Fund, which is in this respect a world central bank, if their own reserves of gold and foreign exchange run down.

In the event of a 'fundamental disequilibrium' in their balance of payments, however, countries are allowed to adjust the price at which their currency is pegged. The system is designed to achieve most of the benefits of certainty and international cooperation that come from fixed rates, while not imposing an unacceptable discipline on a currency which has become seriously out of line.

The adjustable peg system appears to have worked fairly well until the late 1960s. Admittedly, there were a number of monetary crises, but the world nevertheless experienced unparalleled growth of trade and output. For the most part, trade and investment across national frontiers were able to take place with a fair measure of certainty about future exchange rates. At the same time, countries experiencing chronic balance of payments surpluses and deficits were able to rectify their position by devaluing or revaluing their currencies.

But the adjustable peg system has a number of inherent weaknesses, too. It depends on par value changes being sufficiently infrequent to give the advantage of exchange rate certainty, yet taking place promptly whenever countries get into fundamental disequilibrium. (Fundamental disequilibrium, incidentally, is a term of art which has not been precisely defined. It is usually taken to mean a situation where a country's payments position can only be restored to balance by adopting unacceptable and disruptive domestic policies.) It is not easy to strike this delicate balance between too much and too little flexibility in par values. For a long time, changes in par values tended to have a political significance that, in combination with the immediate unfavourable economic consequences for certain segments of society, made countries unwilling to devalue and revalue. Some countries, therefore, suffered unemployment of resources in preference to devaluation, while others accepted unwanted inflation rather than revalue.

Given this political hesitancy in resorting to par value changes, the adjustable peg system tends to stimulate destabilising speculation by providing what amounts to a one-way option for speculators. If a country experiences a balance of payments deficit, some market operators may see its currency as a candidate for devaluation. Others may believe that devaluation will not be necessary; but it will be certain the par value will not be raised. Speculators, therefore, have a very attractive proposition. If they sell the suspect currency, they will either make money (if it devalues) or come out roughly even (if its parity remains fixed). Because the risk of loss does not balance the prospect of gain, heavy speculative pressure can build up out of all proportion to the underlying strength or weakness of the currency concerned.

This problem is exacerbated by the existence of large quantities of internationally mobile capital. One of the consequences of an efficiently functioning international payments system is the increasing integration of the world economy. This results in a growing network of short-term banking and commercial claims which can be shifted easily between currencies to seek profit or avoid loss. The most important and best known of these claims-networks are the deposits and loans that are collectively known as the euro-dollar market; but there are many other forms in which balances can be shifted between countries. The dilemma which is raised by the adjustable peg system is that the growth of international capital markets is beneficial to the worldwide distribution of investments under normal circumstances but, when doubts are raised about the ability of a country to maintain the value of its currency, flows of short-term capital can frustrate the intentions of the government concerned and force a change in parity.

Bands around par values

This device permits each central bank to allow the value of its currency to fluctuate within a certain limited range around a declared 'par value'. Under the original IMF rules, established at Bretton Woods, the permitted band was 1% on either side of parity, though in practice most countries adopted slightly narrower bands. The Washington Monetary Agreement of December 1971 allowed rather wider bands, of $2\frac{1}{4}\%$ either side of the central value.

The advantages of wider bands are twofold. In the first place, by allowing exchange rates to fluctuate to a limited extent, they may discourage speculation. When a currency sinks to the bottom of its band, speculators have a risk of loss if the currency floats up again to balance against the prospect of gain if a devaluation occurs. The balance of prospective gain and loss is far from being equal, but the existence of even a narrow band does tend to reduce somewhat speculative flows of funds, thus reducing the size of reserves needed to make the system work. Secondly, by marginally cheapening a currency, a wider band provides a small stimulus to exports and discouragement to imports. Both of these advantages, it is argued, can be achieved without jeopardising the stability of medium-term expectations about the approximate value of the currency concerned and without, therefore, inhibiting trade and investment flows.

That bands have been found to be of practical use is evidenced by the fact that the Washington Monetary Agreement of 1971 allowed their widening to $2\frac{1}{4}\%$, which was taken full advantage of by most countries. However, the wider bands are allowed to be, the less the advantages of fixed rates, in terms of dealing certainty; while the narrower the bands, the less effective they are in discouraging speculation and permitting balance of payments adjustment.

Crawling peg

The proposal involves the establishment of a par value fixed at a moment in time, but which can change through time. In order to avoid generating an outflow of capital from a depreciating currency, the rate of depreciation has to be very gradual and capable of being matched by an offsetting interest rate advantage. In practice, this probably means that par values would not be able to change by more than about 2% or 3% a year. The loss which would be incurred by holding a depreciating currency could then be offset by higher rates of interest in the depreciating country. The direction and rate of crawl could be the subject of international agreement, or it could be determined by market conditions subject only to a maximum speed.

The principal advantage claimed for the crawling peg is that it allows a process of gradual adjustment to underlying disequilibrium to take place, while limiting annual movements in exchange rates within quite narrow bands. It discourages destabilising speculation, because if countries can rectify their balance of payments disequilibria smoothly and gradually the possibility of step-devaluations, and therefore large overnight gains, is correspondingly reduced.

Crawling pegs are not really suitable for dealing with substantial disequilibria in payments, however. If a currency appears to be overvalued by, say, 10% it would take five years to eliminate the disequilibrium if the maximum rate at which the currency is allowed to 'crawl' downwards is 2% p.a. Speculation may force a step-change in parity at an earlier stage and, even if it does not, it may not be politically acceptable to the country in question to adopt the domestic policies necessary to maintain an overvalued currency in the interim. It can be argued, of course, that with a crawling peg, a currency should not be allowed to get in the position of fundamental disequilibrium—but it is not always easy to spot such a position emerging until it is too late.

The crawling peg does not really solve the problem of eliminating uncertainty from longer-term contracts either. Some of these are planned over a span of several years, and a cumulative change in currency values of 2% p.a. could amount to quite a considerable margin of uncertainty after a lapse of several years.

Finally, the crawling peg has implications for domestic interest rates that may not be compatible with domestic political objectives. If a country is devaluing at 2% p.a., its interest rates will have to be 2% higher than other countries in order to prevent speculative flows of funds. It is quite possible that this will conflict with other aims of policy.

Optimum currency areas

This proposal is that countries whose economies are closely linked should adopt fixed, perhaps rigidly fixed, exchange rates between their currencies, but should allow freely floating rates in exchange between one currency area and another. This proposal recognises that the smaller a country is, the greater the proportion of transactions it is likely to conduct across national boundaries. In 1970, for example, some two fifths of the output of Belgium and Holland was exported. For the UK the equivalent figure was one fifth and for the USA under 5%. The higher the share of foreign trade in the economy, the greater the costs, both in uncertainty and simply in dealing costs, of having a separate currency. On the other hand, the *lower* the share of foreign trade, the greater the relative sacrifice involved in managing the domestic economy in such a way as to keep international payments in balance. The optimum currency area proposal involves organising the world into monetary areas where the advantages for internal trade of further expanding the area of fixed rates are just balanced by the disadvantages of giving up the freedom to devalue and revalue.

The optimum currency area proposal also goes some way to mitigate one of the criticisms of floating rates — that forward markets would not be adequate to provide for traders' needs. With only a few currency areas, the demand for forward accommodation would be concentrated in relatively few markets, instead of being spread around a large number of currencies, each having comparatively few transactions. This would give the markets greater depth and improve the service to traders.

The problem with optimum currency areas is that there can, effectively, be only one monetary authority in each area. This means that a country joining a currency area must surrender a considerable amount of sovereignty to the central policy-making authority. In particular, a country which fears a decline in its competitiveness would risk becoming the 'depressed region' of a monetary area if it gave up its freedom to improve its competitive position through devaluation. For this reason the creation of monetary unions (such as the one envisaged for the Common Market countries) is likely to come about only within the framework of a much more comprehensive agreement on economic and political cooperation.

There is, of course, no reason why several of these compromise proposals should not be put into effect together. Under the Bretton Woods system, for example, the adjustable peg is used with small bands of fluctuation around parity. A crawling peg can also coexist with bands of fluctuation and, though perhaps less easily, with provision for adjustment in discrete jumps. It would, in fact, be possible to have a crawling parity system incorporating bands of fluctuation, with provision for discrete parity jumps, between currency areas.

Liquidity

As can be seen, the possible permutations of exchange rate regimes are almost endless and the number of monetary 'plans' produced in the decade of the 1960s alone runs into three figures. The problem of liquidity, however, is common to all plans which do not involve free floating. All these plans envisage either the compulsory or the discretionary intervention of central banks in exchange markets to maintain the value of their currency at a certain level or within certain limits. This means central banks must stand ready to buy and sell their currency to prevent it moving outside these prescribed limits.

International liquidity is the name given to the assets which central banks use to intervene in markets to preserve the foreign exchange value of their domestic currencies. The problem of liquidity is the problem of providing an acceptable international asset which they can hold as a reserve against fluctuations in their balance of payments.

There are two dimensions to this problem. The first is how much international liquidity should be provided, the second is the form in which it should be provided. There is no foolproof statistical method of deciding how much international liquidity is needed. Liquidity is needed to cover balance of payments deficits, so that the need for it will be related to the normal size of deficits that countries are likely to experience, or, more loosely, to the general level of world trade. If there is too little liquidity, even countries whose international payments are in equilibrium will feel that their reserve against future deficits is inadequate; therefore, they will be seeking to build up their reserves through earning surpluses in their balances of payments and through sharply limiting their deficits.

One of the means of doing so is to tolerate domestic recessions somewhat more and periods of expansion somewhat less. As a result, there would tend be be deflationary bias in economic policy. If there is too much liquidity, so that countries are relatively less concerned about incurring deficits, there will be a persistent bias in the direction of inflationary policies. Whether there is too much or too little liquidity at a point in time is thus a matter of comparing the balance of payments objectives of individual countries to see if they are consistent with one another (i.e., whether those countries who are in surp'us resist the payments disequilibrium as hard as do their trading partners who are simultaneously in deficit).

Turning to the question of the form in which liquidity is provided, there are four broad kinds of international liquidity which have been used in national reserves during the post-war years:

a gold
b national currencies
c balancing facilities
d international reserve assets

Gold has a long history of use as a money-commodity and, for this reason, is highly acceptable. For internal monetary purposes, gold was replaced in most countries during the nineteenth century by paper money and bank deposits. These gold-substitutes were acceptable for internal transactions but of less use in making payments overseas. As gold diminished in importance as a domestic medium of exchange, more gold passed into the hands of central banks which were able to use it as a means of final settlement of international indebtedness.

The great advantage of gold as an international currency is the confidence people have in its continued value. In part, this stems from gold's long history of use as money and, in part, from the knowledge that world supplies of gold cannot easily or quickly be augmented. Gold, in General de Gaulle's phrase, is anonymous and impartial, so that its holders do not fear a decline in value due to mismanagement or the abuse of the printing press.

It is, however, the very scarcity of gold which is its main drawback. If countries peg the value of their currencies in terms of gold, the only way the available stock of gold can be increased is by new mining. Aside from the physical limitations on the quantity of newly mined gold, it is self-evidently wasteful to employ vast resources of men and capital in South Africa, the Soviet Union and other gold-producing countries, merely in order that further resources can be expended storing and guarding the gold in central banks around the world.

It would, of course, be possible to permit the effective quantity of gold to increase by allowing its relative value to rise. This could be achieved either through a fall in the money price of other goods or by allowing the money price of gold to move upwards. Neither of these alternatives is particularly satisfactory, however. A fall in the general price level can usually only be brought about through deflationary policies which also tend to produce unemployment of resources. And to allow the price of gold to fluctuate in terms of currencies would reduce its attractions as a unit of account and means of effecting international settlements. If gold had a fixed value that was subject to periodic revaluations, there would be enormous speculative pressure as the time for revaluation seemed to be drawing near.

It is not, of course, necessary to have a neutral commodity money, such as a gold standard, in order to have currencies whose exchange values are fixed in terms of each other. It is possible to achieve fixed parities by establishing a standard in terms of one or more national currencies, and then holding these currencies as a reserve for market intervention purposes. There are several attractions to using national currencies as reserves and as the medium for intervention in exchange markets. In the first place, it removes the need for a commodity reserve which has positive costs of production and storage. Secondly, it provides the central banks with a reserve having the convenience of being in the same form as the currency used by private traders and investors. Finally, if a national currency is used, its quantity can be increased or contracted to meet the needs of world trade more easily than is the case with a commodity money.

The use of national currencies in reserves has unsatisfactory aspects, however, both for the countries whose currency is being used and for the rest of the world. In the first place, the total of reserves is partly dependent on the balance of payments position of the reserve-currency country. By running a balance of payments deficit, a reserve-currency country will create reserves which will add to world liquidity. But prolongation of that deficit will cast doubt on its ability to maintain the convertibility of its currency into gold or other currencies. The devaluation of a reserve currency imposes a penalty on all those who hold the currency in their portfolios; but equally the attempt to *avoid* devaluation can impose a heavy burden on the country whose currency is being used.

A further political difficulty is presented by the apparent anomaly that a country whose currency is being used in reserves appears to be able to run a balance of payments deficit indefinitely, the deficit being 'financed' by the accretion of its currency in the reserves of other countries. It may seem 'unfair' to other countries that one nation should have the ability to borrow real resources at its own discretion and for indefinite periods of time. As we have just pointed out, this argument overlooks the very real burdens which reserve currency countries have to bear (the UK is a case in point) but it is nonetheless forcibly argued.

Borrowing facilities are different from gold and reserve currencies in that they constitute conditional rather than absolute spending power. That is to say, they are subject to repayment. The difference should not be over-emphasised, however. Countries which run down their reserves to meet a deficit generally aim to reconstitute the old level of reserves when they move back into surplus. The reconstruction of owned reserves is much the same thing, from an economic point of view, as the repayment of borrowed reserves.

Borrowing as a source of liquidity has much to recommend it. It can be expanded by agreement to meet growing needs. It will generally be readily available to countries whose economies are soundly run. And the need to repay provides an incentive to the monetary authorities of the borrowing country to ensure that adequate stabilisation measures are taken. The discipline of conditional liquidity, however, is also its biggest drawback. It places an asymmetrical burden on countries to adjust, since the creditor tends to be in a position to dictate terms to the debtor.

This said, however, there is considerable variance in the freedom of access which countries have to various types of conditional liquidity. Certain drawing rights in the IMF are, as will be seen in the next chapter, quasi-automatic. Once they have been negotiated, drawings under standby facilities and central bank swaps (see pp 233 and 246) are also pretty automatic. On the other hand, the greater the amount borrowed from the IMF the stiffer are likely to be the terms for further drawings.

Because of the disadvantages attendant to using either gold or national currencies, and the objections which are often raised to conditional liquidity, it has for some time been recognised that the world's need for liquidity can most efficiently and equitably be met by an international reserve asset. This would have the advantage of being costless to create and, therefore, not wasteful of real resources. Being internationally controlled, its acceptability could be internationally enforced, and any benefits accruing as a result of reserve creation could be distributed among the international community at large, rather than going to one country. Furthermore, the quantity of reserves would then be a matter for deliberate choice, rather than occurring as a result of the productivity of goldmining or the fluctuations in one country's balance of payments.

While there is a wide measure of agreement that internationally created and controlled liquidity is preferable to haphazard creation through gold production and dollar deficits, there are considerable political hurdles to the detailed implementation of a scheme. The creation of money is an act of political sovereignty, and the creation of international liquidity therefore requires a substantial degree of international agreement at a political level. Progress has therefore tended to be slow, although a substantial step forward was taken in 1969, when agreement was reached on the scheme for special drawing rights, described in the next chapter.

Further reading

Brittan, Sam, *The Price of Economic Freedom—A Guide to Flexible, Rates*, London, Macmillan, 1970.

Hirsch, Fred, *Money International*, Allen Lane, the Penguin Press, 1967.

Krause, Lawrence B., Fixed, flexible and gliding exchange rates, *Journal of Money, Credit and Banking*, May 1971.

Scammell, W. M., *International Monetary Policy*, London, Macmillan, 2nd Edition, 1961, Chapter 2-4.

Tew, Brian, *International Monetary Co-operation 1945-70*, Hutchinson University Press, 10th Edition, 1970, Chapter 1-5.

Questions for discussion

1 In what sense is there a balance of payments problem between England and Scotland, and in what ways can this problem manifest itself?

2 What conditions would have to hold for floating exchange rates to be an efficient system of organising international payments transactions?

3 What are the disadvantages of gold as an international reserve asset? Why has its use persisted?

4 Under the exchange rate system that has existed since the war, there has been more pressure on deficit countries to devalue than on surplus countries to revalue. Why is this, and is such an 'asymmetry' justified?

15

The International Monetary Fund

Origins

The International Monetary Fund had its origins in the desire of members of the international community to avoid the economic mistakes of the 1920s and 1930s. After the First World War, many countries had attempted to return to the old gold standard system, without realising that the conditions under which the gold standard flourished had disappeared. When the worldwide financial crash of 1931 forced Britain, and later other countries, off the gold standard there was a general retreat into purely nationalistic policies. Faced with enormous problems of depression and unemployment, all governments set about erecting tariff barriers to protect domestic industries and trying to force down their exchange rates to give themselves a competitive edge in export markets. The result was the exacerbation of an already catastrophic decline in world trade, and the extension and prolongation of the depression.

Lack of cooperation in matters of trade and payments was seen as the main problem to be tackled in the field of international economic policy. A conference was therefore organised in 1944 under the auspices of the United Nations at Bretton Woods, New Hampshire, to consider various approaches to the problem.

The two principal points of view were represented by Lord Keynes, who was a member of the British delegation, and Harry Dexter White, under-secretary of the US Treasury. Their rival 'plans' had been published before the conference assembled at Bretton Woods. In some respects, the plans had similar objectives; both envisaged a par value system under which exchange rates would be pegged by cooperative central bank action, though with provision for changes in par values in certain circumstances. In other respects, however, there were substantial differences between the Keynes and White plans. Keynes proposed a Clearing Union which would undertake the responsibility for multilateral clearing of balance of payments deficits and surpluses. The various bilateral surpluses and deficits that arose between individual members would be centralised in the Clearing Union, and each member would be responsible only for his net position. The net position of each country in the Clearing Union would be measured in terms of an international union of account, to be known as 'Bancor'. Surplus countries would be obliged to accept 'Bancor' credit balances in specified amounts, while deficit countries would be given substantial overdraft facilities. Indeed, each country would be allowed to borrow (or overdraw) in Bancor to the extent of half the value of its annual trade (exports + imports).

The Keynes plan would in its early stages have given more benefit to the debtor countries of Europe than to the United States. The European countries would have been able to spend their substantial overdraft rights in Bancor in purchasing imports from the United States. On the other hand, there was little immediate prospect of the US being able to spend much of this Bancor it would be receiving on imports from war-damaged European countries.

The principal objection to Keynes' scheme was the inflationary bias which its generous overdraft facilities seemed to impart to the world's payments system. The White Plan therefore proposed that the new institution which it was agreed would be set up should be essentially an intermediary, which would not itself handle the clearing of deficits and surpluses, but would lend strictly limited sums to deficit countries to tide them over difficult periods. Most importantly, under White's plan, the financial operations of the new institution would be on a much smaller scale than Keynes proposed. As a result, countries were bound to be less willing to take the risks involved in abandoning their bilateral payments agreements. Convertibility, under the White plan, was not really achievable in the short term.

Political realities were such that it was inevitable the institution that actually emerged would be closer to White's vision than to Keynes'. The huge excess liquidity, plus pent-up demands for goods and services in the post-war reconstruction period, made US officials very nervous about the danger of inflation. They were thus reluctant to give the Fund powers to lend sums that might exacerbate any inflationary tendencies. Thus, when the International Monetary Fund was eventually set up, it was given only limited powers to mobilise national currencies to be lent, conditionally, to members. (The actual process by which the IMF lends to members is described in more detail later in this chapter.)

The world economic system was to be based in effect on the US dollar, which would be convertible, at a fixed price, into gold. In principle, other countries could also have made their currencies directly convertible into gold, but only Switzerland felt able to do so, and she remained outside the Fund. All other countries fixed their par-values in terms of the dollar. They could, therefore, only change the value of their currency by devaluing or revaluing against the dollar; the dollar was the standard, so that the US was not able unilaterally to devalue or revalue against other currencies.

Aims and constitution

Formally, the IMF comes under the general umbrella of the United Nations, though in practice it has virtually complete autonomy. Its tasks are broadly three: firstly, to promote international monetary cooperation, and establish a code of conduct in international payments practices; secondly to provide financial resources to member countries to enable them to maintain the foreign exchange value of their currencies during temporary balance-of-payments difficulties; and thirdly, to provide for the orderly growth of international liquidity through the Special Drawing Rights scheme.

The membership of the Fund consists of all the countries outside the Comecon group[1] except Switzerland. By the end of 1972 there were 125 members. In principle, the Fund is run by a Board of Governors whose membership consists of the finance ministers or central bank governors of the member countries. In practice, however, this unwieldy body only meets once a year at the annual meetings, and the Fund is run by the Executive Board. The Executive Board consists of executive directors representing member countries or groups of members. The five largest members have an executive director to themselves, while the other members group together on a roughly geographical basis to elect one director to represent the interests of the group. The Managing Director of the Fund, who is an international civil servant, is the non-voting Chairman of the Executive Board.

Unlike the United Nations, the Fund has a system of weighted voting. Each member has a quota (which also determines its subscription and borrowing rights) based roughly on its importance in the world economy. To calculate quotas a formula is used which takes into account the volume of a country's international trade, its importance in relation to the domestic economy, fluctuations in its balance of payments, and sometimes also its level of international reserves. The answer given by the formula (or formulae, for there are

[1] Within Comecon, Romania is the only member of the Fund.

several) is subject to modification where it can be shown that there are other relevant factors which have not been taken into account. At the end of 1972, the quotas of the principal member countries were as shown in Table 15.1.

Each member has a basic allocation of 250 votes plus one vote for each 100,000 SDRs[2] of its quota. Voting is by straightforward majority, but certain important questions, such as amendment of the articles of agreement, a change in the gold price and changes in quotas require larger majorities. In practice, although there are voting provisions, the Fund operates by consensus, and most Executive Board decisions do not have to be put to the vote.

TABLE 15·1

IMF Quotas at End-December 1972

Country		Amount (SDR millions)	%
US		6,700	22.97
UK		2,800	9.60
Germany (Federal Republic)		1,600	5.49
France		1,500	5.14
Japan		1,200	4.11
Canada		1,100	3.77
Italy		1,000	3.43
India		940	3.22
Netherlands		700	2.40
Australia		665	2.28
Belgium		650	2.23
China (Nationalist)		550	1.89
Other countries		9,763	33.47
	Total	29,168	100.00

The Fund as arbiter of international payments practice

The Fund's role as guardian of a code of international conduct is confined to questions of payments practices. The matter of trade restrictions was to have been the responsibility of another body, the International Trade Organisation. In the event the ITO was stillborn, and although the General Agreement on Tariffs and Trade has a secretariat and exercises some policing functions, there is no organisation in the trade field with a regulatory role comparable to the Fund's role on payments questions.

[2] 1 SDR = US $1.00 of the pre-devaluation gold content. At mid-1973, 1 SDR = US $1.20 (approx). SDRs, or Special Drawing Rights, are described later in the chapter.

The Fund's regulatory responsibilities can be divided into those which relate to exchange rate practices, and those which deal with restrictions on international payments. On exchange rates, the IMF is firmly in favour of stability. The very first article of the Fund agreement states that one of the purposes of the IMF is 'to promote exchange stability, to maintain orderly exchange arrangements among members, and to avoid competitive exchange depreciation'. To achieve this, each member is required to agree with the Fund an appropriate par-value for its currency in terms of gold or US dollars. Since the US Treasury at the time the Fund was established stood ready to buy and sell gold to non-US citizens at a fixed price of \$35 per ounce, this requirement was generally met by the establishment of a dollar parity. Thus the system established at Bretton Woods came to be known as the gold-exchange standard. Once a par-value was established, members were required to use their Exchange Equalisation Funds to prevent the market value of their currency moving more than 1% above or below the par value. This provision, for a narrow band of fluctuation, was designed to facilitate the smooth working of exchange markets and also to discourage speculation. It was not intended to promote by itself the adjustments in imports and exports necessary to correct a balance of payments deficit or surplus.

Although the Fund was, and still is, an organisation whose existence is largely predicated on the desirability of an internationally agreed set of exchange rates, it is not wedded to the idea of immovably fixed rates. The question of the appropriate 'adjustment mechanism', whereby balance of payments disequilibria can be corrected without undesirable repercussions on domestic economies, bulks large in both the principles and practice of the Fund. It has always been recognised, for example, that there will be circumstances of 'fundamental disequilibrium' where the balance of payments can only be kept in balance at a given exchange rate through unacceptable restrictions on trade and payments, or through unacceptable domestic policies. In these cases, it is provided in the Fund articles that there should be an agreed move to a new par value.

Under the Articles of Agreement, countries are allowed an initial move of 10% away from their first agreed par value on their own initiative, and thereafter they are expected to seek Fund approval for further changes. In point of fact, however, questions of devaluation and revaluation must of necessity be made in secret, so as not to upset markets, and are usually regarded as matters of national economic sovereignty. Consequently, although there may be private exchanges of view with top management in the Fund, it is usually impossible to undertake a review procedure for par value changes of the kind envisaged at the Bretton Woods conference.

So much for the Fund's role in relation to the question of exchange rate practices. Another explicit objective of Article 1 is 'the establishment of a multilateral system of payments in respect of current transactions between members' and 'the elimination of foreign exchange restrictions which hamper the growth of world trade'. The obligations of member countries in this matter are set out in Article VIII of the Fund Agreement.

The three main strands of Article VIII are the avoidance of restrictions on current payments, the avoidance of multiple currency practices, and current account convertibility. The adoption of these provisions would ensure that traders in goods and services dealing between one member country and another would be able to make or receive payment in their own currency at a rate of exchange fixed within narrow limits. For countries, the provisions would ensure that a current account surplus with one member could be used to offset a deficit with any other.

Although Article VIII sets down this code of good practice, members were allowed, under Article XIV, to retain restrictions during a post-war transitional period. It was hoped that the transitional period could be kept to only five years, and provision was made for the Fund to send annual missions to countries which availed themselves of Article XIV for a longer period. In practice it was some fifteen years after the establishment of the Fund that the principal European countries formally assumed the obligations of Article VIII. Once a country has accepted the obligations of Article VIII, it cannot go back to Article XIV and requires specific Fund approval for any action in breach of its obligations.

Article VIII does not make any mention of controls on capital payments and, in its early years, the Fund seemed to favour the retention of controls over speculative capital movements. More recently, the Fund has tended to favour the liberalisation of capital flows, though recognising that controls may be a useful adjunct to stabilisation policy in certain circumstances.

It is clear that member countries can only maintain convertibility and an absence of exchange restrictions if their balances of payments remain in broad equilibrium over the long term. The Fund is therefore intimately concerned with the correction of balance of payments disequilibria. Consultation missions visit most member countries about once a year and prepare reports covering balance of payments and domestic economic developments. These consultation reports form the basis for a discussion by the Fund's Executive Directors, from which may emerge policy recommendations.

We have already noted that members are allowed and, indeed, encouraged to change the par-value of their currencies if it is apparent that it has become seriously out of line. If the problem is a deficit, the Fund is in a stronger position to make the wishes of the international community felt than when a member is in a persistent surplus position. A country losing reserves will eventually be driven to devalue, to borrow or to impose exchange restrictions. The Fund can outlaw exchange restrictions if the Executive Board does not feel these are justified, and it can make borrowing conditional on the adoption of appropriate domestic policies to deal with the deficit.

A surplus country is under less immediate pressure to adjust its payments position. The Articles of Agreement attempt to tackle this problem of asymmetry in the pressure to adjust in Article VII, the 'scarce currency clause'. Article VII provides that if a currency becomes scarce in the Fund, through debtors borrowing in that currency, the Fund can formally declare it to be a 'scarce currency'. This entitles other members of the Fund to impose restrictions specifically directed at the country whose currency is scarce. The US dollar was in very short supply after the war but, for a number of reasons, other countries did not borrow it. For one thing, the continuance of restrictions on payments to the dollar bloc concealed the underlying shortage of dollars. The combination of continued restrictions against the dollar bloc, with increased freedom to make payments among non-dollar countries, had similar consequences to the invoking of the scarce currency clause.

Thus, the US dollar never became scarce in the technical sense of there being a shortage of dollars available to the Fund. Since the opportunity was not taken to invoke the scarce currency clause against the US dollar, the Fund has not subsequently felt able to justify its use against other currencies.

The Fund's financial operations

As already noted, each member country is required to agree a quota with the Fund, based on its importance in the world economy. It is required to subscribe this quota to the Fund 25% in gold and 75% in its own currency. Since the 75% is in non-interest bearing notes, this element of the subscription involves no immediate real cost to the member country. The real cost comes when the money that has been subscribed by, say, country A is lent to another member of the

Fund, and used by the borrower to acquire real goods or foreign exchange from country A.

For the purpose of subscription, all currencies are valued at their official gold parity. At the time of its establishment in 1946, the Fund had total resources of the equivalent of rather under $9 billion, but since then there have been several large across-the-board increases and, with the addition of new members, the total of quotas at the end of 1971 had grown to the equivalent of over $30 billion.

It is from this pool of currencies that the Fund lends to countries in balance of payments difficulties. Technically, the borrowing country *buys* currencies which are needed to effect settlements and pays for them with a further slice of non-interest bearing notes in its domestic currency. Thus, if the UK wishes to borrow $100 million worth of D Marks, it purchases marks with sterling at the par-value rate. The Fund's total resources are unchanged, but it has $100 million more of sterling and $100 million less of D Marks. When the time comes for the loan to be repaid, the UK 'repurchases' the extra sterling the Fund holds with foreign exchange (not necessarily D Marks).

Before it undertakes any lending, the Fund has 75% of each members quota in the currency of that member. (For the sake of simplicity, the following discussion will be in terms of sterling, but it applies equally to all currencies.) The Fund's holding of sterling will go up as the UK purchases foreign currencies and pays for them with sterling; on the other hand its holding will go down if other countries are drawing sterling to cover their deficits. If the Fund's holdings of sterling are greater than the initial 75% of quota, the UK is a net debtor; if its holdings of sterling are less than 75% the UK is a net creditor, through the Fund, of the rest of the world.

A member's overall right to borrow is limited by Article V which provides that the Fund's holding of its currency should not exceed 200% of quota. Since the Fund starts with 75% of quota as a subscription, this means that net borrowing cannot exceed 125% of quota. The UK, therefore, with a quota of SDR 2,800 million could borrow SDR 3,500 million which together with its sterling subscription of SDR 2,100 million would bring the Fund's holding of pounds to the equivalent of SDR 5,600 million, 200% of the UK quota.

This borrowing right, however, is not automatic or unlimited in time. In the first place, potential borrowers must represent that the drawing is to be used for the purpose of making current payments, since the Fund is precluded under its Articles from providing finance for reconstruction or development, or to offset large and prolonged capital flows. In practice, this representation is little more than semantics, since it is not possible to say that a particular drawing is being used to make one kind of payment rather than another, particularly if the drawing is in a convertible currency.

Drawings are considered in 'tranches' of 25% of the quota, and members are not supposed to borrow more than 25% in any twelve-month period. In practice, however, the Fund has often used special powers under a waiver clause to allow larger drawings. The more tranches which a country draws, the stiffer the conditions on which the Fund has to be satisfied. If the Fund's holdings of sterling were less than 75% of quota, the UK would be a net creditor and would be in the 'super-gold tranche'. Any borrowing here would be automatic and non-repayable. The next tranche, taking the Fund's holding of sterling from 75% to 100% of quota is called the 'gold tranche', because the drawing is effectively backed by the 25% gold subscription. In this tranche, borrowers are given 'the overwhelming benefit of any doubt' in assessing their application, though they must still represent that the drawing is to be used for the purpose of making current payments, and they must undertake to repay. The next 25% is the first credit tranche and in 1955 the Executive Board decided '... in practice the ... attitude towards applications for drawings within the first credit tranche ... is a liberal one'. In the second, third and fourth credit tranches, however, conditions become progressively stricter, and members may have to give undertakings about their domestic policies, to be monitored by performance criteria, before the drawing is agreed to. In a few cases, the Fund has used exceptional powers under a waiver clause to permit countries to borrow beyond the fourth credit tranche.

Certain rules are laid down about which currencies may be borrowed and used to make repayments. Generally speaking, borrowers consult with the Fund before making a drawing in order not to embarrass other members by drawing a currency that is, or might be, in danger of becoming 'scarce'. Repayments (which are technically repurchases by a member of its own currency) must be made in a convertible currency and in one of which the Fund holds less than 75% of quota.

These rules have two interesting and important consequences. Because the Fund will not accept a currency in repayment whenever it already holds 75% of quota, it is impossible for any country to become a net debtor to the Fund as a result of another country's transaction. And because drawings can be made in any currency of which the Fund has a sufficient supply, 'repayment' by Borrower A can be effected by Borrower B drawing A's currency. In general, these arrangements are designed to ensure that the Fund's holdings of each member country's currency return to the 75% level as rapidly as possible.

Because Fund loans are intended to provide short-term assistance to cover seasonal or cyclical fluctuations in the balance of payments, they are repayable as soon as the payments position improves again, and in any event within three to five years. Provision is made for automatic repayments as and when the reserves position of the drawing country improves. Alternatively, repayments will take place according to a schedule agreed between the member and the Fund.

Interest payable on drawings is not related to market rates, but increases according to the size of the drawing and the length of time it is outstanding. Since the maximum rate charged is 5%, this is not really a commercial penalty, but the increasing scale of rates does serve to underline the Fund's concern that recourse to drawings should be limited in time and amount.

Further aspects of the Fund's lending operations which are worthy of note are stand-by facilities and two special schemes, one to finance shortfalls in export receipts for primary producing countries and the other to finance buffer stock payments. Stand-by facilities were introduced so that members could obtain the assurance of being able to draw in advance of the need to do so. The granting of a stand-by serves to enhance the credit-worthiness of a country when seeking to borrow from other institutions and it may also save time when the occasion for a drawing arises. Otherwise, stand-bys, which are usually of six or twelve months duration, are subject to the same sort of conditions as ordinary drawings.

The compensatory financing scheme is designed to allow members to draw to meet temporary shortfalls in receipts from exports of primary products arising from factors beyond the control of the country concerned. Up to 50% of quota may be drawn, and the policy conditions are less strict than for normal drawings. The buffer-stock financing scheme is available to countries who need foreign exchange to cover their subscriptions to approved international buffer stock schemes. Both the compensatory finance and buffer-stock schemes are in addition to the normal borrowing facilities provided by the Fund.

Special drawing rights

Special drawing rights, which were first issued in 1970, are in a rather separate category from the rest of the Fund's financial operations. Under the original articles the Fund had powers to lend sums to member countries, but this lending was conditional, and it was repayable. The special drawing rights scheme involves the Fund in creating what is, in effect, a new reserve asset. For this reason, the use of the term 'drawing right' is confusing. It was employed in deference to the susceptibilities of certain member countries who had expressed reservations about the inflationary aspects of reserve creation.

SDRs are distributed among participating countries in proportion to their Fund quotas.[3] The overall amounts of SDRs to be allocated in a particular period is decided by a weighted 85% majority of members. (Initially 3.5 billion was allocated on 1 January 1970, 3 billion each in January 1971 and 1972.) The value of SDRs is denominated in terms of gold, and 1 SDR is equal to 1/35 oz of gold (i.e., to one dollar at the pre-1971 parity). All participating countries agree to accept SDRs in settlement of international indebtedness at this fixed value.

Any country that can demonstrate a balance of payments need can use its SDRs to buy convertible currency from other participants; but transactions in SDRs are not supposed to be used for the sole purpose of changing the composition of members' reserves. The Fund attempts to ensure that SDRs are only used for approved purposes by channelling transactions through its Special Drawing Account. Under this procedure, a member wishing to use SDRs to acquire convertible currency first applies to the Fund which approves the proposal. The Fund then 'designates' certain countries to provide foreign exchange and credits their balances in the special drawing account. This ensures that no member will be placed in difficulty as a result of its obligation to supply convertible currency in exchange for SDRs.

The other main limitation on the use of SDRs is that a country's holdings of SDRs should not fall below 30% of the quantity it has been allotted, as an average over a five-year period. In practice, what this means is that 70% of the allocation represents unconditional liquidity and the remaining 30% represents a borrowing facility which can only be used over a short period. As a matter of accounting practice, however, all countries add their total SDR allocation to their published reserves.

There is no magic significance in the figure of 30% as the minimum average holding of SDRs—it was arrived at as a compromise between those who wanted new reserves to be mainly conditional (i.e., with an obligation to reconstitute holdings that were run down) and those who wanted them to be entirely at the disposal of members to sell if they wanted.

[3] A few smaller countries do not participate in the SDR scheme.

Countries which hold less than their allocation of SDRs, and are therefore net users of the facility, pay a charge of $1\frac{1}{2}\%$ per annum to the extent of the shortfall; countries holding more than their allocation receive roughly the same rate of interest, with a small charge being levied by the Fund to cover administration costs. The initial allocation of SDRs was made, as noted, in proportion to members quotas. The possibility is being studied, however, of 'linking' reserve creation with the provision of aid to the underdeveloped countries. Under this proposal, SDRs would in the first instance be allocated to underdeveloped countries, or to development agencies. When these were spent on imports from developed countries, they would pass into the reserves of the latter who would hold them as liquidity and stand ready to accept them from each other in settlement of international indebtedness. The underdeveloped countries would pay a low service charge on their net use of SDRs.

The scheme has the attraction of providing a substantial amount of aid to developing countries on 'soft' terms in a manner which is relatively painless to the donor countries. The drawback, however, is that the world's need for development aid and its need for liquidity are two completely separate questions, and to tie them together might risk producing too much liquidity and too little aid or vice versa. Also, there is the question of the willingness of developed countries to accept an asset which, in the event of the SDR scheme being liquidated, is backed only by the promise to pay of the weakest countries.

The future of the IMF

As this book goes to press (early 1973), the future of the international monetary system, and therefore the role of the Fund, is under discussion by a committee of the Fund's Board of Governors (The Committee of 20). It is beyond the purpose of this chapter to speculate about the specific changes in the Fund's aims and functions that will result from the work of this group. However, it seems likely that the Fund will continue to be entrusted with the responsibility of safeguarding orderly payments arrangements among countries. The par-value system is also likely to be preserved, though perhaps in a more flexible form than in the past.

In particular, it seems likely that a reformed monetary system will provide for more participation by the international community in the formulation of policies by which individual countries adjust to balance of payments disequilibrium. If this in fact turns out to be the case, the

Fund will probably have to play an even larger and more active role in the international monetary system than in the past.

Further reading

Fleming, J. M., *The International Monetary Fund, its Form and Functions,* IMF, 1964.

Harrod, R. F., *Money,* op. cit., Chapter 11.

Hirsch, Fred, op. cit., Chapter 13.

Horie, Shigeo, *The International Monetary Fund,* London, Macmillan, 1964.

Scammell, W. M., *International Monetary Policy,* op. cit., Chapter 5-7.

Schweitzer, P.-P., *The IMF and its Role,* Stamp Memorial Lecture, London, 1969.

Tew, Brian, op. cit., Chapters 6 and 7.

Questions for discussion

1 It is often said that the fixing of exchange rates is a question of national sovereignty. Why then should the approval of the IMF be necessary?

2 Is freedom from restrictions more important for current payments than for capital payments?

3 What considerations are important in deciding the quantity of SDRs that should be created?

4 What was the objective of the 'Scarce Currency Clause' in the Articles of Agreement of the IMF?

16

International monetary cooperation since the war

Bilateralism

When the Bretton Woods conference was convened in 1944, there were high hopes on all sides that the end of the war might see a speedy dismantling of payments restrictions and the establishment of free convertibility of currencies and stable exchange rates. Unfortunately, the powers given to the IMF were not sufficient for this to be achieved. The obligations imposed on members of the IMF under Article VIII were virtually nullified by the generous transitional provisions of Article XIV. And the scope of the lending which the Fund was empowered to undertake was nowhere near large enough to give members confidence to free their currencies from the protective restrictions that had grown up during the wartime period.

These limitations on the Fund's powers meant that it played only a minor role in international monetary cooperation in the decade or so following the end of the war. Indeed a prominent expert on international monetary questions, Professor Robert Triffin, wrote in 1956, 'The record of these ten years is a grim and dismal one'. Admittedly, the Fund began operations with a flurry of lending in 1947, but it was apparent that lending at this pace would place strains on its ability to supply dollars, the main currency in demand. After 1947, therefore, many members did not even bother to apply, fearing a rebuff and, until 1956, repayments exceeded drawings every year.

In the absence of firm cooperative action through the IMF, the world payments system in the early peacetime years operated on much the same bilateral basis as it had during the war. Bilateralism was a refined form of barter. Each country entered into individual agreements with each of its trading partners concerning the methods by which two-way trade between them should be financed. These payments agreements were generally accompanied by trade agreements guaranteeing a certain volume of exports and imports. There were also provisions for credit to be extended, so that countries were not forced into a wholly artificial balancing of two-way trade over very short periods.

Nobody pretended that bilateralism was a satisfactory basis for the international payments system. The difficulty was that none of the principal European countries was willing to relinquish the protection it afforded. For one thing, the ending of controls would in many countries have led to an inrush of imports and, in the absence of financial assistance, to devaluation. Devaluation, however, is only a sensible policy if additional resources are available to be channelled into exports. In the early post-war years, there was little hope of European industry, which was only beginning the process of reconstruction, being able to meet extra demand for the kind of goods the United States (the principal customer) would be prepared to import. It was thought better to sell whatever was available for export at the highest possible price, and to balance the payments position by direct controls on imports.

In the case of the United Kingdom, there was another very powerful reason why it was not practicable to abandon restrictions. Much of the war effort had been paid for by payments of sterling to overseas Commonwealth countries who as a result had large accumulations of unconvertible blocked sterling. There was little that these countries wanted to buy from Britain but plenty that they wanted from the US. If the balances had been released, there would have been a massive move to convert this blocked sterling into dollars. The reserves simply would not have been able to stand the strain. This was illustrated in 1947 when, for a short time, sterling was made convertible following a large North American loan to facilitate reconstruction. The attempt to maintain convertibility ended in failure after no more than six weeks.

Approaches to convertibility

The progression from bilateralism to convertibility was achieved through a gradual broadening of areas of multilateral settlement, within which any member's currency would be accepted. One such area, of course, was the sterling area, whose gold and dollar reserves were centralised in the Exchange Equalisation Account, managed by the Bank of England. The sterling area had functioned as such throughout the war. After 1947, various schemes began to be devised in Europe to enable the bilateral surpluses and deficits of European countries to be offset. In the following years considerable progress was made, but the breakthrough came in 1950 with the establishment of the European Payments Union.

The most active years for the EPU were the early 1950s, although it continued in existence until the achievement of full convertibility in 1958. The EPU was a clearing house on the lines of Keynes' proposed Clearing Union, where each member's bilateral surpluses and deficits with other members were recorded as credits or debits. At the end of each month there was a settlement of the net credit or debit position. Settlement could take place in convertible currency (gold or US dollars) or by adjusting the members 'credit' balance—in effect by the issue or redemption of IOUs. These IOUs which debtors issued, and creditors agreed to hold, were expressed in 'units of account' which in practice had the same gold value as the US dollar.

The agency handling the clearing system was the Bank for International Settlements in Basle. This institution had an intriguing history. It was set up as a result of the conference at the Hague in 1929 which produced the Young plan for rephasing the reparation debts of Germany following the First World War. All the European central banks contributed to its establishment and were represented on its Board. As it turned out, however, the reparation payments schedule was quickly in trouble as a result of the worldwide financial crash, and payments lapsed completely after Hitler's accession to power. The BIS was largely inactive from 1933 onwards, but it remained in existence and even did a small amount of commercial business. When an institution was needed to carry out the operations of the EPU the availability of the BIS made it a convenient choice.

The EPU served to widen substantially the area of multilateral settlement. For, in addition to the European countries which were formally members, many of the European currencies were linked in monetary areas with countries in other parts of the world. The sterling area was the largest such system, but the French franc zone was also of substantial size and the Belgian, Dutch and Portuguese currencies formed the basis of the monetary system in their colonies and former colonies. By the early 1950s, therefore, the world had moved away from a predominantly bilateral basis for trading arrangements to a 'two-bloc' system, with the United States and the dollar-bloc countries on the one hand, and the rest of the non-communist world on the other.

Before the establishment of the EPU, a very significant step on the road to convertibility had been taken with the 1949 devaluations. It had been widely recognised that the par-values which had emerged from the war bore little relationship to the values at which currencies could be sustained in a freer trading environment. However, in a world of bilateralism, where many countries had war-shattered economies, the selection of realistic foreign exchange values would have been largely guesswork. By 1949, the initial stages of reconstruction had been completed and the sellers' market for manufactured goods which had existed in the early post-war years seemed to have disappeared (though it was soon to be revived by the outbreak of hostilities in Korea). When faced with a speculative crisis in the autumn of 1949, the UK authorities decided to devalue and they were followed by most of the rest of the non-dollar world. These devaluations, though perhaps greater than were necessary on competitive grounds, established a rough and ready framework of exchange rates within which it made sense to aim at eventual convertibility.

Throughout the 1950s, during the period of EPU, the European countries made gradual steps towards full convertibility by gradually liberalising their restrictions on imports from associated countries and increasing the proportion of any resulting net deficits that had to be settled in gold or dollars. By 1955, the remaining restrictions were only minor and, but for the Suez crisis the following year, convertibility might have come in 1956. As it was, the foreign exchange outflow from Britain and France to which the crisis gave rise made European countries rather nervous of assuming straight away the obligations of Article VIII. Convertibility was therefore delayed until December 1958, and it was not until 1961 that most European countries accepted the obligations of Article VIII.

The revival of the Fund

The financial facilities of the Fund had lapsed almost into disuse, following the initial burst of lending in 1947. The Fund was perturbed about this trend and Executive Board decisions in 1952 and 1955 clarified the criteria on which applications to draw would be treated, in the hope of encouraging greater use of facilities. Even so, the 1955 Annual Report had occasion to regret 'the continued lack of use of the Fund's facilities'.

As the European countries liberalised their payments arrangements, however, the circumstances in which the Fund's assistance might be needed became more likely to arise. The process of liberalisation had encouraged the growth of trade and thus increased the volume of payments settlements. At the same time, it had become easier to build up balances in foreign currencies and, perhaps more significant, to withdraw them again when confidence deteriorated. Thus speculation had become a potential claim on reserves, and individual monetary authorities were much less able to control these claims than hitherto.

The Suez crisis, though it underlined a lack of political cooperation amongst western powers, proved the occasion for a remarkable rebirth of cooperation in the monetary sphere. The outbreak of hostilities in the Middle East caused a substantial outflow of funds from Britain and France, and to cover this both countries drew substantial sums from the IMF. This was the first big lending the Fund had undertaken. It emphasized the importance of the Fund, and was the precursor of many similar operations in the years ahead when member countries' currencies came under speculative pressure. The extent of the growth in Fund operations is illustrated by Table 16.1, showing the amount of IMF lending since 1947.

TABLE 16·1

MF Financial Transactions

| | | $(millions)$ | |
	Gross drawings	Repayments*	Net drawings
1947–49	777	20	757
1949–52	120	200	− 80
1953–55	320	763	−443
1956–58	2,007	546	1,461
1959–61	2,938	2,058	880
1962–64	2,867	2,577	290
1965–67	4,716	2,752	1,964
1968–70	8,863	5,280	3,583

* Including repayments effected by another country's drawing.

The problem of liquidity

IMF lending is a useful source of assistance to tide member countries over temporary balance of payments deficits, but it suffers from two drawbacks. It is limited in amount and it is conditional. These drawbacks were exacerbated by the fact that the need for liquidity grew markedly during the 1950s.

In the first place, as has just been noted, the gradual introduction of non-resident convertibility was adding to the pool of internationally mobile funds, or 'hot money', which might suddenly be withdrawn creating a drain on the reserves. Secondly, the prodigious growth of world trade in the years since the war, and the continuance of inflation, had meant an increase in the value of trade flows and therefore a potential increase in the size of deficits and surpluses to be financed.

The growth of world reserves had nowhere near kept pace with the need for international liquidity. Gold production was adding less than 3% per annum to the world's stock of monetary gold, and there was no prospect of substantially increasing this rate of accretion.

Sterling and dollar balances could be created rather more easily, but their creation had unfortunate side-effects. If these balances were convertible into gold — as dollars always had been, and sterling balances effectively were after December 1958 — they represented a potential claim on the reserves of the UK and the US. If sterling and dollar balances were to grow fast enough to fill the gap left by the much slower growth of gold stocks, the ratio of liabilities to reserves of both the US and the UK would deteriorate. For Britain, indeed, it had always been the case that its international liabilities were greater than available gold and foreign exchange reserves. For the United States, gold holdings were at the beginning greater than foreign-owned dollar balances. But as time wore on, and the US balance of payments deficit persisted, dollar balances became larger and larger relative to US gold stocks. This trend had the consequence that the convertibility of reserve currencies into gold could only be assured so long as the right of convertibility was not exercised on a large scale. This was clearly not a satisfactory basis for the expansion of world liquidity.

Although the problem of liquidity had always been recognised, attention was drawn again to it by an influential book by Professor Robert Triffin, entitled *Gold and the Dollar Crisis*, published in 1959. Triffin pointed out that the need for liquidity was expanding much faster than the supply of gold and that something would have to be done if a shortage of international reserves was not to provoke countries to adopt restrictionist trade policies that might slow down the growth of world trade. His solution was to create an international reserve unit, to be administered by the IMF, which member countries would be obliged to accept in their reserves up to a certain amount. Initially, this reserve unit would be issued in exchange for the sterling and dollar balances held in reserve and for some gold from those countries which did not hold sterling or dollars. Further amounts of the international money would be created by the Fund's open market operations, including loans to member countries.

Although Triffin's analysis of the long-run need to increase reserves met with fairly widespread acceptance, there was considerable dispute as to how soon an increase would be needed, and how these reserves should be created. On the one hand, those who felt inflation was the main danger favoured the 'discipline' of creating 'conditional liquidity'; this could be done by increasing the Fund's lending capacity by the creation of new types of central bank mutual assistance, and possibly even through greater reliance on private markets. On the other hand, some observers felt that conditional liquidity would put disproportionate pressure on the borrowing country to adjust its policies without requiring surplus countries to respond to the same extent.

In the early years following convertibility, international cooperation was principally in the field of increasing conditional liquidity. In September 1959, there was a general increase in quotas in the IMF (and therefore in borrowing rights) of 50%. Apart from increasing quotas, steps were taken to ensure that the IMF should have a sufficient supply of currencies most useful in its lending operations. The General Arrangements to Borrow were established in 1962, to enable the Fund to obtain supplementary supplies of the main currencies direct from member countries. The countries which participate in the facility are known as the 'Group of Ten', and comprise: United States, United Kingdom, West Germany, France, Italy, Japan, Netherlands, Canada, Belgium and Sweden. Since 1963, Switzerland, though not in the IMF, has also been a participant in the GAB, but the title 'Group of Ten' has stuck. The GAB were established with a view to a possible US drawing, but in fact they have never been used for this purpose. They were, however, activated in 1964 to meet the possibility of a large drawing by the UK and have been used on a number of subsequent occasions.

Even with these increases in the Fund's lending capacity, the resources available to member countries were not really adequate to meet the likely demands of the 1960s. It was the emergence of the US deficit, after about 1957, which underlined most pointedly the inadequacy of the Fund's resources.

Since there was no international organisation able to meet the need, the finance of this deficit had to be accomplished by direct cooperation between central banks. One of the principal forms which this took was through the willingness of the European central banks to accumulate reserves in dollars, rather than presenting them for conversion into gold. As an additional safety measure, however, the US authorities took steps to establish an international 'swap network'. In essence, a swap is extremely simple. It involves the exchange of national currencies between central banks at a point of time, coupled with a contract to reverse the transaction, at the same exchange rate, at a fixed future date (usually after 3 months). If, for example, the UK wished to acquire 500 million D Marks to use in its foreign exchange operations to support the pound, it could swap 500 million D Marks worth of pounds with the Bundesbank. The Bundesbank would be fully protected against a possible devaluation of the pound, since the swap would be accompanied by a forward contract to 'unwind' the deal at the same exchange rate.

Swaps were begun in 1961, with informal assistance along these lines for the UK, following the revaluation of the German and Dutch currencies in March of that year. The most significant development occurred later in 1961, when a network of swaps between the dollar and other currencies was negotiated by the Federal Reserve Bank of New York. By 1971, the dollar swap network totalled some $12 billion, with 15 countries and the BIS.

Other swap networks have been established by other countries, notably the UK and France. Normally, swaps are activated by a country losing reserves in order to provide it with foreign exchange for market intervention. They have also been extensively used, particularly by the UK, as a means of window-dressing reserves by borrowing foreign currency for one day only at the end of each month. The purpose of this operation is to conceal the true extent of a reserve loss or gain in order to prevent the monthly reserve announcement setting off a bout of speculative pressure.

In addition to the swap network, the US authorities also tried to maintain confidence in the dollar through the issue of 'Roosa bonds', named after Robert V. Roosa, Under Secretary of the US Treasury during the Kennedy administration. These were bonds issued by the US Treasury to foreign central banks denominated in the currency of the holding country. This was a method of financing the deficit through the issue of longer-term instruments which would offer the holding country complete protection against the possibility of a dollar devaluation.

The expansion of these various methods of providing bilateral support occurred more or less ad hoc, in response to particular crises. Those devices that proved their usefulness were retained and used again. The creation of 'owned' liquidity, on the other hand, raised broader economic and political issues, and agreement took longer to reach.

One suggestion that was canvassed quite widely for a while was that the price of gold should be increased. This would have had the merit of increasing at a stroke the total of liquidity, since the value of gold reserves would go up, and it would also have encouraged mining. It would not have necessitated any change in the existing machinery of cooperation through the IMF and, since the US held the largest stock of gold, it would have increased the scope for dollar-holding in reserves without putting pressure on dollar convertibility.

Despite these advantages, however, the proposal to increase the price of gold had drawbacks. It would have enhanced the importance of gold at a time when it was widely recognised that digging ore out of mines in South Africa only to refine it and bury it again in the vaults of central banks was rather pointless. Also a price increase would have increased expectations of a further change in price at some future date, and thus have stored up problems of speculation for the future. It would have been virtually impossible to get general agreement on the extent to which gold should have been upvalued and the highest figure which would have been generally acceptable would not have been high enough to eliminate speculation about a further change in the near future. Finally, there were political considerations. A change in the price of gold would have been of primary benefit to South Africa and the Soviet Union, the two main producing countries, and to France, the country which in the early 1960s had increased its holdings the most. To help any of these countries would not have been particularly palatable to the US Congress (which had to ratify any change in the gold price) even if it had been prepared to tolerate the loss of face which dollar devaluation would have involved.[1]

From the middle 1960s onwards a greater sense of urgency was injected into the search for a new instrument of liquidity. Payments disequilibria were increasingly accentuated by volatile flows of private short-term capital. The size of these flows had grown rapidly after about 1960 following the establishment of external convertibility for the main European currencies and the development of international markets such as the euro-dollar market. At first, some observers saw in the development of these markets a possible substitute for centrally held reserves. They reasoned that balance of payments fluctuations could be accommodated by increases and reductions in privately owned balances—much in the same way as the Bank of England had protected sterling convertibility in the nineteenth century by using bank rate changes to stimulate movements of private capital rather than by maintaining massive reserves.

Even if it had been possible for central banks to manipulate international markets in this way, such a policy would have meant, in effect, that monetary policy would have to be devoted entirely to balance of

1 It is true that in 1972, the US Congress did agree to devalue the dollar and increase the price of gold, but by this time gold had ceased to occupy a central position in world liquidity, and the dollar had ceased to be convertible. The devaluation represented, therefore, a technical and tactical change rather than an intentional move to increase liquidity.

payments objectives and not at all to the needs of the domestic economy. But in fact, interest rate incentives were not, in themselves, powerful enough to play the role of inducing stabilising capital movements. Too often speculation resulted in movements of private short-term capital that added to the deficit generated by current and long-term investment transactions. Thus, far from diminishing the need for official reserves, the expansion of private capital flows substantially increased it.

In 1963, the Group of Ten countries (i.e., those participating in the General Arrangements to Borrow) set up a working party to discuss 'the functioning of the international monetary system and its probable future needs for liquidity'. The first report of this group recommended an increase in quotas that came into effect in 1965. It also recommended that two further studies should be undertaken, one to investigate the balance of payments adjustment process (described in the next section) and the other to look into proposals for the creation of a new reserve asset. The Report of the Study Group on the Creation of Reserve Assets was published in 1965 and was followed by a further report in 1966, setting out concrete proposals in more detail.

After further modifications, the outline scheme for Special Drawing Rights was put to the assembled IMF members at the 1967 Annual Meeting in Rio de Janeiro. During 1968 and 1969, the slow process of translating the draft scheme into Articles of Agreement and securing ratification was completed, though attention was diverted on a number of occasions by currency crises. The scheme took effect on 1 January 1970 and a total of 9,500 million SDRs were created in the first three years.

The adjustment mechanism

As well as providing international reserves to enable countries to finance deficits and surpluses, the international monetary system must provide a means whereby these deficits and surpluses can be smoothly and quickly eliminated, without generating side-effects which are too painful for the countries concerned. The process of elimination of surpluses and deficits is usually referred to as the adjustment mechanism.

The Bretton Woods system had two major ways of restoring equilibrium: the adjustment of the domestic pressure of demand (inflation or deflation) in order to deal with cyclical disturbances and adjustment of the exchange rate (devaluation or revaluation) to deal with 'fundamental disequilibrium'. In the years following the end of bilateralism the system worked reasonably well. The devaluations of 1949 were used to correct what was self-evidently a fundamental disequilibrium in the exchange rates of European countries with the dollar bloc and during the 1950s deflationary policies were largely successful in righting incipient balance of payments deficits. (There were some grumblings about the stop-go nature of such policies, but in the 1950s at any rate these were muted.)

During the 1960s, however, the shortcomings of the way in which the adjustment mechanism actually worked became more apparent. In the first place, the burden of adjustment seemed to fall more heavily on deficit countries than on surplus countries. Frequently, surplus countries preferred to pile up gold and foreign exchange reserves rather than stimulate domestic demand, which they feared might generate inflation, or revalue, which might hit their export industries. This meant that deficit countries could only get back into balance by devaluation or deflation. The former was difficult for political reasons, since devaluation carried connotations of defeat, while the latter policy involved considerable economic sacrifice through running the economy with a margin of unemployment.

Another difficulty of the way in which the system worked was the fact that, with greater volumes of internationally mobile funds, devaluation was likely to be forced on a country through loss of reserves, whether or not a situation of fundamental disequilibrium existed. And finally, the term 'fundamental disequilibrium' was susceptible of a variety of interpretations. It was impossible to state categorically when a deficit reached the stage of being fundamental, or what size of devaluation would be appropriate to cure it.

The problem of asymmetrical burdens of adjustment was one which the IMF Articles of Agreement had attempted to tackle in the Scarce Currency Clause, but this had become virtually a dead letter by the 1960s. In its place, the principal industrial countries did attempt to concert their policies in the forum of Working Party 3 of the Organisation for Economic Cooperation and Development. Working Party 3 was instituted in 1961 as a sub-committee of the Economic Policy Committee of the OECD. Its purpose was the 'promotion of better international payments equilibrium' and it is required to 'analyse the effect on international payments of monetary, fiscal and other policy measures, both national and international, as they relate to international payments equilibrium'. The working party exercised a form of coordinated moral suasion which could be used to bring pressure on persistent creditor or debtor countries. Under its auspices, the report on the 'Balance of Payments Adjustment Process', referred to above, was published in 1966. This report urged greater international consultation particularly in formulating balance of payments objectives, identifying payments problems, and selecting policy measures aimed at restoring equilibrium.

The Working Party 3 report assumed a continuation of the Bretton Woods par-value system. And although there has been widespread academic advocacy of floating or crawling peg regimes, nearly all official thinking on the adjustment process has been directed towards improving the par-value system rather than changing it. But there was nevertheless a growing feeling that the degree of flexibility which had been envisaged at Bretton Woods was not being fully utilised. It was suggested that the system might work better if there were somewhat more frequent changes in par-value but of a smaller size.

The dollar crisis

The dollar crisis, which culminated in the declaration of the dollar's inconvertibility on 15 August 1971, had been in the making for some time. Indeed, one might say that the central position in which the dollar had been placed after the war was bound, ultimately, to lead to the kind of crisis that occurred in 1971.

The fact that the dollar was the effective standard of the world monetary system, and that other currencies' values were expressed in terms of the dollar, meant that the United States could not unilaterally devalue or revalue its currency. In the 1940s, other currencies were probably over-valued in terms of the dollar, so that there was a tendency for gold reserves to flow to the US, and the universal preoccupation was the dollar shortage. From the mid 1950s onwards, however, and more particularly in the 1960s, many major currencies were undervalued in terms of the US dollar, and as a result the United States ran a balance of payments deficit. For countries in deficit, the normal policy prescription under the 'rules of the game' is to devalue or deflate. The United States could not devalue the dollar in terms of other currencies (at least not without the agreement of the other countries) and deflation would have to have been on an unacceptable scale—producing mass unemployment—to have been effective in improving the balance of payments by the required amount.

What was the United States to do under these circumstances? There was a respectable school of thought which said 'nothing'. If the other countries of the world economy chose to use the US dollar as international money, it was up to them to follow the necessary adjustment policies if the US could not. If a foreign country felt that an inflow of dollars was embarrassing its domestic monetary policy, it had a simple remedy in revaluation. The best policy for the US authorities, in other words, was one of 'benign neglect' of their balance of payments position.

Under certain circumstances, this was a theoretically defensible position but it overlooked the economic and political realities of the situation. So long as the dollar was convertible into gold, it was open to foreign holders of dollars to exercise their option to take gold. The greater the volume of foreign-held dollars, the greater became the suspicion that the US Treasury would not be able to maintain convertibility, and the greater the consequent desire of speculators to get gold while the getting was good. From the early 1960s onwards there was a gradual build-up of speculation on an increase in the gold price.

In 1960 there was a sudden flare-up in the London gold market and the price rose temporarily from the official level of \$35 per ounce to \$41, though it soon fell back when there were official denials of any intention by the US to change the price of gold.[2] There was further speculation at the time of the Cuba crisis in 1962, and during the sterling crisis which began in 1964 and culminated in sterling devaluation in November 1967. But the main speculation built up after sterling devaluation, and during the ensuing months became intense. In March 1968, the United States was forced to abandon unlimited sales of gold at the official price, although convertibility was retained for transactions between central banks. The 'two-tier phase', with a pegged and a free gold price, lasted for a little over three years. It was based on the understanding that countries would not abuse their right on paper to convert their dollar holdings into gold. This was a tenuous basis on which to rest the system and it finally broke down in August 1971 when the dollar was made wholly inconvertible.

Following the declaration of dollar inconvertibility, there was a period of uncoordinated floating of major currencies. Most tended to increase in value vis-à-vis the dollar, but the extent of the rise depended on the intervention of individual countries to prevent what they considered to be an excessive appreciation of their currencies. Most countries felt, however, that the uncertainties to which this situation gave rise might, if prolonged, have adverse consequences for international trade and investment flows to say nothing of the political

2 Following the 1960 flare-up, a 'gold pool' was established among central banks. Under this scheme the participants would contribute agreed amounts of gold to enable their agent, the Bank of England, to stabilise the gold price in the London market. The gold pool ceased to supply gold to the market in March 1968.

frictions which conflicting exchange rate policies might produce. In December 1971, therefore, the Group of Ten countries reached agreement in Washington on a new pattern of exchange rates. As part of this agreement, the US Government undertook to raise the official price of gold from $35 to $38 per ounce. This was really no more than a notional adjustment; it did not involve any commitment on the part of the US to buy or sell gold at the new price.

The reform of the international monetary system

The agreement reached in Washington in December 1971 established an interim regime, which was intended to restore orderly conditions in exchange markets while a more thorough-going reform of the international monetary system was worked out. In practice, the interim regime lasted only a little over a year. Successive speculative crises in February and March 1973 led, first to a further devaluation of the US dollar, then to more general floating among major currencies.

Meanwhile, the longer-term reform of the system has been entrusted to a specially constituted body within the International Monetary Fund, known as the Committee of Twenty. The composition of this committee was based on the groupings of countries in the Fund's Executive Board, and its members were either Ministers or Central Bank Governors. It was therefore in a position to reflect the views of the full Fund membership at a high political level.

Most of the actual negotiations have taken place in a group known as the 'Deputies' of the Committee of 20. This Committee of Deputies, chaired by Mr Jeremy Morse, a former Executive Director of the Bank of England, consists of senior permanent officials in finance ministries and central banks. It began its discussions in late 1972 and at the time of writing (1973) is in the middle of its work.

It would not be profitable to speculate here on the precise nature of the proposals that are likely to emerge from the work of the Committee of 20 and its deputies. It is, however, possible to identify those aspects of the old (pre-1971) system which have not worked particularly well and to which, therefore, the Committee will be particularly addressing themselves.

First comes the manner in which the balance of payments adjustment process should work. It is widely accepted that the world's exchange system should continue to be based on a par-value system though this may well work more flexibly in the future. The Committee and its deputies will be seeking to formulate policy guidelines that can indicate to countries when their balance of payments needs correction, and possibly also suggest the appropriate adjustment policies. In particular, they will be attempting to ensure that the burden of adjustment is equitably shared between deficit and surplus countries.

Next, the negotiators will be attempting to devise a framework within which all countries can accept obligations about converting their domestic currency into other internationally acceptable assets, without this imposing intolerable burdens. This requires a system which can function without the accumulation of large quantities of potentially volatile national currencies in reserves.

The problem of restoring convertibility is tied up, of course, with the question of reserve assets, since convertibility essentially means convertibility into reserve assets. The negotiators will be seeking to provide a basis for world liquidity, which provides for international control over the total quantity of reserves, and which therefore diminishes the role of national currencies in reserves. They will also be seeking to phase gold out of the international monetary system, both because of the inherent wastefulness of using a commodity as a monetary reserve, and because of the problems which are created when there is speculation on a change in the price of gold.

A particularly thorny problem in reform is the question of capital flows. In principle, most countries acknowledge the benefits which can potentially flow from the free movement of capital. To set against these, however, speculative capital movements can force unwelcome policy actions and the freer the movement of capital, the less latitude countries have to undertake independent domestic monetary policies. There is no obvious 'right' answer to this problem. It will be a question of striking the most acceptable balance between freedom of capital movement, to improve the international distribution of investment and aid, and controls to contain the destabilising effects of flows of hot money.

Last, but not least, of the questions facing the reform negotiators is the position of the developing world. The developing countries have a general interest in the smooth functioning of the international trade and payments system, but they also have two more specific interests. They may be particularly affected by adjustment measures affecting trade (such as import surcharges or quotas) and they have an interest in the distribution of the new purchasing power arising from the creation of international liquidity. Since any amendments to the Fund's Articles of Agreement must be ratified by 60 per cent of member countries, it may be expected that the reformed system will have to meet, at least partially, the developing countries' desires in these two matters.

Further reading

Federal Reserve Bank of Boston, *The International Adjustment Mechanism*, 1970.

Hirsch, Fred, *Money International*, op. cit.

International Monetary Fund, *Reform of the International Monetary System*, Report of the Executive Directors, 1972.

Krause, Lawrence B., *Sequel to Bretton Woods*, Brookings Staff Paper, 1971.

Mundell, R. and Swoboda, A. (editors), *Monetary Problems of the International Economy*, University of Chicago, Press, 1969.

Tew, Brian, op. cit., Chapter 8 onwards.

Triffin, R., *Our International Monetary System: Yesterday, Today and Tomorrow*, New York, Random House, 1968.

Questions for discussion

1 Why did it take so much longer than hoped for the main European currencies to become convertible?

2 Why did the Fund play a largely passive rôle for the first ten years of its life?

3 What were the main economic changes of the post-war period which influenced the nature and form of international monetary co-operation?

4 It is sometimes said that the passage of time made the Bretton Woods system obsolete. Do you agree?

5 What were the consequences for the international monetary system of the development of the eruo-dollar market.

Index